FREE TRADE
UNDER FIRE

Princeton University Press   *Princeton and Oxford*

FREE TRADE
UNDER FIRE

SECOND EDITION

DOUGLAS A. IRWIN

Copyright © 2002, 2005 by Princeton University Press

Published by Princeton University Press, 41 William Street, Princeton, New Jersey 08540

In the United Kingdom: Princeton University Press, 3 Market Place, Woodstock, Oxfordshire OX20 1SY

All Rights Reserved.

First Edition 2002

Second Edition 2005

Library of Congress Cataloging-in-Publication Data

Irwin, Douglas A., 1962–

    Free trade under fire / Douglas A. Irwin.—2nd ed.

      p.   cm.

    Includes bibliographical references and index.

    ISBN 0-691-12247-4 (pbk. : alk. paper)

      1. Free trade—United States.   2. United States—Commercial policy.

  3. Globalization.   I. Title.

  HF1756 I68 2005

  382'.71—dc22   2004058683

British Library Cataloging-in-Publication Data is available

This book has been composed in

Printed on acid-free paper. ∞

pup.princeton.edu

Printed in the United States of America

10 9 8 7 6 5 4 3 2 1

_____Contents

List of Figures   vii

List of Tables   ix

Preface   xi

Introduction   1

1   The United States in a New Global Economy?   7

2   The Case for Free Trade: Old Theories, New Evidence   25

3   Protectionism: Economic Costs, Political Benefits?   61

4   Trade, Jobs, and Displaced Workers   94

5   Relief from Foreign Competition: Antidumping
and the Escape Clause   131

6   Developing Countries and Open Markets   160

7   The World Trading System: The WTO
and New Battlegrounds   203

Conclusion   *254*

References   *259*

Index   *283*

Figures

1.1   Merchandise Exports and Imports in the United
      States as a Percentage of GDP, 1869–2002   8
1.2   U.S. Merchandise Exports as a Share of GDP and
      Merchandise Production, Selected Years   10
1.3   U.S. Trade in Goods and Services as a
      Percentage of GDP, 1960–2003   14
1.4   Average U.S. Tariff Rate on Dutiable Imports,
      1869–2003   20
2.1   Relative Productivity in the United States and Japan,
      by Industry, 1990   30
2.2   Employment-Weighted Relative Productivity Level,
      United States and Japan, 1990   33
2.3   Producer Protection and Fertilizer Use in
      Agriculture, 2000   54
3.1   China's Exports and Imports, 1950–2003   73
3.2   Exports and Imports as a Share of GDP, Chile and
      Brazil, 1970 and 1998   74
4.1   Civilian Labor Force and Civilian Employment in the
      United States, 1950–2003   95
4.2   Unemployment and Import Penetration in the
      United States, 1950–2003   96
4.3   U.S. Manufacturing Production and
      Employment, 1970–2003   102
4.4   Change in Production and Imports of
      Manufactured Goods, 1991–2003   104
4.5   Labor Productivity and Labor Compensation
      Costs, 1960–2003   107
4.6   Unemployment and the Trade Deficit, 1960–2003   123
4.7   Savings and Investment as a Percentage of GDP, 1960–2002   128

5.1	Annual Number of U.S. Antidumping Cases, 1970–2003	134
6.1	Real per Capita GDP in China, 1953–2000	167
6.2	Real per Capita GDP in India, 1950–2003	169
6.3	Real per Capita GDP in South Korea, 1953–2002	172
6.4	Labor Costs and Productivity in Manufacturing for 63 Countries, 1995–1999	190
6.5	Labor Productivity, Wages, and Unit Labor Costs in Selected Developing Countries, 1990	191
6.6	Real Wages and Labor Productivity in Manufacturing, South Korea and the Philippines, 1972–1993	192
6.7	Child Labor and GDP per Capita, 2000	198
7.1	Volume of World Trade and World Production, 1925–1938	205
7.2	Volume of World Trade and World Production, 1950–2002	212

Tables

1.1 Composition of U.S. Trade by Category of Commodity, 1960, 1980, 2000   11

1.2 U.S. Imports by Principal End-Use Category   12

4.1 Number of Workers Affected by Extended Mass Layoffs, 1996–2003   97

4.2 Labor Market Outcomes for Displaced Workers in North Carolina, 1986–1992   115

4.3 Reemployment within Same or Another Industry, Displaced Workers in North Carolina, 1986–1992   116

4.4 Status of Workers Displaced from Full-Time Jobs between January 2001 and December 2003   116

5.1 Antidumping Margins by Calculation Method, 1995–1998   136

5.2 Trade Effects of Antidumping Duties   139

5.3 Evidence of Trade Diversion in Antidumping Actions   140

6.1 Average Applied Tariff Rate on Industrial Products, 2001   162

6.2 Trade-to-GDP Ratio in Selected Developing Countries, 2002   165

6.3 Growth in Real per Capita GDP, 1980s and 1990s   175

6.4 Agricultural Support in OECD Countries, 1999–2001   185

7.1 Major Provisions of the General Agreement on Tariffs and Trade   208

7.2 GATT Negotiating Rounds   210

7.3 Post–Uruguay Round Average Applied Tariffs for Selected Countries   218

7.4 Border Protection for Selected Agricultural Goods, 1986–1988, 1995, and 2000   220

7.5 U.S. Regional and Bilateral Trade Agreements   250

Preface

This book was first published in 2002, shortly after the huge antiglobalization protests in Seattle at the 1999 World Trade Organization meeting. Although the antiglobalization movement has been relatively quiet since the attacks of September 11, 2001, trade policy continues, as always, to generate a great deal of controversy.

This book aims to introduce the reader to some basic economic principles and empirical evidence regarding international trade and trade policy. In this second edition, I have added a chapter on developing countries, eliminated some institutional and historical detail on U.S. trade policy, and have otherwise updated the text to deal with new developments such as steel tariffs and outsourcing.

As I noted in the first edition, this book draws together some of the vast amount of economic research on international trade policy. As before, I wish to acknowledge all of the scholars who have made contributions to this field in recent years, for it is their work that has inspired me. I would particularly like to thank Brink Lindsey, Michael Knetter, Anne Krueger, Arvind Panagariya, Nina Pavcnik, Phillip Swagel, and Alan Winters for providing valuable comments. I am especially indebted to Meir and Becky Kohn for convincing me to undertake the project and for making significant improvements in the organization and clarity of the text. I also wish to thank my editor at Princeton University Press, Peter Dougherty, for his enthusiasm and good sense, both of which encouraged and guided me through two editions. Finally, I am grateful as always for the forbearance of my wife, Marjorie, and our daughters, Ellen and Katie. This book is for them.

FREE TRADE
UNDER FIRE

Free trade, one of the greatest blessings which a government can confer on a people, is in almost every country unpopular.
—Thomas Babington Macaulay, 1824

Introduction

Nearly two centuries after Macaulay made it, this observation by one of Britain's great historians still rings true. Growing world trade has helped lift standards of living around the world, and yet today, as in Macaulay's time, free trade does not win many popularity contests. Trade policy remains a highly controversial subject, a source of never-ending public debate.

In every country, international trade invariably brings out anxieties and insecurities. With each passing decade, some of the old fears about trade recede and new ones take their place. In the 1980s, many Americans were convinced that Japan would achieve economic dominance by wiping out industry after industry in the United States, from automobiles to semiconductors to supercomputers, and thereby diminish America's position in the world. In the 1990s, many feared that the North American Free Trade Agreement (NAFTA) would result in a "giant sucking sound" of jobs lost to Mexico due to its low wages. Others protested in the streets of Seattle in late 1999 against the World Trade Organization (WTO) for its promotion of free trade and alleged indifference to the world's workers and environment. Now, in the first decade of the twenty-first century, concern has shifted to China and India. China is becoming a goliath in the production of manufactured goods, while the outsourcing of white-collar jobs (from software programming to radiology) to India has sparked new worries of a "service sector sucking sound."[1]

[1] Perhaps not surprisingly, many people in Japan, Mexico, China, India, and the rest of the world have seen things very differently. They fear economic domination by the United States and wonder how local producers can ever compete against large, wealthy, and technologically sophisticated American companies.

Fears of trade exist in good times and in bad. The 1990s were a period of robust economic growth and the lowest U.S. unemployment in thirty years, yet NAFTA and the WTO generated heated debates. Economic downturns invariably bring out cries that foreign countries are stealing our jobs and therefore protectionist trade policies are required. And opponents of free trade are not confined to one segment of the political spectrum. From Patrick Buchanan on the right to Ralph Nader on the left, trade skeptics can be found everywhere.

Although free trade has always been the subject of complaint, the rhetorical charges against it have stepped up in recent years, as the protests in Seattle and elsewhere have made clear. A wide range of groups, from environmentalists to religious organizations to human rights activists, have joined in marching against free trade. These groups rail against free trade and the WTO as a system that serves the interests of corporations rather than people, harms workers, decimates manufacturing industries, sweeps aside environmental regulations, and undermines America's sovereignty.

The litany of complaints placed on the doorstep of free trade is quite impressive and goes well beyond the perennial objection that trade forces painful economic adjustments such as plant closings and layoffs of workers. Ralph Nader charges that "the Fortune 200's GATT and NAFTA agenda would make the air you breathe dirtier, and the water you drink more polluted. It would cost jobs, depress wage levels and make workplaces less safe. It would destroy family farms and undermine consumer protections." Patrick Buchanan chimes in with the claim that 'broken homes, uprooted families, vanished dreams, delinquency, vandalism, crime—these are the hidden costs of free trade."[2] The organization Public Citizen says that "the real-life devastation being caused by the implementation of the WTO's terms—and the growing social and political backlash this pain is generating worldwide—is the reason the WTO is wracked by the severe crisis that burst into view in Seattle and Cancún."[3]

Why is such hostility directed at free trade policies and the World Trade Organization? The rapid increase in international trade in recent decades may have unleashed a "globalization backlash." In this view,

---

[2] Nader 1993, 1; Buchanan 1998, 286.
[3] Wallach and Woodall 2004, 283.

increased global integration has accelerated the pace of economic change and has brought with it painful economic adjustments. Meanwhile, the reach of world trade rules has gone beyond trade barriers to encompass internal regulatory policies regarding health, safety, and the environment. As a result, groups disturbed by these changes, whether directly in terms of their jobs or indirectly in terms of the community values they believe are at stake, have questioned the effects of integration and the institutions associated with it. These groups have raised legitimate concerns about commerce and the community and about whether sovereignty has shifted from elected representatives at home to faceless and unaccountable bureaucrats abroad.

Clearly, the debate over trade policy is intense and shows little prospect of abating. The debate has raised many fundamental questions. Why is free trade considered to be a desirable policy? Do the most frequently made criticisms of free trade, such as its adverse impact on employment and the environment, have merit? Do the economic circumstances of developing countries qualify the case for free trade in any way? What is the World Trade Organization, and do world trade rules erode a country's sovereignty and undermine its health and environmental regulations?

This book aims to answer these basic questions and demystify some of the complex issues that surround discussions of trade policy. These questions will be examined mainly through the lens of economics. Despite widespread popular skepticism about free trade, economists generally take a positive view of international trade and believe that reducing government-imposed trade barriers is desirable. In the eyes of economists, trade between countries is mutually beneficial, just like the exchange of goods within a country, even though the goods happen to cross national boundaries. While some groups lose from trade, people around the world are generally better off with trade than they would be without it.

Trade skeptics often accuse economists of having a religious faith in free trade, of blindly clinging to the doctrine in the face of contrary evidence. But the economic case for free trade is based not on faith, but on logic and evidence. As Paul Krugman has written, "The logic that says that tariffs and import quotas almost always reduce real income is deep and has survived a century and a half of often vitriolic criticism nearly intact. And experience teaches that governments that imagine or pretend that their interventionist strategies are a sophisticated improvement on free trade nearly always turn out, on closer examination, to be engaged in largely irrational policies—or worse, in policies that are rational only in the sense that they benefit key interest groups at the expense of everyone else."[4]

Still, the logic and evidence behind the case for free trade deserves to be put under searching scrutiny, as does the logic and evidence behind alternative policies. Even advocates of free trade need to be reminded of the case, lest they simply restate stale arguments that fail to persuade. As John Stuart Mill argued, "even if the received opinion be not only true, but the whole truth; unless it is suffered to be, and actually is, vigorously and earnestly contested, it will, by most of those who receive it, be held in the manner of a prejudice, with little comprehension or feeling of its rational grounds." Thus, "however true [a proposition] may be, if it is not fully, frequently, and fearlessly discussed, it will be held as a dead dogma, not a living truth."[5]

So the views of economists deserve critical scrutiny, but first they deserve a fair hearing. Economists have studied trade for a very long time and have noticed that the same worries and fears about trade tend to get repeated generation after generation. "With America's high standard of living, we cannot successfully compete against foreign producers because of lower foreign wages and a lower cost of production." This claim is heard today, but this particular quote comes from President Herbert Hoover in 1929 as he urged Congress to pass what became known as the Smoot-Hawley tariff. (Such statements can be found in abundance in the nineteenth century as well.) Among the claims heard yesterday and today are that trade will destroy jobs and lead to unemployment and falling incomes, and that trade deficits will siphon away a country's wealth. To economists, these are economic fallacies that history and experience have refuted time and again. As one observer quipped, "free traders are trapped in a public policy version of [the movie] 'Groundhog Day,' forced to refute the same fallacious arguments over and over again, decade after decade."[6]

[4] Krugman 1995, 31.
[5] Mill 1982, 116, 97.
[6] Sanchez 2003.

Chapter 1 in this book, "The United States in a New Global Economy?" sets out basic facts about international trade and the U.S. economy. World trade has expanded rapidly in recent years, and this development provides the context in which to consider questions of trade policy. This chapter discusses the reasons for the increase in trade and the state of public opinion on the question of globalization.

Chapter 2, "The Case for Free Trade: Old Theories, New Evidence," examines the economic logic of free trade and recent empirical evidence reinforcing the case for it. Ever since Adam Smith and David Ricardo described the gains from trade in a systematic way, economists have stressed the higher income that results from improved resource allocation as the main advantage of trade. But economists have found mounting evidence that trade not only helps to allocate existing resources properly, but also makes those resources more productive. These productivity gains from trade, overlooked in the standard calculations, appear to be substantial. The welfare benefits of a greater variety of products as a result of trade have also been ignored until recently, and yet preliminary evidence suggests that they are quite important.

Chapter 3, "Protectionism: Economic Costs, Political Benefits?" considers the flip side of the case for free trade—that trade interventions are usually misguided and often costly. Tariffs and quotas on imports redistribute income from consumers to producers, but do so inefficiently with a net economic loss because the costs to consumers are much greater than the benefits to producers. The chapter raises the question of why, despite its costs, trade protectionism is often politically attractive. Finally, the chapter examines situations in which protection may be justified in theory, even if governments are often ill equipped to take advantage of those situations.

Chapter 4, "Trade, Jobs, and Displaced Workers," focuses on the most frequent argument in favor of limiting trade: that jobs will be saved in industries that compete against imports. As we shall see, reducing trade saves those jobs only by destroying jobs elsewhere in the economy. Opponents of free trade have also argued that imports have replaced good, high-wage jobs with bad, low-wage jobs. The truth turns out to be quite the opposite: jobs in industries that compete against imports are mainly low-skill and consequently low-wage jobs. This chapter also evaluates government assistance to help workers displaced by imports.

Chapter 5, "Relief from Foreign Competition: Antidumping and the Escape Clause," describes the legal framework that allows firms to petition the government for the imposition of tariffs on competing imports. The antidumping law is the most commonly used measure to block so-called unfair imports. The government's definition of "dumping" is a lower price charged in the United States than in a foreign exporter's home market, but it is not clear that this is a problem requiring trade restrictions, or that the government calculates the dumping margin in a fair manner. This chapter also examines the case for providing domestic industries with temporary relief from imports so that they can adjust to the competition.

Chapter 6, "Developing Countries and Open Markets," takes a look at the special circumstances of developing countries. Is free trade always beneficial in the case of poor countries? What type of trade policy is most likely to promote economic development? Did countries such as Japan and Korea grow rich by rejecting free trade and instead pursuing closed markets and industrial policies? The chapter also addresses how rich-country agricultural subsidies and import tariffs harm developing countries, as well as how developing countries harm themselves with their own antitrade policies.

Chapter 7, "The World Trading System: The WTO and New Battlegrounds," focuses on the current controversies about the multilateral trading system, particularly the World Trade Organization. Since its inception, the WTO has come under intense criticism from nongovernmental organizations (NGOs), which attack it as an antidemocratic institution that has struck down domestic environmental regulations by ruling them inconsistent with world trade laws. This chapter examines the WTO's rules and dispute settlement system, the leading trade and environmental cases that have come before it, and the impact of regional trade arrangements such as NAFTA.

As Macaulay so aptly noted long ago, there is a fundamental incongruity about free trade: despite its palpable benefits, it is frequently the object of condemnation rather than approbation. That condemnation is often the result of misconceptions about the benefits of international trade, the impact of trade policies, and the role and function of the WTO. This book seeks to dispel these misconceptions and is offered in the modest hope that it may improve our understanding of the issues of trade policy that confront us.

1

The United States in a New Global Economy?

International trade has become an integral part of the U.S. economy over the past few decades. The United States imports toys from China, clothing from Costa Rica, and steel from Korea, and exports aircraft from Washington, wheat from Kansas, and machinery from Illinois. The United States sells financial services to customers around the world and subcontracts data entry, software programming, and call center services from India. There is hardly a sector of the economy or a region of the country that is unaffected by international markets. As the twenty-first century begins, the United States may even have achieved a historically unprecedented degree of economic integration with the rest of the world. Perhaps it is not surprising, therefore, that the rapid growth of trade has been accompanied by a intensified debate over U.S. trade policy. To establish a context in which we can later examine current trade policy, this chapter briefly looks at the role of trade in the U.S. economy.

_____The Increasing Importance of Trade

How important is trade in merchandise goods to the U.S. economy? The simplest way to answer this question is to look at its share in gross domestic product (GDP). In 2003, for example, merchandise exports amounted to about $725 billion, about 6.6 percent of GDP. At the same time, merchandise imports were about $1,283 billion, about 9.3 percent of GDP.

By looking at these numbers in a historical perspective, we can determine whether they are high or low. Figure 1.1 presents U.S. merchandise exports and imports as a share of GDP from 1869 to 2003. As

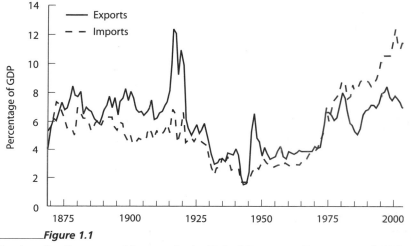

_____Figure 1.1
Merchandise Exports and Imports in the United States as a Percentage of GDP, 1869–2003
Source: Merchandise trade (1869–1970) from U.S. Bureau of the Census 1975, and (1971–2000) from Council of Economic Advisers 2004, table B-103. GDP (1869–1928) from Balke and Gordon 1989 and (1929–2003) from U.S. Bureau of Economic Analysis at http://www.bea.gov.

the figure shows, merchandise trade was fairly stable at about 7 percent of GDP in the period just after the Civil War until the outbreak of World War I in 1914. Exports surged during the war, but the trade shares declined sharply during the period from 1919 to 1939 and on through World War II. Between the world wars, many countries pursued inward-looking economic policies, including protectionist trade policies, restrictions on international labor migration, and limitations on international capital flows. These policies substantially reduced world economic integration. Since the end of World War II, many of these restrictions have been relaxed, and trade has slowly responded. For about a quarter century after 1945, exports and imports remained lower than they had been prior to World War I, but both began to rise in the early 1970s. Thus, in some sense, the United States has gone back to the future, returning to the degree of integration that prevailed before World War I.

Economists have interpreted these data in two conflicting ways. One interpretation—the "fin de siècle déjà vu" view—is that trade is about as important now as it was a century ago. This view points out that merchandise exports stood at about 7 percent of GDP in the late nineteenth century and are about the same today, although the share of merchandise imports is now much higher. A second interpretation—the "new global economy" view—stresses that the rapid rise in trade's share of GDP since the mid-1970s has put trade at a level unprecedented in recent history.[1] Evidence discussed below suggests that this second interpretation is a more accurate description of the current state of trade.

Will the current trend toward a higher trade share continue? There is certainly no law in economics that dictates an inexorable rise in the ratio of trade to GDP over time. In fact, many economists, from Robert Torrens in the early nineteenth century to Dennis Robertson in the mid–twentieth century, have expounded a "law of diminishing international trade." They believed that the spread of industrial technology around the world would result in smaller differences in industrial efficiency across countries. Each country would eventually come to produce manufactured goods just as efficiently as any other, and so international trade would diminish. But this theory has been proven false: over time, the division of labor in manufacturing and in other sectors has become more refined, increasing trade even between those countries with comparable technology. For example, the spread of industrial technology has enabled an increasing number of countries to produce automobiles. Rather than reducing international trade in cars, this development has stimulated a large amount of trade in automobile products, especially parts and components.[2]

A more plausible version of the idea of diminishing international trade is that the trade share would fall as countries grew richer because the composition of demand would shift away from traded goods (such as food, clothing, and manufactures) toward nontraded goods (such as housing, health care, education, and other services). And to some extent, this has taken place in the United States: the share of personal consumption expenditures devoted to services has risen steadily in recent decades at the expense of expenditures on durable and nondurable goods. This shift in demand has contributed to a change in the U.S.

---

[1] Bordo, Eichengreen, and Irwin (1999) compare global integration now and a century ago and conclude that, despite similarities, the current period exhibits much greater integration.

[2] Furthermore, Clark and Feenstra (2003) note that international differences in technology have not narrowed over time but have widened.

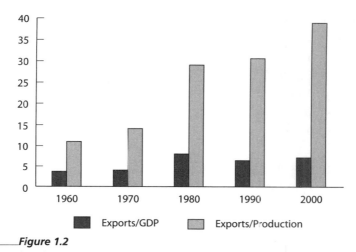

_____Figure 1.2
U.S. Merchandise Exports as a Share of GDP and Merchandise Production,
Selected Years
Source: Council of Economic Advisers 2004, tables B-12 and B-103.

economy away from the production of merchandise goods and toward
the production of services. (The more rapid productivity growth in goods-
producing sectors, which has reduced the prices of goods relative to those
of services, has also contributed to this result.) As a result, the traded-goods
sectors of the economy—agriculture, mining, and manufacturing—have
declined from 33.5 percent of current-dollar GDP in 1960 to 16.4 percent
in 2002.[3] The service sectors of the economy, comprising transportation
and public utilities; wholesale and retail trade; finance, insurance, and
real estate; and government have grown more rapidly than the traded-
goods sectors. Although in the past many of these service activities could
not be traded internationally, an increasing number of services are now
tradable, as will be discussed shortly.

Even though the merchandise goods share of the economy has
fallen significantly, the overall merchandise trade share has not. The
gradual rise in the share of merchandise trade to GDP therefore masks
the vastly increased importance of trade within the traded-goods sector.
This is seen most strikingly by comparing merchandise exports to merchandise production rather than to total GDP. As figure 1.2 indicates,
merchandise exports as a share of merchandise production soared from

[3] Council of Economic Advisers 2004, table B-12.

_____*Table 1.1*
Composition of U.S. Trade by Category of Commodity, 1960, 1980, 2000 (percentage distribution)

	1960		1980		2000	
	Exports	*Imports*	*Exports*	*Imports*	*Exports*	*Imports*
Food, animals, etc.	16	23	14	8	6	4
Crude materials	16	20	12	5	4	2
Mineral fuels	2	11	4	33	2	11
Chemicals and manu- factured goods	32	36	31	30	36	38
Machinery and transport equipment	35	10	39	25	53	45

Source: United Nations 1962, 574–75. Organization for Economic Cooperation and Development 1981, 30–31; 2001, 32–33.
Note: By SITC category.

about 15 percent in 1970 to nearly 40 percent in 2000, while relative to GDP it has changed only modestly. This implies that the increase in the size of the nontraded sector can sharpen the degree to which countries specialize in the traded-goods sector and therefore increase trade.[4] Thus, a close analysis of the merchandise trade figures indicates that trade is substantially more important now than in the recent past for those sectors engaged in trade.

The rise in trade relative to production is also evident in the case of specific commodities. Both the share of domestic production shipped to other markets and the ratio of imports to domestic consumption are much more pronounced today than just a few decades ago, especially for perishable products, such as fruits, flowers, and vegetables, which only recently have become widely traded across countries.

Two final points should be made about U.S. merchandise trade. First, the composition of both exports and imports has shifted toward manufactured goods over the past few decades. Table 1.1 presents the commodity composition of these exports and imports. The United States is a net exporter of agricultural commodities and a net importer of fuels. But manufactured goods constitute the overwhelming majority—over 80 percent—of both exports and imports. Many of these manufactured goods fall in the same general categories; the value of both exports and imports is large in the case of machinery (electrical, general industrial,

[4] This is precisely what the analysis by Flam (1985) predicted.

_____Table 1.2
U.S. Imports by Principal End-Use Category (percent distribution)

	Consumer Goods	Industrial Materials and Supplies	Capital Goods	Automotive Goods
1960	36	55	4	5
1980	22	53	13	12
2003	32	26	24	18

Source: U.S. Bureau of the Census 1975, 895 and http://www.ita.doc.gov.

Note: Consumer goods include consumer durables and nondurable goods (except automobiles), and foods, feeds, and beverages; industrial supplies and materials include crude and processed materials such as fuels and lubricants, paper, building materials, and the like; and capital goods include machinery, equipment, apparatuses, instruments, as well as parts, components, and accessories. Automotive goods includes assembled automobiles, automobile engines, and parts.

power generating, and scientific), motor vehicles, and office equipment. In other categories, there is less overlap in trade: leading manufactured exports also include airplanes and parts and a variety of chemicals, while leading manufactured imports include televisions and consumer electronics, clothing and footwear, iron and steel mill products, and toys and sporting goods.

Second, most of this trade in manufactured goods is not in final consumer goods, but rather in intermediate components and parts. Table 1.2 classifies imports based on their final actual use for several categories: consumer goods, industrial supplies and materials, capital goods, and automotive products. The most striking change is the rise of capital goods as a share of U.S. imports. Capital goods include machinery, equipment, instruments, parts, and various other components to production. (Many imports categorized under automotive products are also capital goods, such as engines and parts.) About half of all imports are either intermediate components or raw materials. These imports are sold as inputs to domestic businesses rather than as goods consumed directly by households. As chapter 3 will explain, this fact has important implications for trade policy: protectionist policies will directly harm employment in other domestic industries by raising their production costs, in addition to forcing consumers to pay a higher price for the products they buy.

Though trade is more important than ever for the merchandise-producing sector, this is not necessarily the case for the overall economy. Production and employment have shifted toward the service sector, in which international trade does not play as large a role. In fact, only about

15 percent of American workers are directly exposed to international competition by being employed in the goods-producing sectors of the economy (agriculture, mining, and manufacturing). In contrast, about 40 percent of workers were employed in those sectors in 1960.[5] This means that a smaller part of the U.S. economy, in terms of output and employment, is directly affected by fluctuations in merchandise trade.

Yet this statement must also be qualified. Many previously non-traded services are now becoming more tradable. In 2003, the value of these U.S. service exports (excluded from the merchandise trade figures considered so far) amounted to about $325 billion, nearly a third of the value of merchandise exports. The United States is a large net exporter of services, having only imported $260 billion in that year. The major categories of services trade include shipping and tourism, royalties and fees (receipts from intellectual property rights, such as trademarks, patents, and copyrights), and military transfers.

The addition of trade in services has raised the overall economic significance of trade. In 2003, exports of goods and services were 9.5 percent of GDP, of which merchandise exports were 6.6 percent and service exports were 2.9 percent. (In 1970, by contrast, service exports were only about 1 percent of GDP.) Also in that year, imports of goods and services stood at 11.7 percent of GDP, of which merchandise imports were 9.3 percent and service imports were 2.4 percent.[6] Figure 1.3 provides a closer look at exports and imports of goods and services as a percentage of GDP since 1970. (The trade deficit will be discussed in chapter 4.)

The most rapidly growing category of U.S. service exports are those listed as "other private services," which include education, finance, insurance, telecommunications, and business, professional, and technical services. Despite recent fears that "outsourcing" will harm the employment prospects of white-collar workers, the United States continues to export more than it imports in these "other private services." In 2003, the value of U.S. exports of legal work, computer programming, engineering, management consulting, and other private services was $131 billion. U.S. imports of such services, including call centers and data entry to developing countries, among other things, was $77 billion. This is true even in

[5] Council of Economic Advisers 2004, tables B-46 and B-100.
[6] From the Bureau of Economics Analysis, Department of Commerce.

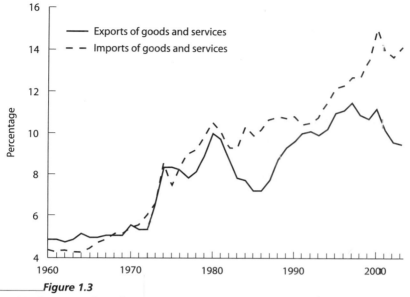

_____Figure 1.3
U.S. Trade in Goods and Services as a Percentage of GDP, 1960–2003
Source: Bureau of Economic Analysis, http://bea.gov.

the narrower category of "computer and data base processing service," in which the United States exported over $5 billion and imported just over $1 billion in 2002.[7]

Unlike the case of merchandise, trade in services tends to be a small part of total service production, although the share is rising. In 1960, the ratio of service exports to services value-added was 1.7 percent, but by 2002 that ratio had risen to 4.9 percent.[8] While small in comparison to the merchandise sector, this ratio has been rising and portends even greater trade in services in the future.

Yet even services that are not subject to trade are increasingly subject to international competition. This is because direct investments enable U.S. firms to enter foreign markets and allow foreign service providers to compete in the U.S. market. U.S. direct investments abroad increased from 6 percent of GDP in 1960 to 19 percent in 2003, and many

[7] Lindsey 2004. See also Borga and Mann 2003.
[8] Council of Economic Advisers 2004, table B-12.

of these investments were in the service sector. For example, in the 1990s the University of Chicago's Graduate School of Business built small campuses in Barcelona and Singapore to bring education services directly to Europeans and Asians who are not able to travel to Chicago. Similarly, foreign direct investment in the United States increased from 1 percent of GDP in 1960 to 19 percent in 2003. For example, many foreign banks have established a presence in the U.S. market to provide financial services, and many foreign automobile firms (such as Honda, Toyota, BMW, Mercedes, and Volkswagen) have set up plants to produce in the U.S. market. In addition, domestic service firms are increasingly the target of mergers and acquisitions as foreign firms seek entry into the U.S. market. As an indication of the increased foreign presence in the U.S. economy, the foreign-owned affiliates' share of gross product originating in private industry in the United States increased from 2.3 percent in 1977 to 6.4 percent in 2001.[9]

As a result, firms have a choice in how they can sell products to foreign residents: either by exporting domestically produced goods, or by producing and selling directly in the foreign country. This gives us another way to look at international commerce—based on company ownership rather than production location. In 2002, U.S. companies sold $974 billion worth of goods and services to foreign consumers through exports and earned $143 billion in net income from sales to foreign consumers through their foreign affiliates. Meanwhile, foreign companies sold $1,392 billion to U.S. consumers through exports to the United States and earned nearly $50 billion in net income through sales by their U.S. affiliates. The resulting U.S. deficit in goods, services, and net receipts from sales by affiliates in 2002 was almost $100 billion less than the deficit in goods and services in the conventional international accounts based solely on location of production. The ownership-based deficit was smaller because U.S. companies earned more in net income from sales to foreign consumers through their foreign affiliates than foreign companies earned in net income selling through their U.S. affiliates.[10]

[9] Zeile 2003a. Direct investment figures are from the Bureau of Economic Analysis (www.bea.gov).

[10] Lowe 2004.

_____Trade and the Fragmentation of Production

Is the recent rise in the trade share misleading? The increased trade in intermediate components requires that we ask this question. Every time a component is shipped across a border, it gets recorded by customs officials as an export or an import. When components are repeatedly shipped across the border at different stages of production, the official recorded value of trade rises with each crossing, but there may be no more final goods output than before. Thus, the value of trade relative to production may be inflated if intermediate products cross national borders multiple times during the production process. For example, there is substantial two-way trade between the United States and Canada in automobiles and parts. About 60 percent of U.S. auto exports to Canada are engines and parts, whereas 75 percent of U.S. auto imports from Canada are finished cars and trucks.[11] The increase in automobile trade between the United States, Canada, and other countries does not itself indicate that more and more cars are being built; rather, various parts and components that used to be produced domestically are now produced in other countries and traded multiple times across international borders.

This phenomenon is known as *vertical specialization*. Vertical specialization refers to the fragmentation of the production process as intermediate goods and components become a greater part of world trade. According to one estimate, vertical specialization accounts for about a third of the increase in world trade since 1970.[12]

As the Canada auto trade example suggests, a nonnegligible portion of the value of U.S. imports is simply the value of U.S. exports of domestically produced components that are shipped abroad for further processing or assembly and then returned to the United States for

[11] Hummels, Rapoport, and Yi 1998, 84. The coordination involved in this cross-border movement of auto parts is mind-boggling. To keep a Ford factory in Toronto producing 1,500 Windstar minivans a day, a logistics subcontractor "organizes 800 deliveries a day from 300 different parts makers. . . . Loads have to arrive at 12 different points along the assembly lines without ever being more than 10 minutes late. Parts must be loaded into trucks in a pre-arranged sequence to speed unloading at the assembly line. To make all this run like clockwork takes a team of ten computer-wielding operations planners and 200 unskilled workers, who make up the loads in the right sequence at a warehouse down the road." *Economist*, December 5, 2002.

[12] Hummels, Ishii, and Yi 2001.

additional work before sale or export. Imports that incorporate U.S.-made components are often given duty-free or reduced-duty treatment under the "production sharing" provision of the tariff code.[13] In 2002, imports entering the United States under the production-sharing provision amounted to $54 billion, or almost 6 percent of total merchandise imports. The value of U.S.-produced components in these imports was about $9 billion, or 16 percent of the total value of imports entered under this provision. In other words, a significant portion of the value of U.S. imports actually represents the value of domestic products that have been exported and then returned to the United States.[14]

This phenomenon is a particularly striking aspect of U.S. trade with Mexico. In 2002, the United States imported $134 billion in goods from Mexico. Of this, $11 billion (9 percent) entered under the production-sharing provision, and $5 billion represented the U.S. content of these imports. Thus, nearly half (47 percent) of the value of goods that entered the United States under the production-sharing provision actually reflects the value of U.S.-made components.

These official figures grossly understate the magnitude of production sharing in U.S. trade. A majority of imports from Canada and Mexico incorporate U.S.-made parts but no longer enter the United States under the production-sharing provisions of the tariff code because they are already eligible for duty-free treatment under NAFTA. Nearly a third of U.S. imports from Canada, Mexico, and the Caribbean Basin consisted of motor vehicles, televisions, and apparel, the sectors in which production-sharing or outsourcing arrangements are extensive. This tariff provision, along with communication and transportation technology, has significantly deepened cross-border integration in North America and the Caribbean Basin, enabling firms to subcontract some operations to neighboring countries. For example, most apparel imported from Mexico and the Caribbean Basin is sewn from U.S.-made fabrics, whereas apparel imports from Asia are not.

---

[13] This provision of the tariff (chapter 98 of the Harmonized Tariff Schedule) dates back to 1964 and was designed to enable U.S. companies to reduce their costs by outsourcing labor-intensive assembly operations to neighboring countries, and thereby compete more effectively against European and Japanese companies, which take advantage of lower labor costs in eastern Europe and Asia for assembly operations.

[14] These statistics come from Watkins 2003, table B-2.

Such production sharing and outsourcing means that the origin of any particular manufactured product cannot be attributed to a single country. An Airbus aircraft imported from France may have engines produced in the United States by General Electric or Pratt & Whitney. For one particular car produced by an American manufacturer, 30 percent of the car's value is due to assembly in Korea, 17.5 percent due to components from Japan, 7.5 percent due to design from Germany, 4 percent due to parts from Taiwan and Singapore, 2.5 percent due to advertising and marketing services from Britain, and 1.5 percent due to data processing in Ireland. In the end, 37 percent of the production value of this American car came from the United States even though the car was imported.[15] Similarly, one type of Barbie doll is manufactured with $0.35 in labor from China, $0.65 in materials from Taiwan, Japan, the United States, and China, $1.00 in overhead and management from Hong Kong. The export value from Hong Kong is $2.00, and, after shipping, ground transportation, marketing, and wholesale and retail profit, the doll is sold in American stores at $9.99.[16] Most of the cost is incurred in the United States.

Such specialization in the production process, which may account for the fact that world trade has grown much more rapidly than world output, is only partly related to the role that multinational firms have played in international trade. Of course, a sizable part of U.S. trade is simply the exchange of goods between affiliated units of a multinational company: in 2000, 30 percent of U.S. exports of goods and 36 percent of U.S. imports of goods were "intrafirm" transactions between affiliated companies.[17] But this share has not changed much since the late 1970s, when the Commerce Department started collecting this data. In fact, the share of U.S. trade accounted for by multinationals has declined significantly. The overall share has been stable only because the intrafirm-share of the multinationals' trade has increased.

Thus, by simply looking at the sheer volume of goods leaving and entering the country, one can say that the United States engages in significantly more international trade today than in the recent or distant past. But the statistics on trade can also be misleading for two reasons:

[15] World Trade Organization 1998, 36.
[16] Tempest 1996.
[17] Zeile 2003b, table 1.

a final good may be produced with inputs that cross national borders multiple times, each time getting recorded as an export or an import, and imports may have a large degree of U.S. content.

_____Why Is Commercial Integration Greater Today?

International trade has increased rapidly during the postwar period, particularly in the last two decades. What accounts for this growth in trade? One simple answer is that the costs previously inhibiting trade, and preventing exchanges from taking place, are now lower than before. These impediments to trade include transportation costs, transactions costs, and government policies.

Although the expansion of international trade in the late nineteenth century was propelled by a significant decline in shipping costs, the postwar period has apparently not experienced a comparable reduction in the costs of moving goods between markets. Yet such costs have remained low and have changed in qualitative ways. Technological innovations have expanded the array of delivery mechanisms. Containerization, bulk shipping, and other innovations have cut loading times and resulted in more efficient transportation. The rise of air transport as a means of moving goods between countries has cut delivery times in ways that have brought an ever-increasing variety of perishable goods (cut flowers from Central America, lobsters from Maine) into world commerce. According to one estimate, each day saved of shipping time is worth 0.5 percent of the value of the products. Trade in intermediate goods is the most time sensitive, and according to one calculation faster methods of transport over the past fifty years have been equivalent to reducing tariffs from 20 percent to 5 percent.[18]

Other transactions costs are harder to quantify, but are lower in potentially important ways. These transactions costs are any expense that must be incurred to bring about exchange. The costs of acquiring information, for example, can limit the extent of market integration. A century ago, before the age of mass communications, obtaining information about distant markets was more difficult than today. Producers are now more likely to have better information about local tastes and demands

[18] Hummels 2000.

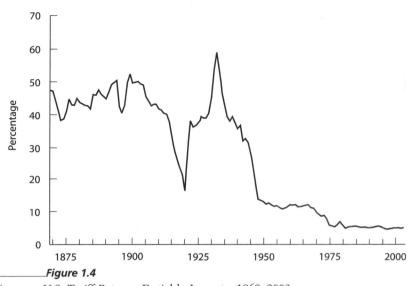

_____Figure 1.4

Average U.S. Tariff Rate on Dutiable Imports, 1869–2003
Note: Calculated as customs revenue divided by dutiable imports.
Source: U.S. Bureau of the Census 1975 and U.S. International Trade Commission's
dataweb (http://www.usitc.gov).

than they did in the past, which makes them able to service demand in those markets more efficiently. In addition, consumers used to have good information only about the attributes of locally produced goods, but now they are likely to be equally well informed about the products of foreign firms.

Trade has also expanded because government trade restrictions have been reduced. Tariffs, import quotas, and exchange controls that originated in the interwar period have been gradually relaxed in the decades after World War II. Average tariffs on manufactured goods dropped from roughly 40 percent to less than 5 percent in most developing countries over the postwar period. In the case of the United States, average tariffs fell sharply during World War II and have continued to fall over the postwar period. Figure 1.4 illustrates that high tariffs were the norm prior to the 1940s, but that taxes on imports have been very low in recent decades.

Furthermore, whole geographic areas, such as western Europe and North America, have abolished customs duties and become free trade areas. Although some nontariff measures have been adopted to protect domestic producers from import competition, it is nonetheless true that, overall, trade barriers have fallen substantially over the postwar period.

Quantifying the precise contribution of these factors in the rapid growth in world trade is difficult. One study finds that about two-thirds of the postwar growth in the trade of countries belonging to the Organization for Economic Cooperation and Development (OECD) is due to income growth, a quarter to tariff reductions, and about 10 percent to transportation cost reductions.[19] This calculation, however, does not take into account production sharing or vertical specialization.

Even though world economic integration has increased rapidly in recent decades, the world remains far from fully integrated. Within-country trade dominates between-country trade by an order of magnitude, suggesting that there is a strong "home bias" in the pattern of trade. The United States is more integrated with the rest of the world than in the recent past, but we are far from the point at which trade between New York and Rio de Janeiro is carried on as easily as trade between New York and Los Angeles. It remains the case that about 85 percent of what the United States consumes is produced in the United States.

One economist has used the following analogy to illustrate how far we are from perfect trade integration: if Americans were just as likely to purchase goods and services from foreign producers as from domestic producers, then the U.S. import-to-GDP ratio should equal the non-U.S. share of world GDP. In other words, the United States would spend as much on foreign products as the average foreign resident, or roughly 75 percent, which is about the non-U.S. share of world GDP. Since the current trade share is about 12 percent, while that hypothetical trade share would be 75 percent, one can conclude that we are only about one-sixth of the way to the point at which "it would literally be true that Americans did business as easily across the globe as across the country."[20]

Empirical models of bilateral trade (the so-called gravity equations) show that there are numerous factors that shape international trade: distance between countries; geographic location; language, currency, and political ties; and so on. In these empirical models, the mere

[19] Baier and Bergstrand 2001.
[20] Frankel 2000.

presence of a national border acts as a powerful impediment to trade. The implication is that even when countries share a common language and a common border, similar institutions and a similar culture, the mere existence of a national border creates a significant bias in favor of intranational trade as opposed to international trade, even if trade barriers are low.[21]

Public Views on Globalization: The Trade Policy Controversy

What are the views of the American public on the "globalization" of the U.S. economy in general and on trade policy in particular? According to an exhaustive survey carried out by the University of Maryland's Program on International Policy Attitudes in 2004, Americans broadly favor global economic integration. A majority of 59 percent believe that the U.S. government should either "actively promote" globalization (19 percent) or "allow it to continue" (40 percent). Yet 38 percent of respondents favored trying to "slow it down" (29 percent) or trying to "stop or reverse it" (9 percent).[22]

When it comes to international trade, however, there is greater skepticism. When asked if the growth of trade is a good thing or a bad thing for the United States, 36 percent say it is positive, 38 percent say it is equally positive and negative, and 23 percent say it is negative. These views have shifted by a few percentage points in the negative direction since 1999. However, support for reciprocal trade liberalization is strong. When asked if the United States should reduce its trade barriers on goods from another country that agrees to lower its trade barriers on U.S. exports, 67 percent of those polled agreed, while 24 percent disagreed, a slightly wider margin of support than in 1999.

When the public is asked about specific trade policy initiatives, however, public support is considerably lower. The public is much more

---

[21] Anderson and van Wincoop (2003) find that the border effect (the difference between intranational and international trade) implies a 45 percent reduction in trade, after controlling for other factors affecting trade, such as size, distance, language, and currency. On the issue of trade costs, see Anderson and van Wincoop 2004.

[22] Kull 2004. This is down slightly from a 1999 PIPA poll in which 61 percent favored promoting or allowing globalization to continue. In that poll, however, 28 percent favored promoting it, while 33 percent favored allowing it to continue.

divided over the North American Free Trade Agreement (NAFTA) and other free trade initiatives than it is over international trade in general. Skepticism about trade initiatives is driven by the perception that businesses benefit more than workers from these trade agreements, leading to an increasing gap between rich and poor in the United States. While those interviewed in the survey were skeptical about using trade barriers to protect workers from foreign competition, they gave overwhelming support to the idea of helping workers adjust to import competition through government programs for education and worker retraining. Only a quarter of those polled believed that government efforts to help displaced workers was adequate, and almost two-thirds thought those efforts are inadequate. When asked whether measures protecting the environment and labor standards should be a part of trade agreements, over 90 percent of respondents answered yes.

In the 1999 poll, these general findings were consistent across almost all demographic and socioeconomic categories.[23] The greatest variation in responses was linked to years of formal education: individuals with at least some college education were much more likely to have positive attitudes about globalization and trade than those with a high school degree only.[24] As we will see in chapter 4, this association could arise because individuals with less education are more likely to be employed in sectors that compete against imports and have greater difficulty becoming reemployed once displaced than those with a higher level of education.

Public opinion polls, therefore, suggest the following dichotomy: there is a willingness to accept increased international trade driven by the anonymous force of technology, but a hesitation to support integration driven by specific policy initiatives. Even though economists have not untangled the precise degree to which recent trade integration has been technology-driven or policy-driven, the public appears to view this distinction as important. This is consistent with the finding that the public appears to care about jobs destroyed because of imports,

---

[23] Political affiliation and region made little difference in the responses. Women were slightly more skeptical of the benefits of free trade and more sensitive to its costs than men; younger people were more positive about globalization and trade than older people; and minorities had a somewhat more positive view of trade than nonminorities. Kull 2000, 61–70.

[24] Scheve and Slaughter 2001a, 2001b.

but not care as much about jobs destroyed due to the invisible hand of technological change.

This divergence, support for trade in the abstract and skepticism about trade policy in the particular, gets to the root of the controversy over free trade. Trade policy has always been contentious, but trade policy has come to involve complex economic, political, and legal factors, making it increasingly difficult to understand. This book aims to examine how these factors affect U.S. trade policy. The appropriate place to begin is the economic case for free trade.

2

The Case for Free Trade: Old Theories, New Evidence

For more than two centuries, economists have pointed out the benefits of free trade and the costs of trade restrictions. As Adam Smith argued more than two centuries ago, "All commerce that is carried on betwixt any two countries must necessarily be advantageous to both," and therefore "all duties, customs, and excise [on imports] should be abolished, and free commerce and liberty of exchange should be allowed with all nations."[1] The economic case for free trade, however, is not based on outdated theories in musty old books. The classic insights into the nature of economic exchange between countries have been refined and updated over the years to retain their relevance to today's circumstances. More importantly, over the past decade economists have gathered extensive empirical evidence that contributes appreciably to our understanding of the advantages of free trade. This chapter reviews the classic theories and examines the new evidence, noting as well the qualifications to the case for free trade.

Specialization and Trade

The traditional case for free trade is based on the gains from specialization and exchange. These gains are easily understood at the level of the individual. Most people do not produce for themselves even a fraction of the goods they consume. Rather, we earn an income by specializing in certain activities and then using our earnings to purchase various goods and services—food, clothing, housing, health care—produced by others.

[1] Smith 1978, 511, 514.

In essence, we "export" the goods and services that we produce with our own labor and "import" the goods and services produced by others that we wish to consume. This division of labor enables us to increase our consumption beyond that which would be possible if we tried to be self-sufficient and produce everything for ourselves. Specialization allows us to enjoy a much higher standard of living than otherwise and gives us access to a greater variety of goods and services.

Trade between nations is simply the international extension of this division of labor. For example, the United States has specialized in the production of aircraft, industrial machinery, and agricultural commodities (particularly corn, soybeans, and wheat). In exchange for exports of these products, the United States purchases, among other things, imports of crude oil, clothing, and iron and steel mill products. Like individuals, countries benefit immensely from this division of labor and enjoy higher real incomes than they would by forgoing such trade. Just as there seems no obvious reason to limit the free exchange of goods within a country without a specific justification, there is no obvious reason why trade between countries should be limited in the absence of a compelling reason for doing so. (Popular arguments for limiting trade will be examined in subsequent chapters to see if they are persuasive.)

Adam Smith, whose magnificent work *The Wealth of Nations* was first published in 1776, set out case for free trade with a persuasive flair that still resonates today. Smith advocated the "obvious and simple system of natural liberty" in which individuals would be free to pursue their own interests, while the government provided the legal framework within which commerce would take place. With the government enforcing a system of justice and providing certain public goods (such as roads, in Smith's view), the private interests of individuals could be turned toward productive activities, namely, meeting the demands of the public as expressed in the marketplace. Smith envisioned a system that would give people the incentive to better themselves through economic activities, where they would create wealth by serving others through market exchange, rather than through political activities, where they might seek to redistribute existing wealth through, for example, legal restraints on competition. Under such a system, the powerful motivating force of self-interest could be channeled toward socially beneficial activities that would serve the general interest rather than socially unproductive activities that might advance the interests of a select few but would come at the expense of society as a whole.[2]

Free trade is an important component of this system of economic liberty. Under a system of natural liberty in which domestic commerce is largely free from restraints on competition, though not necessarily free from government regulation, commerce would also be permitted to operate freely between countries. According to Smith, free trade would increase competition in the home market and curtail the power of domestic firms by checking their ability to exploit consumers through high prices and poor service. Moreover, the country would gain by exchanging exports of goods that are dear on the world market for imports of goods that are cheap on the world market. As Smith put it:

> What is prudence in the conduct of every family can scarce be folly in that of a great kingdom. If a foreign country can supply us with a commodity cheaper than we ourselves can make it, better buy it of them with some part of the produce of our own industry, employed in a way in which we have some advantage. The general industry of the country . . . will not thereby be diminished . . . but only left to find out the way in which it can be employed with the greatest advantage. It is certainly not employed to the greatest advantage, when it is thus directed towards an object which it can buy cheaper than it can make.[3]

Smith believed that the benefits of trade went well beyond this simple arbitrage exchange of what is abundant in the home market for what is abundant in the world market. The wealth of any society depends upon the division of labor. The division of labor, the degree to which individuals specialize in certain tasks, enhances productivity. And productivity, the ability to produce more goods with the same

[2] Rosenberg (1960) provides an excellent discussion of this aspect of Smith's work.

[3] Smith 1976, 457. Free trade made this possible: "The interest of a nation in its commercial relations to foreign nations is, like that of a merchant with regard to the different people with whom he deals, to buy as cheap and to sell as dear as possible. But it will be most likely to buy cheap, when by the most perfect freedom of trade it encourages all nations to bring to it the goods which it has occasion to purchase" (464).

resources, is the basis for rising living standards. But, as he put it, the division of labor is limited by the extent of the market. Smaller, more isolated markets cannot support a high degree of specialization among their workforce and therefore tend to be relatively poor. Free trade enables all countries, but particularly small countries, to extend the effective size of their market. Trade allows such countries to achieve a more refined division of labor, and therefore reap a higher real income, than if international exchange were artificially limited by government policies.[4]

_____Comparative Advantage

In 1799, a successful London stockbroker named David Ricardo came across a copy of *The Wealth of Nations* while on vacation and quickly became engrossed in the book. Ricardo admired Smith's great achievement, but thought that many of the topics deserved further investigation. For example, Smith believed that a country would export goods that it produces most efficiently and import goods that other countries produce most efficiently. In this way, trade is a mutually beneficial way of increasing total world output and thus the consumption of every country. But, Ricardo asked, what if one country was the most efficient at producing everything? Would that country still benefit from trade? Would disadvantaged countries find themselves unable to export anything?

To answer these questions, Ricardo arrived at a brilliant deduction that became known as the theory of comparative advantage.[5] Comparative advantage implies that a country could find it advantageous to import some goods even if it could produce those same goods more efficiently than other countries. Conversely, a country would be able to export some goods even if other countries could produce them more efficiently. In either case, countries stand to benefit from trade. Ricardo's conclusions about the benefits of trade were similar to Smith's, but his approach contains a deeper insight.

[4] For a more complete discussion of Smith's ideas about trade and trade policy, see Irwin (1996a).

[5] For speculation on how Ricardo discovered the theory, see Ruffin (2002).

At first, the principle of comparative advantage seems counterintuitive.[6] Why would a country ever import a good that it could produce more efficiently than another country? Yet comparative advantage is the key to understanding the pattern of international trade. For example, imagine that you were hired to examine the factors explaining international trade in textiles. You might start by examining the efficiency of textile producers in various countries. If one country was found to be more efficient than another in producing textiles, you might conclude that this country would export textiles and other countries would import them. Yet this conclusion could well be wrong because simply comparing the efficiency of production across countries is insufficient for determining the pattern of trade.

According to Ricardo, international trade is not driven by the *absolute* costs of production, but by the *opportunity* costs of production. The country most efficient at producing textiles might be even more efficient than other countries at producing other goods, such as shoes. In that case, the country would be best served by directing its labor to producing shoes, in which its margin of productive advantage is even greater than in textiles. As a result, despite its productivity advantage in textiles, the country would export shoes in exchange for imports of textiles. In the absence of other information, the absolute efficiency of one country's textile producers in comparison to another country's is insufficient to determine whether that country produces all of the textiles it consumes or imports some of them.

To put it differently, a country can obtain textiles either *directly* through domestic production, or *indirectly* by producing something else and exporting it in exchange for imports of textiles. The most efficient way of getting textiles is whichever way yields the country the greatest quantity of such goods at the least cost. So returning to the textile question, one must first recognize that the real choice facing a country is whether it should devote its resources to producing textiles, or to producing other goods that can be exported in exchange for textiles. The

[6] When challenged by a distinguished mathematician to name "one proposition in all of the social sciences which is both true and non-trivial," the Nobel laureate economist Paul Samuelson (1972, 683) famously replied by mentioning the theory of comparative advantage. In a lucid essay, Krugman (1998a) examines why many noneconomists have difficulty grasping the essential logic of comparative advantage.

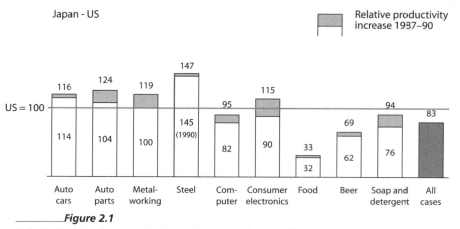

Japan - US

Relative productivity
increase 1987–90

____*Figure 2.1*

Relative Productivity in the United States and Japan, by Industry, 1990
Source: McKinsey Global Institute 1993, exhibit S-1.

efficiency of domestic and foreign textile producers is not the sole determining factor.[7]

    Although the concept of comparative advantage can be counter-
intuitive when applied to countries, individuals base their actions on it
every day. The neighborhood teenager may take three hours to mow
your lawn when you could do it in one, but given the amount you have
to pay the teenager for the chore, you might have a much better way to
spend your time. Without information on alternative activities, your absolute efficiency in this one activity should not determine where you
choose to direct your (scarce) labor time. Yet absolute efficiency is still
frequently discussed as if it alone determines the pattern of international
trade. Domestic steel and textile producers insist that they are the world's
most efficient producers of their products, implying that something must
be wrong or unfair because they are beset by competition from imports.

    Figure 2.1, which compares industry-level productivity in the
United States and Japan in 1990, illustrates the concepts of comparative

    [7] As James Mill, as close friend of Ricardo's, explained: "When a country can ei-
ther import a commodity or produce it at home, it compares the cost of producing at home
with the cost of procuring it from abroad; if the latter cost is less than the first, it imports.
The cost at which a country can import from abroad depends, not upon the cost at which
the foreign country produces the commodity, but upon what the commodity costs which it
sends in exchange, compared with the cost which it must be at to produce the commodity
in question, if it did not import it" (quoted in Irwin 1996a, 91).

and absolute advantage. In comparison with the U.S. industry, Japan has an absolute advantage in producing steel, automobiles, and consumer electronics and an absolute disadvantage in producing computers, soap and detergent, and food. It should come as no surprise that Japan's export success has been greatest in steel, automobiles, and consumer electronics, and weakest in the other goods. But a few decades ago, there was *no* industry in which Japan's productivity exceeded that of the United States. For example, the figure indicates that in 1987 Japan's productivity in metalworking and consumer electronics, where Japan has been a strong exporter for many decades, was less than or equal to that of the United States. Although it lacked an absolute advantage in these goods, Japan still had a strong comparative (i.e., relative) advantage in exporting them in comparison to other goods.

From the standpoint of the domestic industry, the trade patterns dictated by comparative advantage can sometimes seem unfair. Lee Iacocca, the charismatic chief of Chrysler in the 1980s, once admitted that American automakers had fallen behind their Japanese rivals in the past, but proudly proclaimed that the U.S. auto industry had met the competitive challenge and had finally matched the efficiency of Japanese producers. (This claim may stretch the truth, as figure 2.1 shows, but let us accept it for the sake of argument.)

Unfortunately, the theory of comparative advantage indicates that Iacocca has a problem: it may not be enough for an industry that competes with imports merely to match or even to exceed the productive efficiency of foreign producers to overcome that competition and recapture market share. The reason is that Chrysler and other U.S. automakers were not really competing against Japanese automakers as much as they were against other American industries that enjoyed an even greater productive superiority over their counterparts in Japan. U.S. auto producers might be able to match the productive efficiency of Japanese auto producers, but if American farmers and telecommunications equipment producers remain vastly more efficient than their Japanese counterparts, the United States will continue to export agricultural and telecom products to Japan in exchange for imports of automobiles.

It seems wrong that an American industry can be as efficient as, or even more efficient than, any of its foreign competitors in absolute terms and yet fail to export—and even struggle against imports. But comparative advantage tells us that those sectors with the greatest *relative* efficiency advantage will be the ones that export with the greatest success. And the resulting trade will be mutually beneficial for the countries involved.[8]

For developing countries, the theory of comparative advantage is good news as well. Even if a developing country lacks an absolute productive advantage in any field, it will always have a comparative advantage in the production of some goods. Most countries, from Argentina to Zambia, are unable to match the productive efficiency of any U.S. industry, and yet still they are able to export some goods to the United States. Such countries will export goods where their relative disadvantage is least and use those export revenues to improve their standard of living by purchasing other foreign-produced goods, from fuel to capital equipment to medicine. There is no country whose economic circumstances prevent it from engaging in mutually beneficial trade with other countries. (Chapter 6 examines developing countries in more detail.)

What determines a country's comparative advantage? There is no single answer to this question. Sometimes specialization is based on climate or natural resources, sometimes on accumulated skills and capital, sometimes on an abundance of cheap labor, sometimes on government promotion of a particular industry. Some sources of comparative advantage are relatively immutable, while others—based on technology, education, and worker skills—can evolve over time. Entrepreneurship and the business environment can be critical factors. A country could have an ideal climate for producing wine, but unless someone invests in the capital and skills necessary for production, that climatic advantage will remain latent and unexploited. Whatever the underlying reasons, these differences across countries are the primary driving force behind trade.

Critics of free trade sometimes insist that the theory of comparative advantage is obsolete because Ricardo did not consider capital mobility or technology transfer between countries. But modern economists have altered many of the assumptions underlying Ricardo's analysis, and

---

[8] Crude but informative empirical tests of the Ricardian theory of comparative advantage show that it does a reasonably good job of explaining trade patterns. See Golub and Hsieh 2000.

Relative productivity levels, U.S.-Japan

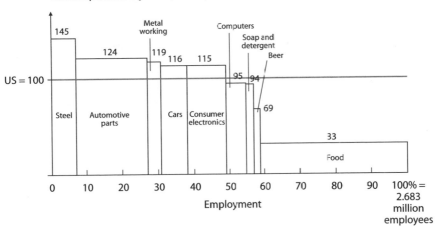

_____*Figure 2.2*
Employment-Weighted Relative Productivity Level, United States and Japan, 1990
Source: McKinsey Global Institute 1993, exhibit S-2.

the main result—that international exchange is mutually advantageous—
remains intact.[9]

Thus, an absolute productive advantage in any good is not required to participate in and reap the benefits of international trade. But
an absolute productive advantage is enormously beneficial for another
reason: it translates into higher per capita income. Even though the productivity of several Japanese manufacturing industries exceeds that of the
United States, per capita income in Japan was only about 80 percent of
that in the United States in 1990. As figure 2.2 indicates, this can be explained by looking at the employment-weighted average of Japanese productivity. Japan's weighted average productivity was only about 80 percent
of that in the United States because it was dragged down by low productivity in the food sector. Food processing employs 11 percent of manufacturing workers in Japan, but their total factor productivity is just 40 percent
of that in the United States.

[9] In fact, the United States is a large free trade area with labor and capital mobility and transferable technology across regions. Yet despite lower wages in the South for
much of the late nineteenth and early twentieth centuries, high-wage regions of the country did not suffer from a "race to the bottom," and the South did not get rich at the expense
of the North, but rather a slow process of convergence to higher incomes occurred across
regions. See McLean and Mitchener 1999.

This low productivity is due to the small scale of Japanese firms in this sector; Japan has six times more food-processing firms per capita than the United States. Insufficient domestic competition in this sector means that there has not been enough pressure to consolidate production and improve efficiency. Trade protection limits competition and encourages this inefficiency. Japan's vegetable oil sector is protected by just a 5 percent tariff, and its level of productivity is 85 percent of the United States', whereas the dairy industry gets protected by a stiff 227 percent tariff and its level of efficiency is less than half of that in the United States.[10] While Japanese steel producers may be vastly more efficient than their American counterparts, that advantage alone does not make Japan a rich country because that sector is a small part of the overall economy. Japan will match U.S. per capita income only when the average productivity of its overall workforce matches that of the United States.

The Gains from Trade

While the idea that all countries can benefit from international trade goes back to Smith and Ricardo, subsequent research has described the gains from trade in much greater detail. In the *Principles of Political Economy* (1848), John Stuart Mill, one of the leading economists of the nineteenth century, pointed to three principal gains from trade. First, there are what Mill called the "direct economical advantages of foreign trade." Second, there are "indirect effects" of trade, "which must be counted as benefits of a high order." Finally, Mill argued that "the economical benefits of commerce are surpassed in importance by those of its effects which are intellectual and moral."[11] What, specifically, are these three advantages of trade?

The "direct economical advantages" of trade are the standard gains that arise from specialization, as described by Smith and Ricardo. By exporting some of its domestically produced goods in exchange for imports, a country engages in mutually advantageous trade that enables it to use its limited productive resources (such as land, labor, and capital)

---

[10] These data are from a 1990 McKinsey study; see "Rotten," *Economist*, August 17, 2000. See also Lewis 2004.

[11] Mill 1909, 580ff.

more efficiently and therefore achieve a higher real national income than it could in the absence of trade. A higher real income translates into an ability to afford more of all goods and services than would be possible without trade.

Economists suspect that these static gains from specialization are sizable. But it is difficult to measure the overall gains from trade because most countries have always been open to world trade in some degree. We usually do not observe countries moving abruptly from situations of no trade to trade, or vice versa, so that we can calculate the benefits of trade. Fortunately, history provides a few examples of such changes that allow us to get a glimpse of the total static gains from trade.

The classic illustration of the direct gains from trade comes from Japan's opening to the world economy. In 1859, as a result of American pressure, Japan opened its ports to international trade after two centuries of self-imposed economic isolation (autarky). The gains from trade can be estimated by examining the prices of goods in Japan before and after the opening of trade. For example, the price of silk and tea was much higher on world markets than in Japan prior to the opening of trade, while the price of cotton and woolen goods was much lower on world markets. With the introduction of trade, prices of those goods in Japan converged to the prices on the world market. As a result, Japan exported silk and tea in exchange for imports of clothing and other goods. According to one calculation, Japan's national income was 4 percent higher as a result of the static reallocation of resources in response to the opportunity to trade.[12] (Of course, the long-run dynamic gains from acquiring better technology and improving its productivity were many multiples of this, and will be discussed shortly.)

The early United States provides another example, this time of a country that was open to trade and then deliberately shut its borders for a short period. In 1807, President Thomas Jefferson ordered an economic embargo to prevent the harassment of American shipping by British and French forces that were engaged in a bitter military conflict. When America's ports were closed to international commerce, the domestic price of imported goods rose 33 percent and the domestic price of exported goods fell 27 percent. The static welfare loss from this

---

[12] Bernhofen and Brown 2004.

embargo was about 5 percent of U.S. GDP. It is little wonder that the embargo was highly unpopular and, as a result, abandoned after just fifteen months.[13]

Today, economists estimate the gains from increased trade as a result of the reduction in trade barriers. Computable general equilibrium models, which are complex computational models used to simulate the impact of various trade policies on specific industries and the overall economy, calculate the gains that arise from shifting resources between various sectors of the economy. Specifically, these models examine the shift of labor and capital away from industries that compete against imports toward those in which the country has a comparative advantage as a result of changes in trade policy.

For example, one study projects that an agreement in the current Doha Round of multilateral trade negotiations to reduce agricultural protection, tariffs on manufactured goods, and service barriers by one-third would yield a $686 billion welfare gain (in 1995 dollars) to the world, or about 2 percent of world GDP. For the United States, the net welfare gain would be $164 billion, or 1.8 percent of its GDP. This gain combines the benefits of reducing U.S. trade barriers and the benefits to the United States of lower foreign trade barriers. Most of the gains to the United States arise from lower barriers to services trade; dropping barriers in that sector alone would generate a $135 billion welfare gain for the United States. Because most tariffs on manufactured goods in developed countries are already quite low, the gains from lower tariffs on such goods would be just $37 billion for the United States.[14]

As these examples indicate, the calculated welfare gains that emerge from these simulations are sometimes small as a percentage of GDP. Even some economists have interpreted these calculations to mean that trade liberalization is not especially valuable. But the small numbers arise partly because these agreements usually lead to modest policy changes for the United States. For example, what the United States undertook in signing the North American Free Trade Agreement (NAFTA) or might undertake as a result of the current multilateral trade negotiations,

[13] Irwin 2001.

[14] Brown, Deardorff, and Stern 2003. Also see Francois, van Meiji, and van Tongeren 2003.

essentially making already low import tariffs somewhat lower, cannot be compared to Japan's move from autarky to free trade or Jefferson's embargo on shipping. These numbers do not reflect the entire gains from trade, just the marginal gains from an additional increase in trade as a consequence of a partial reduction in trade barriers. A complete elimination of global barriers to trade in goods and services would bring much larger gains. According to the study mentioned in the previous paragraph, removing all barriers to world trade would generate $497 billion in gains for the United States (5.5 percent of GDP) and $2,080 billion in gains for the world (6.2 percent of world GDP).

More importantly, the reallocation of resources across industries as calculated in the simulation models does not take into account the other channels by which trade can improve economic performance. What are these other channels? One view is that greater openness to trade allows firms to sell in a potential larger market, and that firms are able to reduce their average costs of production by expanding the size of their output. The lower production costs resulting from these economies of scale are passed on to consumers and thereby generate additional gains from trade. In evaluating the impact of NAFTA through general equilibrium simulations, for example, moving from the assumption of constant returns to scale to increasing returns to scale boosted the calculated U.S. welfare gain from 1.67 percent to 2.55 percent of its GDP, Canadian welfare gain from 4.87 percent to 6.75 percent of its GDP, and Mexican welfare gain from 2.28 percent to 3.29 percent of its GDP, according to one study.[15]

These numbers are more impressive, but there are also reasons to be skeptical. Evidence from both developed and developing economies suggests that economies of scale at the plant level for most manufacturing firms tend to be small relative to the size of the market. As a result, most plants have attained their minimum efficient scale. Average costs seem to be relatively unaffected by changes in output, so that a big increase in a firm's output does not lead to lower costs, and a big reduction in output does not lead to higher costs. For example, many firms are forced to reduce output as a result of competition from imports, but these firms' production costs rarely increase significantly. This suggests

[15] Roland-Holst, Reinhardt, and Schiells 1992.

that the importance of scale economies may be overstated, and yet the simulation models sometimes build in such scale effects.[16]

There is much better, indeed overwhelming, evidence that free trade improves economic performance by increasing competition in the domestic market. This competition diminishes the market power of domestic firms and leads to a more efficient economic outcome. This benefit does not arise because foreign competition changes a domestic firm's costs through changes in the scale of output, as just noted. Rather, it comes through a change in the pricing behavior of imperfectly competitive domestic firms. Firms with market power tend to restrict output and raise prices, thereby harming consumers while increasing their own profits. With international competition, firms cannot get away with such conduct and are forced to behave more competitively. After Turkey's trade liberalization in the mid-1980s, for example, price-cost margins fell for most industries, consistent with a more competitive outcome. In fact, a survey of several studies concludes: "In *every* country studied, relatively high industry-wide exposure to foreign competition is associated with lower [price-cost] margins, and the effect is concentrated in larger plants."[17] Numerous studies confirm this finding in other countries, providing powerful evidence that trade disciplines domestic firms with market power. Yet the beneficial effects of increasing competition are not always taken into account in simulation models discussed above because they frequently assume that perfect competition already exists.

Another problem with the standard estimates of the gains from trade is that they largely overlook the benefits to consumers from exposure to a greater variety of goods. This neglect comes from the traditional emphasis on the easily calculated effects of trade on production, whereas the gains to consumers from choice among a wider variety of goods are more difficult to quantify. (Consumer utility is an amorphous concept, and detailed product-level data are difficult to come by.) Yet the few intriguing attempts to explore this benefit have suggested that it is tremendously important. For example, tariffs may affect not just the amount but

[16] As Tybout and Westbook (1995, 134) argue, "the simulation literature has created a mirage of large potential gains from unexploited scale economies by ignoring plant heterogeneity and, in some cases, by using market structure assumptions that lead to implausible adjustments in plant size." See also Tybout 2000, 2003.

[17] Roberts and Tybout 1996, 196. On Turkey, see Levinsohn 1993.

the range of foreign goods imported. When the selling of a product in a market has a fixed cost, a tariff reduces the size of the market and therefore the potential profits of engaging in trade. Because the smaller size would not allow firms to recoup the fixed costs of selling in that market, some varieties of goods would be excluded from it. In this way, barriers to trade can reduce the range of goods available to an economy and limit the availability of specialized consumer and producer intermediate goods.

When restrictions reduce the number of traded goods, the welfare costs of trade restrictions are much larger than in the standard analysis, where the number of traded goods is assumed to be fixed. The reason is this: if a tariff eliminates imports of a particular variety of good, then all the consumption benefits are lost with no offsetting gains. Although the standard computable models do not account for this loss, we know that variety is highly valued. For example, consider consumers in East Germany and Poland who, after the collapse of Communism, found exotic and affordable fruits such as bananas and oranges in the marketplace for the first time in their lives. Or consider their newfound ability to purchase apples and cabbages without worms and rot. The effect of such changes on aggregate output and income was minuscule, but the welfare gains from the availability of new and improved goods was not insignificant at all.

If a tariff simply reduces the quantity of an imported good, the loss to consumers is a much smaller, second-order loss to overall welfare, because most of what consumers lose is transferred to producers or paid to the government in the form of tariff revenue. If a computable model assumes that a tariff just reduces the quantity of existing goods, when it actually reduces the range of imported goods, the welfare cost is understated—by as much as a factor of ten, according to one calculation.[18] Another study simulated the experience of a small open economy that reduces its import tariff from 20 percent to 10 percent. With constant returns to scale and no product variety, the welfare gain is 0.5 percent of the present value of consumption. With product variety, the welfare gain is about 10 percent of the present value of consumption over the infinite horizon. This is because the tariff reduction induces entry into the

---

[18] See Romer 1994.

production of intermediate goods, and the resulting increase in variety, reduces the cost of intermediates to final goods producers.[19]

These welfare effects need not imply an enormous change in national income: domestic output (measured GDP) may not change much as a result of the tariff. But the cost to consumer welfare is substantial when consumers value the consumption of different varieties of goods. To the extent that economists focus only on trade's effect on production or income, they understate the gains from trade.[20]

Is there systematic evidence that tariffs reduce the range of consumer and intermediate varieties available to an economy? Can we be sure that this reduction in variety is costly to economic welfare? A growing body of evidence suggests that the answer is yes. Trade is responsive to tariff reductions, especially on the variety dimension. After trade barriers are reduced, countries do not simply trade more of the same goods, but rather trade expands most rapidly in goods that were previously not traded or only traded at low levels. In other words, goods on the margin are those that respond most to reduced costs of exchange. The high sensitivity of trade flows to reductions in trade barriers may be due to this factor.[21]

A study of detailed import data from Costa Rica, which liberalized its trade policy in the mid-1980s, found a strong negative relationship between the product-level tariff and the number of countries that Costa Rica imported that product from. A 1 percent increase in the tariff rate resulted in the importation of 0.34 percent fewer varieties of intermediate goods and 0.73 percent fewer varieties of consumer goods. Taking account of the expanded variety of goods made available by trade increased the standard welfare gains from reducing tariffs by 50 percent.[22] By overlooking effects on variety, the standard calculations of

[19] Rutherford and Tarr 2002.

[20] This point was recognized some time ago by the Nobel laureate John Hicks (1969, 56): "The extension of trade does not primarily imply more goods; its main function is not to increase the quantity of goods produced, but to reshuffle them so that they are made more useful. The variety of goods available is increased, with all the widening of life that that entails. This is a gain which 'quantitative economic history,' which works with index numbers of real income, is ill-fitted to measure, or even describe."

[21] Kehoe and Ruhl 2002.

[22] Klenow and Rodríguez-Clare 1997. Since even detailed import data do not reveal product characteristics, they use the number of countries from which Costa Rica purchased specific imports as a proxy for product variety.

gains from trade clearly understate the true advantages of international commerce.

Variety is just as valuable for producers as it is for consumers. Free trade expands the range of intermediate goods available for domestic firms to use as inputs. The availability of different specialized inputs can increase the productive efficiency of the industry that produces the final goods. For example, the use of new inputs by Korean business groups (chaebol) helped to promote total factor productivity growth at the industry level, even after controlling for other factors such as research-and-development expenditures.[23]

Even countries that did not dramatically change their trade policy have, as a result of expanding international trade, experienced welfare benefits as a result of the expansion of variety. For example, over the past three decades, the number of varieties imported by the United States has increased by a factor of four. The number of countries supplying each imported good has doubled. As a result, according to one study, welfare is almost 3 percent of GDP higher over this period simply due to the gains from variety.[24]

_Productivity Gains

Trade improves economic performance not only by allocating a country's resources to their most efficient use, but by making those resources more productive in what they are doing. This is the second of John Stuart Mill's three gains from trade, the one he called "indirect effects." These indirect effects include "the tendency of every extension of the market to improve the processes of production. A country which produces for a larger market than its own can introduce a more extended division of labour, can make greater use of machinery, and is more likely to make inventions and improvements in the processes of production."[25]

In other words, trade promotes productivity growth. The higher is an economy's productivity level, the higher is that country's standard of living. International trade contributes to productivity growth in at least

[23] Feenstra, Markusen, and Zeile 1992.
[24] Broda and Weinstein 2004.
[25] Mill 1909, 581.

two ways: it serves as a conduit for the transfer of foreign technologies that enhance productivity, and it increases competition in a way that stimulates industries to become more efficient and improve their productivity, often by forcing less productive firms out of business and allowing more productive firms to expand. After neglecting them for many decades, economists are finally beginning to study these productivity gains from trade more systematically.

The first channel, trade as a conduit for the transfer of foreign technologies, operates in several ways.[26] One is through the importation of capital goods. Imported capital goods that embody technological advances can greatly enhance an economy's productivity. For example, the South Carolina textile magnate Roger Milliken (an active financier of anti-free-trade political groups) has bought textile machinery from Switzerland and Germany because domestically produced equipment is more costly and less sophisticated.[27] This imported machinery has enabled his firms to increase productivity significantly. Between a quarter and half of growth in U.S. total factor productivity may be attributed to new technology embodied in capital equipment. To the extent that trade barriers raise the price of imported capital goods, countries are hindering their ability to benefit from technologies that could raise productivity. In fact, one study finds that about a quarter of the differences in productivity across countries can be attributed to differences in the price of capital equipment.[28]

Advances in productivity are usually the result of investment in research and development (R&D), and the importation of foreign ideas can be a spur to productivity. Sometimes foreign research can be imported directly. For example, China has long been struggling against a devastating disease known as rice blast, which in the past destroyed millions of tons of rice a year, costing farmers billions of dollars. Under the direction of an international team of scientists, farmers in China's Yunnan province started planting a mixture of two different types of rice in the same paddy. By this simple technique of biodiversity, farmers nearly eliminated rice blast and doubled their yield. Foreign R&D enabled the

[26] Keller 2004.

[27] Lizza 2000.

[28] Eaton and Kortum 2001. Lee (1995) finds that the ratio of imported to domestically produced capital goods is significantly related to growth in per capita income, particularly in developing countries, and Mazumdar (2001) reaches similar conclusions.

Chinese farmers to increase yields of a staple commodity and to abandon the chemical fungicides they had previously used to fight the disease.[29]

At other times, the benefits of foreign R&D are secured by importing goods that embody it. Countries more open to trade gain more from foreign R&D expenditures because trade in goods serves as a conduit for the spillovers of productive knowledge generated by that R&D. Several studies have found that a country's total factor productivity depends not only on its own R&D, but also on how much R&D is conducted in the countries that it trades with. Imports of specialized intermediate goods that embody new technologies, as well as reverse-engineering of such goods, are sources of R&D spillovers. Thus, developing countries, which do not conduct much R&D themselves, can benefit from R&D done elsewhere because trade makes the acquisition of new technology less costly.[30] These examples illustrate Mill's observation that "whatever causes a greater quantity of anything to be produced in the same place, tends to the general increase of the productive powers of the world."

The second channel by which trade contributes to productivity is by forcing domestic industries to become more efficient. We have already seen that trade increases competition in the domestic market, diminishing the market power of any firm and forcing them to behave more competitively. Competition also stimulates firms to improve their efficiency; otherwise they risk going out of business. Over the past decade, study after study has documented this phenomenon. After the Côte d'Ivoire reformed its trade policies in 1985, overall productivity growth tripled, growing four times more rapidly in industries that became less sheltered from foreign competition.[31] Industry productivity in Mexico increased significantly after its trade liberalization in 1985, especially in traded-goods sectors.[32] Detailed studies of Korea's trade liberalization in 1980s, Brazil's during 1988–90, and India's in 1991 reached essentially the same conclusion: trade not only disciplines domestic firms and forces them to behave more like a competitive industry, but helps increase their productivity.[33]

[29] Yoon 2000.
[30] Keller 2002.
[31] Harrison 1994.
[32] Tybout and Westbrook 1995.
[33] Kim 2000; Ferreira and Rossi 2003; Krishna and Mitra 1998; and Sivadasan 2003.

Competition can force individual firms to adopt more efficient production techniques. But international competition also affects the entry and exit decisions of firms in a way that helps raise the aggregate productivity of an industry. In any given industry, productivity is quite heterogeneous among firms: not all firms are equally efficient. Trade promotes high-productivity firms and demotes low-productivity firms. On the export side, exposure to trade allows more productive firms to become exporters and thereby expand their output. In the United States, plants with higher labor productivity within an industry tend to be the plants that export; in other words, more efficient firms are the ones that become exporters.[34] The opportunity to trade, therefore, allows more efficient firms to grow.

On the import side, competition forces the least productive firms to reduce their output or shut down. For example, when Chile began opening up its economy to the world market in the 1970s, exiting plants were, on average, 8 percent less productive than plants that continued to produce. The productivity of plants in industries competing against imports grew 3 to 10 percent more than in non-traded-goods sectors. Protection had insulated less productive firms from foreign competition and allowed them to drag down overall productivity within an industry, whereas open trade weeded out inefficient firms and allowed more efficient firms to expand.[35] Thus, trade brings about certain firm-level adjustments that increase average industry productivity in both export-oriented and import-competing industries.

The impact of the U.S.-Canada Free Trade Agreement on Canadian manufacturing is also suggestive. Tariff reductions helped boost labor productivity by a compounded rate of 0.9 percent per year in manufacturing as a whole and by 1.9 percent per year in the most affected (i.e., high tariff) industries. These are astoundingly large effects. This amounts to a 15 percent increase in productivity in the post-FTA period in the highly affected sectors, and a 5 percent increase for manufacturing overall. These productivity effects were not achieved through scale effects or capital investment, but rather due to a mix of plant turnover

[34] Bernard and Jensen 1999. Clerides, Lach, and Tybout (1998) show that this selection mechanism operates in developing countries (such as Mexico, Columbia, and Morocco) as well. See also Bernard et al. 2003.

[35] Pavcnik 2002.

and rising technical efficiency within plants. By raising productivity, the FTA also helped increase the annual earnings of production workers, particularly in the most protected industries.[36]

To sum up, traditional calculations of the gains from trade stress the benefits of shifting resources from protected industries to those with an international comparative advantage. But new evidence shows that, because large productivity differences exist between plants within any given industry, shifting resources between firms within an industry may be even more important. Trade may affect the allocation of resources among firms within an industry as much as, if not more than, it affects the allocation of resources between different industries. In doing so, trade helps improve productivity.

While difficult to quantify, these productivity effects of trade may be an order of magnitude more important than the standard gains. Countries that have embarked upon the course of trade liberalization over the past few decades, such as Chile, New Zealand, and Spain, have experienced more rapid growth in productivity than previously. Free trade contributes to a process by which a country can adopt better technology and exposes domestic industries to new competition that forces them to improve their productivity. As a consequence, trade helps raise per capita income and economic well-being more generally.

_____Can We Measure the Gains from Trade?

We have seen that trade raises aggregate income through a variety of mechanisms. But can this be empirically verified in studies using cross-country data? Do countries engaging in more trade also have a higher per capita income? This question may seem straightforward, but it is deceptively difficult. Until recently, empirical analysis of the issue was unsatisfactory. The usual approach was to examine the statistical relationship between trade (typically measured by the ratio of exports to GDP) and income across many countries. Although studies usually uncovered a positive correlation between trade and income, the meaning of this result is uncertain. Perhaps countries that trade more have higher incomes, or perhaps countries with higher incomes engage in more trade, because

[35] Trefler 2004.

they have better ports and other infrastructure that support trade or because they have better economic policies in general.

Fortunately, creative research by Jeffrey Frankel and David Romer has overcome this ambiguity. They demonstrated that the reason higher incomes are associated with more trade is not simply because high-income countries trade more.[37] Indeed, they find that the effect of trade on income is strikingly higher once the part of trade that is not driven by income is isolated: the standard estimates suggest that a 1 percent increase in the trade share increases per capita income by about 0.8 percent, but using only geographic determinants of trade raises the estimated effect to about 2 percent (although this is imprecisely estimated). Frankel and Romer find that the effect of trade on income works mainly through higher productivity, but also by increasing the capital stock.[38]

Although differences in trade resulting from policy may not affect income the same way as differences resulting from geography, these results are suggestive for trade policy. One study therefore used dozens of statistical specifications to examine the link between various indicators of a country's trade policy and its per capita income. Almost invariably, more open trade policies are associated with higher per capita income,

---

[37] The fundamental problem is that trade affects income and income affects trade. To isolate the effect of trade on income, a measure of trade that is unrelated to income must be found. Noting that distance from trade partners is a key determinant of trade but is unrelated to income, Frankel and Romer (1999) used a country's geographic attributes to identify the relationship between trade and income. Using a cross-section of countries in 1985, they found that the effect of trade on income is considerably higher in instrumental variables estimation than in an ordinary least squares regression. Irwin and Terviö (2002) confirm that the Frankel-Romer findings are not unique to 1985, but hold in most periods from 1913 to 1990. Rodríguez and Rodrik (2001) suggest that the Frankel-Romer result disappears once one controls for distance from the equator, but other research, such as Hall and Jones (1999), finds that inclusion of latitude does not undermine the positive effect of trade on income.

[38] Trade policies that increase the domestic relative price of imported capital goods can prove harmful to investment and therefore to growth as well (Lee 1995). Tariffs and other trade barriers that raise the domestic price of capital goods mean that each investment dollar buys less capital, reducing the efficiency of investment spending. Levine and Renelt (1992) uncovered an indirect link between trade and growth: the share of investment in GDP is positively correlated with growth in per capita income, and trade is positively correlated with investment. This means that while trade may not be directly correlated with growth, it may stimulate growth indirectly through investment.

although the magnitude and significance of the relationship varied considerably depending upon the indicator used.[39]

In the theories discussed earlier in this chapter, freer trade can be expected to lead to higher level of income or consumer welfare, but not necessarily a higher rate of economic growth. Yet in the transition from a lower to a higher level of income, the growth rate should increase. What sort of growth effect from trade liberalization is plausible? Suppose trade barriers are reduced such that the share of imports in GDP rises from 10 percent to 14 percent. This move to free trade allows the economy to purchase an additional 4 percent of GDP's worth of imports. If we assume that the average surplus gain from these imports is half the export cost, then the real value of consumption rises 2 percent. If the reduction in trade barriers is phased in over a decade, this corresponds to an increase in growth of about 0.2 percent annually.[40]

In this case, the trade policy change would not have a decisive, or even noticeable, impact on the overall rate of economic growth in any given year. But the magnitude of the impact on growth does not need to be large to generate substantial welfare benefits over time. A permanent increase in the steady state growth rate of an economy of just 0.2 percent can yield a welfare gain equivalent to 5 percent increase in the present value of consumption over a long horizon.[41]

What is the empirical link between trade liberalization and economic growth? While several studies have a found positive relationship between lower trade barriers and more rapid economic growth in the postwar period, others have questioned these results.[42] One obstacle that hampers these empirical studies is the absence of a single variable that accurately measures trade policy.[43] The relationship between trade policy

[39] Jones 2001. However, Rodríguez and Rodrik (2001) have countered that reverse causality precludes this conclusion because richer countries generally choose to have lower trade barriers.

[40] I owe this example to Brad DeLong.

[41] Rutherford and Tarr 2002, 268.

[42] Sachs and Warner (1995) are notable for finding that open economies grow faster than closed economies. Rodríguez and Rodrik (2001) have dissected this and other studies and suggest that many results are not robust or do not directly address whether trade barriers are responsible for the observed growth performance.

[43] There is no single metric that ideally describes the stance of a country's trade policy. Import tariffs can be measured imperfectly, but they are not necessarily the most

and economic growth may be hard to pin down in the context of cross-country growth comparisons, partly because trade policy is poorly measured, and partly because the effects of trade policy may be swamped by other factors that are difficult to measure.

One recent study addresses many of the flaws that have plagued previous research. Most previous studies estimated the growth effects of trade liberalization by examining a cross-section of countries, that is, by comparing country X's experience with country Y's. But the difference in these countries' growth rates could be due to a host of reasons that economists cannot adequately control for. Instead, Romain Wacziarg and Karen Welch used a panel of data from 1950 to 1998 to estimate the *within*-country response of per capita income, investment, and trade share to the date of major trade policy changes.[44] After controlling for time-invariant country characteristics, they find that the average within-country growth rate is 1.5 percentage points higher after periods of trade liberalization in comparison to the no-reform period.[45] However, they find considerable heterogeneity in the growth effect—although the average effect is positive and statistically significant, in about half of the countries growth was zero or negative in the postliberalization period. The within-country effect of trade reform on the investment rate is also positive and around 1.5 to 2.0 percentage points.[46] And the ratio of exports and imports to GDP is found to rise about 5 percentage points as a result of trade liberalization.

What should be concluded from this research? While there is no guarantee that trade liberalization will increase the level of income or the rate of economic growth under all circumstances, the repeated finding of a positive relationship between them is more than just coincidence. Despite shortcomings in method and measurement, cross-country and within-country studies support the conclusion that economies with more open trade policies tend to perform better than those with more restrictive

---

important feature of trade policy today. Nontariff barriers can be an even more important impediment to trade in many countries, but they cannot be measured precisely.

[44] Wacziarg and Welch 2003.

[45] They are also able to control for the fact that many reforms are undertaken during periods of economic crisis and therefore growth may rebound after a stabilization that includes trade reform.

[46] See also Wacziarg 2001.

trade policies. Additional, striking evidence comes from individual country experiences. These event studies clearly dramatize the benefits of deregulating imports, and the experience of countries such as China, Chile, South Korea, India, and Vietnam will be considered in chapter 6.

Additional Benefits of Trade

The economic gains from trade are substantial, but they are not the only benefits that come to countries with a policy of open trade. John Stuart Mill's third and final claim was that "the economical advantages of commerce are surpassed in importance by those of its effects which are intellectual and moral."[47] Mill did not elaborate, but he may have been referring to the idea of *doux commerce*, exemplified by Montesquieu's observation in *The Spirit of the Laws* (1748) that "commerce cures destructive prejudices."[48] Trade brings people into contact with one another and, according to this view, breaks down the narrow prejudices that come with insularity. Commerce can also force merchants to be more responsive to customers, as greater competition gives consumers a wider choice. This may be a quality margin on which producers compete for the patronage of consumers.

For example, a study on the effects of McDonald's on Asian culture noted that rest rooms in Hong Kong previously had the reputation for being unspeakably filthy. When McDonald's opened in the mid-1970s, it redefined standards, setting a new, higher benchmark for cleanliness that other restaurants were forced to emulate. In Korea, McDonald's established the practice of lining up on first-come, first-serve basis to purchase food, rather than the rugby scrum that had been the norm. When McDonald's first opened in Moscow, a young woman with a bullhorn stood outside its doors to explain to the crowd that the servers smiled not because they were laughing at customers but because they were happy to serve them. Sanitation, queuing, and friendly service have their

---

[47] "It is hardly possible to overrate the value . . . of placing human beings in contact with persons dissimilar to themselves, and with modes of thought and action unlike those with which they are familiar," Mill continues, because "there is no nation which does not need to borrow from others, not merely particular arts or practices, but essential points of character in which its own type is inferior" (1909, 581).

[48] Montesquieu 1989, 338.

advantages and surely make for more pleasant living, whatever your opinion of McDonald's food.[49]

There is also a long-standing idea that trade promotes peace among nations. Many Enlightenment philosophers in the eighteenth century and classical liberals in the nineteenth century expressed this view. Montesquieu argued that "the natural effect of commerce is to lead to peace" because "two nations that trade with each other become reciprocally dependent." In his essay "Perpetual Peace," Immanuel Kant suggested that durable peace could be built upon the tripod of representative democracy, international organizations, and economic interdependence. A burgeoning political science literature now examines whether economic interdependence mitigates conflict between nations. Most of that work affirms that there is indeed a positive link between trade and peace.[50]

While the link between trade and peace is intriguing, there are also reasons for being skeptical of any attempt to establish a statistical relationship between them.[51] The methodological obstacles include making political concepts operational and representing them numerically, as well as establishing causal relationships. For example, countries that are at peace with one another are also more likely to be trading partners; which is the cause and which is the effect? Countries that are less aggressive are probably more likely to join international institutions, raising the same question. One must avoid reading too much into these findings. After all, on the eve of World War I, Norman Angell proclaimed that, in view of the extensive trade that existed between Germany and Britain and France, economic interdependence had rendered war obsolete.

[49] See Watson 1997. Some globalization critics revile McDonald's for destroying local cuisine and foisting homogeneous, unhealthy, processed food on the public. Yet Watson (1997) points out that McDonald's restaurants located in foreign countries are locally owned and highly attuned to local culture and tastes. One recent survey indicated that nearly half of all Chinese children under the age of twelve identified McDonald's as a domestic brand. See Rosenthal 2002.

[50] Oneal, Russett, and Berbaum (Oneal and Russett 2000; Oneal, Russett, and Berbaum 2003) examine Kant's hypothesis concerning the effect of democracy, trade, and membership in international institutions on the use of military force using a data set that spans country-pairs for the years 1885 to 1992. Barbieri (2002) is critical of the view that trade promotes peace, although much of her argument is that trade does not always promote peace and that the effect of trade on peace is overwhelmed by other factors

[51] See Gates, Knutsen, and Moses 1996.

If the trade-peace link is plausible though uncertain, a stronger finding is that democracies are more peaceful than autocratic countries. While we do not know whether democratic regimes are inherently more peaceful than other types of government, overwhelming evidence shows that democracies rarely go to war against one another. Does increasing trade contribute to peace indirectly, by promoting political reform and democratization? This view of nineteenth-century classical liberals appears to have new support: as Chile, Taiwan, South Korea, and Mexico have been integrated into the world economy, they have also moved toward more democratic political systems. The link between trade liberalization and political liberalization was a contentious issue in the debate over extending Permanent Normalized Trade Relations (PNTR) to China in early 2000. Proponents of normalized trade argued that expanding commerce would enhance the power and influence of the private sector in China at the expense of the government. Opponents disagreed. Those opposed to U.S. economic sanctions against Cuba believe that greater trade with that country would increase the prospects of political reform there too.

Untangling the links between trade and democratization is difficult because each is related to the other. Trade may indeed promote democracy, but democracies are also more likely to pursue open trade policies and therefore trade more.[52] But new work suggests that, after accounting for this effect, trade does indeed promote democracy. Examining the period after 1870, this study detects a positive impact of openness on democracy from about 1895 onward. Late-nineteenth-century globalization may have helped to generate the "first wave" of democratization. Between 1920 and 1938 countries more exposed to international trade were less likely to become authoritarian. These results hold for the post–World War II period as well. However, there is some variation in the impact of openness by region, and commodity exporters and petroleum producers do not seem to become more democratic by exporting more of such goods.[53]

Even if trade fails to generate a movement toward democracy, it can still promote better performance among other domestic institutions. For example, countries that are more open also tend to be less corrupt,

[52] Mansfield, Milner, and Rosendorff (2000) examine this relationship.
[53] Lopez-Cordova and Meissner 2004.

a finding that holds even after accounting for the fact that less corrupt countries may engage in more trade.[54]

While the statistical relationships between trade, peace, and democracy are difficult to sort out, the existing evidence suggests that there are beneficial links between them. In sum, Mill's observations about the noneconomic benefits of trade—such as peace and political reform—appear to be valid.

_____Free Trade and the Environment

Free trade has many critics, among the most vocal of whom are those who worry about its impact on the environment. Some environmentalists believe that freer international trade will lead to more economic activity, and more economic activity will lead to greater environmental degradation. In other words, with trade comes more logging, more fishing, more soil erosion, more industrial pollution, and so on. But what, in fact, is the relationship between trade and the environment? Must trade lead to environmental damage, or might it in some ways actually benefit the environment?

To answer these questions, we must recognize that the link between trade and the environment is indirect. The greatest environmental disasters in recent years have taken place in eastern Europe and the former Soviet Union. The horrible air pollution caused by state-run, coal-burning, capital-intensive industries and the killing of lakes and streams with toxic chemicals owed nothing to free trade but resulted from a system of centralized decision-making that valued resources less wisely than a system of decentralized markets with well-established property rights and prudent government regulation. In other countries as well, trade is not the underlying cause of environmental damage. The burning of the Amazon rain forests is largely motivated by local inhabitants clearing land for their own use, not international trade. And simple observation demonstrates that more trade and commerce does not always create more pollution: air quality in Delhi and Mexico City prior to economic liberalization was much worse than in most

[54] Ades and Di Tella 1999. This finding makes sense for several reasons. Trade restrictions can breed corruption, particularly when bureaucrats are responsible for allocating import licenses among those who wish to import goods.

industrialized countries, even though those cities had fewer cars and generated less electricity.

Environmental damage results from poor environmental policies, not poor trade policies. Environmental damage results from the inappropriate use of our natural resources in the land, sea, and air. The overuse of these resources is commonly related to the lack of well-defined property rights. When property rights are not well established, that is, when no one has ownership rights and control over a resource, then open access to the resource frequently leads to its exploitation beyond the socially optimal level. For example, if ownership of a forest is not well defined, then anyone can chop down trees for his or her own use without paying the costs associated with utilizing the resource.[55] If control of the forest were established through property rights, then the owners would regulate and charge for the use of the timber. Obviously, the ownership and overuse problems are particularly acute for the air and ocean, where government regulation of the right to use the resource, reflecting public ownership of it, may be called for.

In many such cases, because environmental problems stem from the failure to clearly establish and enforce private or public property rights, trade policy is not the first-best means by which to achieve environmental objectives. Trade is only indirectly related to environmental problems, and therefore trade policy is an indirect, inefficient, and often inefficacious way of addressing environmental problems. Fortunately, the objectives of free trade and the environment do not always conflict; in fact, they often work together. Many government policies that are harmful to the environment are also those that international trade negotiators are attempting to limit. Three cases provide an illustration: fisheries, agriculture, and forestry trade.

Ocean fishing is a classic example of a common resource that is overutilized, and yet fishing is a heavily subsidized activity. The Food and Agriculture Organization estimates that world fishing subsidies are on the order of $54 billion annually, nearly 80 percent of the total value of the world's harvested fish.[56] Many of these subsidies have led to

[55] Ferreira (2004) finds that openness to trade alone does not promote deforestation, but that it can do so in countries with poor government institutions that fail to define and protect property rights.

[56] Milazzo 1998.

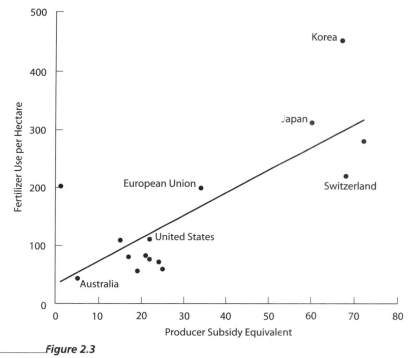

_____*Figure 2.3*
Producer Protection and Fertilizer Use in Agriculture, 2000
Source: Organization for Economic Cooperation and Development 2004,
table III.3, and Food and Agriculture Organization 2002, table 14.

excess capacity in fishing fleets, which in turn promotes overfishing. In this way, such subsidies directly harm efforts to conserve fishing stocks and promote sustainable development. Clearly there is no trade-off in eliminating fishing subsidies and preserving the environment. In fact, the United States, Iceland, Australia, and New Zealand have pressed the membership of the World Trade Organization to discuss an international agreement to limit or abolish fishing subsidies, not just because such subsidies distort trade, but to prevent further depletion of ocean resources.

In the agricultural sector, import restrictions, domestic price supports, and export subsidies are widespread among the industrialized countries. These trade barriers and price subsidies tend to intensify agricultural production in countries that do not have a comparative advantage in such goods. As figure 2.3 indicates, the more a country protects its

[56] Milazzo 1998.

domestic agricultural producers, the more those producers rely on pesticides and fertilizers. Korea, Japan, Switzerland, and, to a lesser extent, the European Union heavily protect agriculture and must rely on chemicals to boost yields because these regions are not particularly well suited for all types of agricultural production.[57] As a result, trade barriers and production subsidies have "intensified land use, increased applications of agrochemicals, [and caused] adoption of intensive animal production practices and overgrazing, degradation of natural resources, loss of natural wildlife habitats and bio diversity, reduced agricultural diversity, and expansion of agricultural production into marginal and ecologically sensitive areas."[58] Countries that have a comparative advantage in agriculture, whether they are industrialized, such as Canada and Australia, or developing, such as Argentina and Brazil, do not depend as heavily on fertilizers and pesticides to maintain output.

Liberalizing trade in agricultural products would therefore benefit the environment by allowing countries with a comparative advantage in agriculture to expand production and forcing countries with a comparative disadvantage to contract output. One economist has noted that "an international relocation of cropping production from high-priced to low-priced countries would reduce substantially, and quickly, the use of chemicals in world food production."[59] In addition, the relocation of meat and milk production from intensive grain-feeding enterprises in densely populated rich countries to pasture-based enterprises in relatively lightly populated poorer countries would reduce the use of growth hormones and medicines for animals.

With regard to forest products, the United States sought without success to eliminate all tariffs on such goods in recent multilateral trade negotiations. Environmental critics have charged that liberalizing trade in forest products will merely accelerate an unsustainable rate of

[57] As Anderson (1998, 74) notes, "land-scarce Western Europe and Japan crop twice as much of their total land area as does the rest of the world on average, so the extent of contamination of their soil, water, and air from the use of farm chemicals is even greater [than figure 2.6 suggests]." Thus, "the relocation of crop production from densely populated protectionist countries to the rest of the world would cause a much larger reduction in degradation in the former compared with any increased degradation in the latter, where chemical use would expand from a low base and to still-modest levels."

[58] Sampson 2000, 55

[59] Anderson 1992, 163.

deforestation around the world. Yet trade in timber and timber products is a minor cause of deforestation in tropical countries. Almost all the annual logging in developing countries is for the domestic production of fuel and charcoal—for the simple reason that fuel and charcoal are the cheapest source of energy for poor people. About 77 percent of forest timber production in Asia, 70 percent in South America, and 89 percent in Africa is for domestic fuel and charcoal.[60] As with all open-access resources, better forestry management is the key to reducing the rate of deforestation.

In fact, not only are policies that reduce trade in forest products ineffective in reducing deforestation, limiting trade in forest products may exacerbate the problem. Without the timber trade, which raises the value of forests by providing external demand for its products, the investment value of these forests would fall. This smaller value would give local users less of an incentive to conserve the resource. In addition, eliminating trade restrictions would directly improve the efficiency of wood use. For example, Indonesia maintains high export taxes on logs to promote domestic forest-based industrialization. These export taxes have generated a large but inefficient domestic lumber industry. Every cubic meter of Indonesian plywood produced requires the cutting of 15 percent more trees than if plywood mills elsewhere in Asia had processed the logs. Indonesia's policy of protecting plywood mills has not only failed to reduce total log demand, but gross operational inefficiencies have also led to a much higher rate of logging than if log exports were allowed.[61] Thus, a ban on imports of raw tropical forest lumber by developed countries would not only fail to counter the underlying cause of deforestation, but might accelerate it due to the inefficiency of local processors.

Finally, there is the issue of whether free trade exacerbates industrial pollution. Once again, trade itself is not a direct cause of pollution, so one must examine the indirect links. Numerous studies have traced the relationship between pollution emissions and a country's per capita income. They have generally found a relationship shaped like an inverted U: as per capita incomes rise from low levels, pollution increases,

[60] World Resources Institute 1999, table 11.3.
[61] Barbier et al. 1995, 419.

but beyond a certain point, further increases in income tend to diminish pollution. The initial increase in pollution is due to industrialization, while the decrease is due to more effective environmental regulation and cleaner production technologies that come with higher incomes. Both Delhi and New York City have traffic jams, for example, but the locally made cars and scooters in developing countries tend to belch out worse fumes than the cleaner exhaust systems in the United States.

A recent study examined three channels by which trade can affect sulfur dioxide (SO_2) emissions: the scale effect (increases in economic activity increase SO_2 emissions), the technique effect (increases in income lead to cleaner production methods and reduce emissions), and the composition effect (trade alters the composition of activity and hence the average pollution intensity of national output). The authors were surprised to conclude that free trade is good for the environment because, as an empirical matter, the technique effect outweighs the scale and composition effects.[62] The effect of income growth on pollution depends largely on the underlying source of growth: growth achieved through capital accumulation tends to raise pollutants, while growth achieved by trade and technological change appears to reduce pollutants. This could also account for the inverted-U-shaped relationship of pollution to income— developing countries tend to achieve growth through (dirtier) capital accumulation, whereas growth in developed countries is based on human capital accumulation and technology (cleaner methods).

Controversy about the environmental impact of free trade was particularly intense during the debate over NAFTA in 1993. There are several reasons to expect that, with time, NAFTA will lead to environmental improvements. One study found that pollutant emissions increase until per capita income reaches about five thousand dollars and diminish thereafter. Because Mexico is near that watershed, NAFTA will improve the environment if it increases Mexico's income.[63] Because Mexico has a comparative advantage in unskilled labor-intensive goods rather than in capital-intensive goods, freer trade may force dirtier capital-intensive

---

[62] Antweiler, Copeland, and Taylor 2001. Their empirical estimates of the scale effect indicate that a 1 percent increase in the scale of economic activity increases SO_2 emissions by 0.3 percent, but that the technique effect suggests that a 1 percent increase in income decreases emissions by 1.4 percent.

[63] Grossman and Krueger 1993.

industries in Mexico to contract as a result of competition. With protective tariffs eliminated, these industries are forced to shut down or adopt better technology to stay in business. Furthermore, the "dirty industry migration" hypothesis, that polluting industries will migrate to developing countries where environmental regulations are lax, has received no empirical support. There is no "race to the bottom" in environmental standards because the costs of abating pollution are not a significant determinant of industries' location, and consequently not a significant determinant of trade flows.[64]

The mainstream environmental community recognizes that free trade and the environment can go hand in hand. For example, once the environmental side agreements to NAFTA were negotiated, environmental groups that represented approximately 80 percent of the membership of the entire environmental community agreed to support the agreement.[65] Other more militant organizations, such as the Sierra Club, Friends of the Earth, Greenpeace, and Public Citizen, continued to oppose NAFTA. But these groups generally oppose any growth-oriented trade policy, regardless of its environmental provisions. Steward Hudson of the National Wildlife Foundation testified before Congress that "a fair and objective reading of the NAFTA leaves you with one uncompromising conclusion: the environment is far better off with this NAFTA than without . . . those who want to kill NAFTA are hiding behind the environment. The environmental critics of NAFTA, those who would forever be holding out for more, even at the expense of making progress on the environment in dealing with problems that concern all of us, are out to kill trade. . . . No amount of fine tuning or renegotiation will satisfy these opponents of NAFTA. The bar will continue to be raised because the goal is to kill NAFTA."[66]

[64] See Jaffe et al. 1995 and Kahn 2000.

[55] These groups included the World Wildlife Fund, the National Wildlife Federation, the Environmental Defense Fund, the National Audubon Society, and others (Audley 1997, 90).

[56] U.S. House of Representatives 1994, 368–70. In the end, the major congressional critics of NAFTA, such as Richard Gephardt, David Bonior, and Marcy Kaptur, made no reference to the environment in their floor speeches against the agreement, but rather focused on job loss in the United States (Audley 1997, 106). The more extreme opponents of NAFTA were prone to exaggeration and hyperbole. The Sierra Club, for instance, said that NAFTA would be "a major step toward ending democracy" in America.

This evidence should not be taken as minimizing the importance of taking effective measures to improve the environment. But free trade and a cleaner environment are not incompatible. Because trade in itself is not a driving force behind pollution, a policy of free trade rarely detracts from such goals, and in many instances may help. (The link between world trade rules and environmental regulation is also considered in chapter 7.)

Free Trade in Perspective

The benefits of free trade appear to be substantial, although precise quantification of those benefits is sometimes difficult. In extreme cases, governments that force their citizens to forgo the advantages of international trade, particularly in developing countries (as discussed in chapter 6), do not sacrifice just a couple of percentage points of national income, but risk impoverishing their people. The higher real income that comes with trade is valuable not just to allow the consumption of more goods for crass material reasons, but to help people afford food and medicine. With free trade comes higher income, which gives people access to better health care, better education, and better technologies that will help improve the environment. Regrettably, the United States imposes stiff import barriers on agricultural products and labor-intensive manufactured goods, such as clothing and leather, in which developing countries have a comparative advantage. This not only harms consumers in the United States, but reduces income in developing countries as well.

But several caveats should be offered. Free trade is beneficial because it allows a country to take advantage of the opportunity to trade, but it is not the only—or even the most important—determinant of whether a country's achieves economic prosperity. Free trade is not a "magic bullet" that can solve all economic problems. The real and substantial gains from free trade should not be exaggerated when other fundamental economic problems are pressing. Stable macroeconomic policies, the rule of law, and the protection of property rights that enable the market mechanism to function properly are preconditions for reaping the full benefits of international trade.[67] As Thomas Macaulay stated

---

[67] According to Adam Smith, "Commerce and manufactures can seldom flourish long in any state which does not enjoy a regular administration of justice, in which the people do not feel themselves secure in the possession of their property, in which the faith of

back in 1845, "It is not one single cause that makes nations either prosperous or miserable. No friend of free trade is such an idiot as to say that free trade is the only valuable thing in the world; that religion, government, police, education, the administration of justice, public expenditure, foreign relations, have nothing whatever to do with the well-being of nations."[68]

At the same time, restricting trade entails real economic costs. These losses may appear to be abstractions, but they are in fact harm for real individuals. And yet many protectionist policies are maintained, and new ones are always being proposed. This is because most trade restraints have a superficially plausible justification. These rationales are often more apparent than real, however, and the next two chapters will address them.

---

contracts is not supported by law, and in which the authority of the state is not supposed to be regularly employed in enforcing the payments of debts from all those who are able to pay. Commerce and manufactures, in short, can seldom flourish in any state in which there is not a certain degree of confidence in the justice of the government" (1976, 910).

[68] Macaulay 1900, 89.

3

Protectionism: Economic Costs, Political Benefits?

Economic analysis has long established free trade as a desirable economic policy. This conclusion has been reinforced by mounting empirical evidence on the benefits of free trade, and yet protectionism is far from vanquished in the policy arena. Of course, this is nothing new: as Adam Smith observed more than two hundred years ago, "not only the prejudices of the public, but what is much more unconquerable, the private interests of many individuals, irresistibly oppose" free trade.[1] Indeed, interest groups opposed to free trade often have a political influence that is disproportionate to their economic size. This chapter describes the economic costs of trade restrictions and examines why, despite these costs, protectionism is often a seductive and politically attractive policy. The chapter concludes by considering instances in which trade protection might actually be beneficial.

The Costs of Tariffs and Quotas

In the *Wealth of Nations*, Adam Smith not only developed a powerful case for free trade, but he also issued a scathing attack on contemporary mercantilist policies that restricted trade. The ostensible purpose of these government policies was to promote national wealth, but Smith argued that such policies were ill-conceived and detracted from that objective. Smith observed that policymakers too frequently equated the interests of producers with the interests of the nation as a whole. Under mercantilism, almost any policy that helped existing producers expand output,

[1] Smith 1976, 471.

such as limits on imports or restrictions on competition, was deemed beneficial. But Smith pointed out that this approach confused the means with the end:

> Consumption is the sole end and purpose of all production; and the interest of the producer ought to be attended to only so far as it may be necessary for promoting that of the consumer. The maxim is so perfectly self-evident that it would be absurd to attempt to prove it. But in the mercantile system the interest of the consumer is almost constantly sacrificed to that of the producer; and it seems to consider production, and not consumption, as the ultimate end and object of all industry and commerce.[2]

Furthermore, Smith argued that policies such as trade barriers would not expand total output but merely divert resources to less productive uses. As he put it, "No regulation of commerce can increase the quantity of industry in any society beyond what its capital can maintain. It can only divert part of it into a direction into which it might not otherwise have gone; and it is by no means certain that this artificial direction is likely to be more advantageous to the society than that into which it would have gone of its own accord."[3]

While governments often justified trade restrictions as serving the public interest, Smith noted that such restrictions did not benefit the public as much as they served the private interests of influential merchants who had captured government policy for their own advantage. In fact, he believed that trade restrictions "may . . . be demonstrated to be in every case a complete piece of dupery, by which the interests of the State and the nation is constantly sacrificed to that of some particular class of traders."[4]

> In every country it always is and must be the interest of the great body of the people to buy whatever they want of those who sell it cheapest. The proposition is so very manifest that it seems ridiculous to take any pains to prove it; nor could it ever

[2] Smith 1976, 660.
[3] Smith 1976, 453.
[4] Smith 1977, 272.

have been called in question had not the interested sophistry of merchants and manufacturers confounded the common sense of mankind. Their interest is, in this respect, directly opposite to that of the great body of the people. As it is the interest of the freemen of a corporation to hinder the rest of the inhabitants from employing any workmen but themselves, so it is the interest of the merchants and manufacturers of every country to secure to themselves the monopoly of the home market.[5]

Policies that give preferential treatment to domestic producers in the home market still exist today. For example, in rebuilding the San Francisco–Oakland Bay Bridge, the California transit authority is finding it difficult to hold down costs. "Buy America" rules, which give preference to domestic producers in government procurement contracts, dictate that foreign steel can be used only if it is more than 25 percent cheaper than domestic steel. A domestic bid came in at 23 percent above the foreign bid, and so the more expensive domestic steel had to be used. Because of the large amount of steel used in the construction project, this preference means that California taxpayers must pay a whopping $400 million more for the bridge.[6] While this requirement may be good for domestic steel firms, it is hard to see the benefit to California taxpayers, who might wish to devote the nearly half a billion dollars to other uses, such as schools or health care, or even fiscal deficit reduction.

Despite the gradual decline in trade barriers over the past half century, the array of protectionist policies around the world is still quite large. The principal means of blocking trade is through tariffs (taxes) and quotas (quantitative restrictions) on imports. These policies reduce trade and distort economic activity, leading to inefficient outcomes. Their effects can be separated into two parts.

---

[5] Smith 1976, 493–94. "That this monopoly of the home-market frequently gives great encouragement to that particular species of industry which enjoys it, and frequently turns towards that employment a greater share of both the labour and stock of the society than would otherwise have gone to it, cannot be doubted. But whether it tends either to increase the general industry of the society, or to give it the most advantageous direction, is not, perhaps, altogether so evident." Smith 1976, 453.

[6] Renaud 2004.

First, import barriers redistribute income from domestic consumers to domestic producers. When imports of a product are restricted, it becomes more scarce in the domestic market. Scarcity drives up the price, benefiting domestic producers of the product because consumers are forced to pay more for it. This redistribution is often hard to justify. For example, because of restrictions on imports, the U.S. price of sugar is roughly twice that on the world market. Domestic sugar producers reap about $1 billion annually as a result of this policy. However, 42 percent of the total benefits to sugar growers goes to just 1 percent of all farms.[7] The rationale for rewarding a few large sugar producers with hundreds of millions of dollars every year at the expense of consumers has never been made clear.

Second, and even worse, protectionist policies distort prices and therefore economic incentives. This distortion leads to wasted resources, known as a deadweight loss. As import restrictions push the domestic price of a good above the world price, domestic firms produce more, while consumers reduce their overall purchases and suffer a real income loss as a result of the higher prices. The inefficiency associated with these distortions of incentives imposes a deadweight loss on the overall economy. The income transfer from consumers to producers is therefore akin to taking ten dollars from one group while giving only eight dollars to another, resulting in a two-dollar loss to the economy as a whole. The sugar policy benefited producers of sugar to the tune of $1 billion, but it imposed far greater costs—about $1.9 billion, according to the General Accounting Office—on consumers. The result is a net (or deadweight) loss to the economy of $900 million.

Economists make rough estimates of the income transfers and the deadweight losses associated with trade barriers. The U.S. International Trade Commission (ITC) calculated that the net cost—that is, the deadweight loss—of existing U.S. trade barriers was about $16.4 billion in 2002.[8] (The overall costs to consumers, and transfers to producers, of course, is much larger than this figure.) Elimination of these barriers would increase U.S. imports by 2 percent (or $28 billion).

---

[7] U.S. General Accounting Office 2000a; 1993, 32–33. See also Beghin et al. 2003.
[8] U.S. International Trade Commission 2004, 120. This figure excludes the cost of antidumping duties, which will be considered in chapter 5.

In comparison with most other countries, U.S. import restrictions are relatively modest, and the U.S. market is generally quite open to international trade. In 2002, the average U.S. tariff was just 1.6 percent, whereas the world average tariff on agricultural products was 17 percent and on industrial products 9 percent.[9] Yet the low average tariff belies significant trade barriers in certain product categories, including textiles and apparel, footwear and leather, and agriculture, as well as antidumping duties (to be discussed in chapter 5). The United States essentially has a two-tiered tariff system: average tariffs of 10.5 percent on light consumer goods (clothes, shoes, suitcases) and 0.8 percent on everything else. For example, clothes and shoes account for less than 7 percent of all imports yet bring in nearly half of all tariff revenue.[10]

Indeed, U.S. import restrictions on textiles and apparel were by far the most costly of all sectoral measures in 2002, accounting for $12 billion of the $16 billion deadweight loss due to import barriers as calculated by the ITC. This is due to something called the Multi-Fiber Arrangement (MFA), the biggest piece of protectionist cholesterol blocking the arteries of world trade until its demise in January 2005. The MFA restricted imports of foreign textiles and apparel through a complex maze of country- and product-specific quotas. Under the MFA, the United States maintained more than three thousand separate quotas on imports from more than forty nations. The narrowly defined quotas include cotton diapers from China, men's and boys' cotton coats from Sri Lanka, women's and girls' wool coats from Czech Republic, women's bras from Mexico, men's trousers from Guatemala, women's and girls' man-made-fiber woven blouses from the United Arab Emirates, and so on. In 1989, the Treasury Department's Customs Service prohibited the import of thirty thousand tennis shoes from Indonesia because the boxes contained an extra pair of shoelaces, which, it was decided, fell in a separate import quota category.[11]

---

[9] U.S. International Trade Commission 2004, 79. Developing countries tend to maintain more extensive barriers to trade, as will be seen in chapter 6.

[10] Gresser 2002.

[11] Customs later decided that an extra pair of shoelaces would be permitted so long as they were laced into the shoes and color-coordinated with the shoes (Bovard 1991, 45). See also Faini, de Melo, and Takacs 1995.

The result has been severely distorted trade and significantly higher prices of clothing for U.S. consumers.[12] The combined effect of tariffs and quotas raised domestic prices of apparel by 18 to 24 percent and prices of finished textile products by about 14 percent in 2002.[13] Indeed, according to virtually every study on the matter, the economic benefits to the United States from eliminating the MFA are enormous. The direct consumer cost of this protection amounts to $24.4 billion in 1990, a burden of over $260 per household.[14] The tax is generally believed to be quite regressive, because lower-income households devote a greater share of their expenditures to clothing than those with higher incomes.

Under the Uruguay Round trade agreement of 1994, the United States and other countries vowed to abolish the MFA in January 2005. Like most trade reforms, the trade barriers are phased out over time. Unfortunately, the phaseout is "back-end loaded," meaning that most of the reforms take place late in the transition period. (This is akin to a diet plan that calls for losing twenty pounds over twelve months: none in the first ten months and then ten pounds in each of the last two months.) The United States was supposed to implement about half of the liberalization in the last three years of the ten-year transition period. But provisions in the MFA phaseout allow the deferment of these plans for the most sensitive import sectors. As a result, nearly 90 percent of apparel imports and 47 percent of textile imports were due for liberalization in January 2005.[15] As a result, the domestic textile and apparel industries lobbied strongly but unsuccessfully for postponing the MFA expiration. The abolition of the MFA in January 2005 eliminated the country quotas, but not the existing high tariffs, or the ability of import-competing firms to seek antidumping duties on imports (see chapter 5).

The high costs of the MFA illustrate an important difference between an import tariff and an import quota. When the United States imposes a tax on imports, the government collects as tariff revenue the

---

[12] The restrictiveness of the MFA varies considerably across commodity products, ranging from 7 to 12 percent for apparel overall, 12 to 28 percent for women's and girls' cotton knit shirts, 44 to 47 percent for cotton bed sheets, etc. U.S. International Trade Commission 2004, 70.

[13] U.S. International Trade Commission 2004, 71.

[14] Hufbauer and Elliott 1994.

[15] U.S. International Trade Commission 2004, 61.

difference between the world price and the higher, tariff-inclusive domestic price charged to consumers. But when a country limits the quantity of imports with a quota, the difference between the world price and the higher domestic price becomes a scarcity rent rather than tariff revenue. This scarcity (or quota) rent is captured by foreign exporters as a markup if they have obtained the right to export a certain amount under the quota in the import-restricting market, where they get to charge a higher price than on the world market.

The transfer of quota rents is a national loss because money is taken from consumers and handed to foreign exporters (in the form of a higher markup) instead of the government (in the form of tax revenue), as would have happened if a tariff had been imposed. According to most studies, almost all of the roughly $12 billion net cost to the United States of the MFA was due to the transfer of quota rents to foreign exporters and very little due to domestic deadweight efficiency losses. The transfer of quota rents also distorts the incentives of the exporters, particularly in developing countries. When the United States imposes an import quota, foreign governments are usually responsible for determining which exporters will be allowed to sell in the U.S. market (and thus receive the quota rent) and which exporters will be prohibited from exporting. The allocation of quota rights, except when those rights are auctioned off, is inherently arbitrary and increases the power of government bureaucrats, thereby fostering corruption. The politically well-connected firms, who perhaps are not averse to sharing the quota rents with the bureaucrats, are most likely to obtain export licenses, whereas other firms are shut out. This gives entrepreneurs in developing countries the wrong signal: the way to get rich is to invest in political influence, not to invest in productive efficiency.

As the MFA example indicates, the quota rents can be extremely valuable. In other cases, the quota rent received by foreign producers helps them compete against American firms. For example, when the United States limited the quantity of Japanese black-and-white televisions sold in the U.S. market in the early 1970s, the quota rent transfer is said to have given Japanese producers the financial resources to enter the market for color televisions and videocassette recorders more quickly. When the United States persuaded Japan to limit its automobile exports in 1981, Japan's auto exporters were able to raise the average price of their cars by about one thousand dollars, part of which they invested in product improvements that enabled them to compete even more effectively against their American rivals.[16]

Another example comes from the mid-1980s, when the United States forced Japan to maintain high minimum prices on its semiconductor exports. Some of Japan's electronics producers were pleased that the American government, acting to help domestic semiconductor producers, was also helping them raise their prices in the U.S. market. Japan's exporters reaped billions of dollars in higher profits as a result. According to one account, Japanese companies producing one-megabyte dynamic random access memories (DRAMs) made an additional $1.2 billion in profits in 1988 because of the U.S. trade intervention.[17]

As these examples suggest, the textiles and apparel industry is not the only sector of the U.S. economy that has been protected by special import barriers at one point or another. As already noted, the United States assists the domestic sugar industry through price supports and import restrictions in the form of a tariff-rate quota. Under a tariff-rate quota, sugar-exporting countries are given a certain (small) quantity that they can bring into the United States at the regular tariff rate, and any exports beyond that specified quantity are subject to a tariff rate of nearly 150 percent. As already noted, the sugar import restrictions and price supports cost domestic users of sweeteners $1.9 billion in 1998. Domestic sugar beet and sugarcane producers reaped $1 billion as a result of these policies, with most of the benefit accruing to sugar beet growers. The net loss to the economy is $900 million annually, $500 million due to economic inefficiency bred by the policy and $400 million in the transfer of quota rents to foreign exporters.

The United States maintains other protectionist policies. High tariffs and tariff-rate quotas impede trade in dairy products, tobacco, beef, tuna, and peanuts, while average tariffs are quite high for footwear and leather goods. The steel industry, among others, has succeeded in getting high antidumping duties imposed on imports. According to an estimate discussed in chapter 5, the welfare cost of antidumping tariffs amounted to $4 billion in 1993. The Jones Act restricts trade in maritime

[16] Feenstra 1984.
[17] Flamm 1996, 277.

services and cargo shipments within the United States and is estimated to have a welfare cost of $656 million in 1999.[18] A 1996 softwood lumber agreement between the United States and Canada imposed high duties on any imports of Canadian lumber above a certain threshold and, according to one study, raised the average cost of a new home by eight hundred to thirteen hundred dollars, thus pricing some three hundred thousand families out of the housing market.[19] After the agreement expired early in 2001, the lumber industry accused Canadian firms of dumping their products in the U.S. market. After finding the domestic industry was "threatened" with material injury, the government imposed tariffs of 10 to 20 percent on Canadian lumber once again.

Yet simply documenting the economic costs of protection often has a limited impact on policy. One reason could be that the calculated welfare gains from additional trade liberalization are quite small as a share of GDP. The International Trade Commission's estimate of $16.4 billion in gains from unilaterally removing U.S. import restraints in 2002, for example, amounts to only 0.15 percent of that year's GDP. This is almost a trivial sum—it is equivalent to an extra $75 pay for a worker who earns $50,000 a year—even though it is an annual gain that accrues in perpetuity. In other countries, particularly many developing countries, trade barriers are much more pervasive and restrictive, and therefore the potential gains from liberalization are much more substantial.[20]

But as we already know from chapter 2, such estimates understate the true costs of trade barriers. These estimates fail to consider the productivity and variety benefits of trade. The estimates are also understated because they do not take into account the resources devoted to political pressure. Expenditures on campaign contributions and lawyer fees may generate private benefits for those making the expenditures, but they can be socially unproductive because they aim at redistributing wealth rather than creating it.

---

[18] U.S. International Trade Commission 2004.

[19] Lindsey, Groombridge, and Loungani 2000.

[20] Messerlin (2001) reports that the costs of protection in the European Union are equivalent to about 6 to 7 percent of the EU's GDP, or about the same as the annual value of output in Spain. The net cost of trade protection in Japan (circa 1989) has been estimated to be anywhere from $8 billion to $17 billion, according to Sazanami, Urata, and Kawai (1995).

Indeed, the impact of trade barriers can be significantly understated if the political determinants of those barriers are not taken into account. A standard statistical method of gauging the effect of trade restraints on imports is to examine the determinants of import demand, such as the relative price of imports, domestic income, and other explanatory variables. To the extent that trade restrictions increase the price of imports, the detrimental effect on the volume of trade can be calculated. But this approach ignores the simultaneity of imports and protection: higher tariffs may reduce imports, but more imports also lead to greater political pressure for higher tariffs. This confounds any attempt to isolate the effect of tariffs on imports and, unless corrected for, leads one to understate the effect of tariffs on imports. When one economist confronted this problem by examining the political-economic determinants of trade barriers in the United States and using the results to help explain imports, the statistical coefficient representing the negative impact of non-tariff barriers (such as quantitative restrictions) on imports was increased by a factor of ten. The conventional estimate suggests that removing non-tariff barriers would increase manufactured imports by $5.5 billion (in 1985), whereas after controlling for the political determinants of those barriers, the impact was estimated to be closer to $50 billion.[21]

Even when we can accurately state the welfare costs of trade barriers, the resulting numbers have a surreal magnitude that makes them hard to fathom. It is questionable whether these welfare costs have much political significance: if the welfare losses were to double or triple, would that make any difference to policy? Perhaps not, but the seamier details of the protectionist racket are rarely exposed and might create more of a stir.

The sugar program is a classic example. Sugar imports are restricted to maintain domestic price supports for sugar beet and cane producers. The benefits of these restrictions are highly concentrated because Congress has not limited the amount of support that large firms can receive. For example, one farm received over $30 million in benefits from the sugar program in 1991, and just 0.2 percent of all sugarcane farms—thirty-three in total—received 34 percent of the entire program benefits.[22] The family of Alfonso Fanjul single-handedly supplies the

[21] Trefler 1993.
[22] U.S. General Accounting Office 1993.

United States with about 15 percent of its sugarcane through its land holdings in south Florida and the Dominican Republic, collecting somewhere between $52 to $90 million in benefits from the price supports on U.S. production and the quota rents on Dominican sugar exports.[23] Not surprisingly, the Fanjul family could afford to make nearly three hundred thousand dollars in campaign contributions in 1988.[24] At the same time, the Fanjul farms were being investigated for chronic violation of U.S. labor laws. Government support for the sugar industry has also harmed the environment because chemical runoff from the intensive farming of sugarcane in south Florida has seeped into the Everglades.

The sugar program is not just an economic, political, and environmental inequity, but it prevents desperately poor sugar-producing countries from exporting to the United States. Countries such as Colombia and Guatemala are deprived of valuable foreign exchange earnings that could be spent on food, fuel, and medicine. Congressional opponents of the sugar policy have suggested that Andean farmers, prevented from selling their sugar in major markets such as the United States, have turned their cropland toward the production of coca used in cocaine production and other illegal drugs. The Caribbean and Latin American farmers who find themselves cut out of the American sugar market may be forced to turn to illegal crops as a way to make a living.

When examined up close, trade policy is not a pretty sight. Steel industry lobbyists, for example, have induced members of Congress to change U.S. trade laws for the specific benefit of their industry, which has received pension bailouts, loan guarantees, environmental exemptions, decades of trade restrictions—and continues to press for more. When powerful industries push politicians to intervene on their behalf, the picture is often an ugly one.

So far we have examined the direct costs of import barriers. But the indirect effects of import barriers are also important, though not always readily apparent. The indirect consequences of import restrictions include a reduction in exports and lower employment in downstream industries, and we consider each in turn.

[23] Mayer and de Cordoba 1991.

[24] Alfonso Fanjul is so politically powerful that President Bill Clinton interrupted a "meeting" with Monica Lewinsky to take a phone call from him. This is according to Lewinsky's testimony as presented in the Kenneth Starr report.

_____*Import Barriers Harm Exports*

Imagine taking a poll of Americans and asking: "Should the United States impose tariffs on foreign goods to prevent imports from low-wage countries from harming American workers?" A sizable fraction of the respondents would probably answer "yes." If asked to explain their position, they would probably reply that import tariffs would create jobs for Americans and thereby reduce unemployment. (The validity of this opinion will be examined in chapter 4.)

Then suppose you asked the same people: "Should the United States levy an export tax on domestically produced goods such as aircraft, grains, machinery, software, and the like?" The answer would probably be a resounding and unanimous "no!" After all, they would argue, export taxes would destroy jobs and harm important industries.[25]

Yet according to an important proposition known as the Lerner symmetry theorem, these two policies are equivalent in their economic effects.[26] The Lerner symmetry theorem holds that a tax on imports is functionally equivalent to a tax on exports. In other words, any restriction on imports also operates as a restriction on exports. This theorem helps us understand another aspect of import tariffs—how they destroy jobs in export industries.

Some participants in the debate on trade tend to believe that a country's exports and imports are independent of one another, and therefore one can reduce imports without having an adverse effect on exports. In fact, exports and imports are the flip side of the same coin. Exports are the goods a country must give up in order to acquire imports. Exports are necessary to generate the earnings to pay for imports. The past century illustrates the close relationship between exports and imports in the United States. Looking back at figure 1.1, which plots U.S. merchandise exports and imports as a percentage of GDP from 1869 to

[25] In addition to being unconstitutional under Article 1, section 9 of the Constitution.

[26] The theorem is named after Abba Lerner, who published a short but brilliant paper on the subject as a graduate student at the London School of Economics in 1936. Lerner's paper established the formal truth of the proposition, but it had been a feature of trade policy debates long before then. The converse proposition, that an export subsidy is equivalent to an import subsidy, does not exactly hold except under certain circumstances (Casas 1991). It remains the case that when a government undertakes policies to expand exports, it cannot help but expand imports as well.

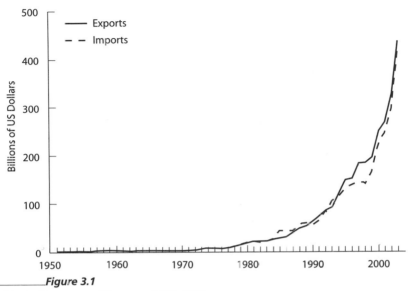

_____*Figure 3.1*

China's Exports and Imports, 1950–2003
Source: International Monetary Fund, International Financial Statistics

2003, we see that exports and imports are highly correlated. (The trade deficit will be discussed in chapter 4.)

Additional evidence of the Lerner symmetry theorem comes from the recent experience of developing countries. Figure 3.1 depicts China's exports and imports. Most people are well aware that China has become a major exporter. Few realize that China's astounding growth in exports has been matched by astounding growth in imports. This simply demonstrates that trade is indeed a two-way street, not a one-way flow.

As another example, consider two South American countries, Chile and Brazil. These countries have pursued quite different types of commercial policies in recent decades. Chile undertook an extensive liberalization of its trade policy in the 1970s, dramatically cutting its import tariffs. As figure 3.2 indicates, this change in policy helped Chile's imports surge from about 15 percent of GDP in 1970 to 30 percent of GDP in 1998. And yet this period also witnessed a surge in exports on the same order of magnitude: the import expansion was matched by an export expansion. As in the case of other countries, Chile's experience

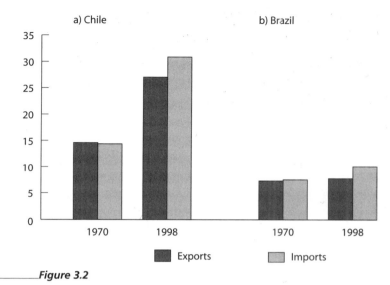

a) Chile

b) Brazil

Exports   Imports

_____*Figure 3.2*

Exports and Imports as a Share of GDP, Chile and Brazil, 1970 and 1998
Source: International Monetary Fund 2000.

also suggests that export diversification is an additional benefit that comes
with lifting the implicit export tax that is inherent in import tariffs.[27]

By contrast, Brazil has pursued "import substitution" policies
since the 1960s. These policies aimed to promote industrialization by severely restricting imports. In 1970, Brazil's exports and imports amounted
to about 7 percent of its GDP. Brazil's trade policy did not change dramatically in the subsequent twenty-eight years, and thus, Brazil's exports
and imports remained at 7 percent of GDP in 1998 despite the tremendous growth in world trade over this period. The Brazilian government
has made great efforts to expand exports, but substantial import barriers
have indirectly constrained exports and undermined those efforts.

At one level, the idea that import restraints will reduce exports is
straightforward. If foreign countries are blocked in their ability to sell

[27] By reducing import taxes, a country is lifting an implicit tax on the export sector. This tax relief allows marginal exports, previously squelched by the tax, to become
profitable. As a result, countries do not simply export more of the same things, but other
goods that were previously unprofitable to export. This implies that trade liberalization allows exports to become more rather than less diversified, thereby reducing the risk of adverse export price shocks. Chile, for example, reduced its export dependence on metals
(mainly copper) from 64 percent of exports in 1980 to 46 percent in 1996.

their goods in the United States, they will be unable to earn the dollars they need to purchase U.S. goods. The mechanisms that link a country's exports and imports to one another are complex and not always readily apparent, but can be illustrated by focusing on the foreign exchange market. If the United States unilaterally reduces its tariff on Japanese goods, for example, one would expect U.S. demand for Japanese goods to increase. To make these purchases, consumers in the United States will (indirectly) have to sell dollars on the foreign exchange market to purchase yen. In response to the increased demand for yen from those holding dollars, the value of the dollar will fall in terms of yen, or conversely the yen's value will rise in terms of dollars. This change tends to raise the price of Japanese goods in the United States, dampening demand for those goods.

But here is the flip side: although it was the United States that lowered its tariffs while Japan left its tariffs unchanged, Japan will now purchase more goods from the United States. This is because the cheaper dollar tends to lower the yen price of U.S. goods, stimulating Japanese demand for them. Therefore, the foreign exchange market is one of several mechanisms that link exports and imports, ensuring that a country's exports increase when it unilaterally reduces its own import tariffs.[28]

The pattern of U.S. exports and imports shown in figure 1.3 also illustrates this relationship. The ratio of exports and imports to GDP was fairly stable in the 1950s and 1960s, but in the early 1970s and again in the late 1970s there was a pronounced jump in both of these ratios. These jumps coincide with large increases in world oil prices. (As late as 1980, almost 30 percent of U.S. imports by value were mineral fuels.) The big increase in the import bill is seen in the higher ratio of imports to GDP, but—since those imports must be paid for with something—the export ratio also rose in each case. In both instances the increase in exports was brought about by a depreciation in the value of the dollar.

This link between exports and imports also explains why the employment effects of trade intervention tend to cancel each other out. Throughout U.S. history, large tariff increases have failed to stimulate

---

[28] A change in the exchange rate is only one of several mechanisms by which symmetry will hold; for example, it still holds for countries with fixed exchange rates or in single currency areas such as Europe.

greater employment because any increase in employment in import-competing industries is offset by a decrease in employment in export-oriented industries. The Smoot-Hawley tariff of 1930, for example, significantly reduced imports but failed to create jobs overall because exports fell almost one-for-one with imports, resulting in employment losses in those industries.

Thus, the connection between imports and exports cannot be overlooked when evaluating trade policy. Governments that undertake policies to reduce imports will find themselves also reducing exports. This reduction in imports may expand employment in industries that compete with them, but the reduction in exports contracts employment in those industries. An appreciation of the Lerner symmetry theorem is particularly important when assessing the claim that import tariffs have a beneficial effect on overall employment.

Import Barriers Harm Downstream Industries

Not only do import restrictions reduce the number of jobs required to produce exports, but they also destroy jobs in downstream industries that use the imports. Recall from table 1.2 that the majority of U.S. imports are not final consumer goods, but intermediate goods used by domestic firms in their production. Any trade restriction that raises the price of an intermediate good directly harms downstream user industries and thus adversely affects employment in those industries. In other words, when domestic firms have to pay a premium on their productive inputs, particularly when they are competing with foreign rivals who do not pay those taxes, employment in those industries suffers.

Restrictions on imported sugar, for example, have produced sour results for those employed in the sugar-refining and candy-making industries. When food manufacturers who produce sugar-intensive products are forced to pay a higher price for sugar than their foreign rivals, their competitive position suffers. In 2002, a LifeSavers candy plant that employed 650 workers in Michigan was closed and relocated to Canada. Before the shut down, the plant produced about 3 million rolls of Life-Savers per day using 250,000 pounds of sugar. Due to the high price of sugar in the United States, the company will save over $10 million a year in sugar costs just by relocating across the border.

Limits on sugar imports have had repercussions throughout the American food manufacturing industry. According to Mayor Richard Daley, Chicago's confectionary industry has lost 11 percent of its jobs since 1991. "The continuation of domestic sugar price supports," Daley said, "is a key reason these companies [confectioners] are considering leaving Chicago and relocating their facilities outside of U.S. borders."[29] In 1990, Brachs Candy Company announced that because of the high domestic price of sugar, it would close a factory in Chicago that employed three thousand workers, and expand production in Canada.[30] Canada is the location of choice for large sugar-using food manufacturers because the country does not have any sugar farmers and hence does not artificially inflate the price of sugar on their behalf.

There are numerous examples of the adverse effect that trade restrictions have on employment in related industries. In 1991, the United States imposed antidumping duties on imported flat panel displays, used by domestic manufacturers of laptop computers: specifically, 62.67 percent duties on active matrix LCD displays and 7.02 percent duties on electroluminescent displays. Producers of laptops could no longer afford to purchase the expensive displays in the United States and still compete effectively against overseas rivals, who could buy the same displays at much lower prices on the world market and then export their laptops freely to the United States. To avoid the higher domestic prices, several manufacturers decided to shift production abroad. Immediately after the imposition of the antidumping duties, Toshiba announced that it would

[29] Groombridge 2001, 5.

[30] Bovard 1991, 75–76. In 1988, the Department of Commerce estimated that the high price of domestic sugar cost almost 9,000 jobs in food manufacturing (because of increased imports of cheaper sugar-containing products) and 3,000 jobs in the sugar-refining industry (due to lower demand for sugar). At the time of the Commerce study, sugar-producing farms employed about 35,000 workers, but the sugar-processing sector employed about 8,000 workers, and industrial users of sugar (soft drink, baking, confectioneries industry) employed over 700,000 workers. A great many workers in the sugar-using industries were put at risk to save the jobs of the few workers in the sugar-producing industry (U.S. Department of Commerce 1988). Of course, when the domestic price of sugar is forced up, jobs are created producing sugar substitutes, such as high-fructose corn syrup. But even if the overall effect on employment is zero, we have to ask: it is good government policy to reshuffle employment so much in this sector, creating jobs in the sugar industry but destroying them in the confectioneries industry, creating jobs in the corn syrup industry but destroying them in the baking industry?

cease production of laptops in California and shift production to Japan, Sharp announced that it would cease production of laptops in Texas and move production to Canada, and Apple announced that it would relocate its assembly of laptops from California to Ireland or Singapore.[31] Similarly, after the United States imposed price floors on Japanese DRAM semiconductors, computer manufacturers shifted their assembly operations outside of the United States to take advantage of the lower prices for memory chips in other markets. In these and numerous other cases, import restrictions benefiting one industry have only harmed another industry.

When the purchasers of imported intermediate goods organize politically, they can alter the debate over the desirability of protection on employment grounds. In the case just mentioned, firms that used semiconductors (particularly computer manufacturers, IBM, Hewlett-Packard, Sun Microsystems, and others) formed a coalition to oppose the renewal of the price floors on Japanese memory chips. As a result of this consumer coalition, U.S. trade officials no longer heard a single voice—that of semiconductor producers—regarding America's trade policy. The government did not know how to deal with the sharply conflicting domestic interests, so it simply let the price floor agreement expire.[32]

The same political process played out in the steel industry. In 1984, the United States negotiated voluntary restraint agreements (VRAs) that limited steel imports from all major foreign suppliers. The VRAs raised the domestic price of steel and helped steel producers, but harmed the production, employment, and exports of the far more numerous domestic users of steel, including the automobile, machine tool, and construction industries. To fight the VRAs, these downstream industries formed the Coalition of American Steel-Using Manufacturers (CASUM), led by Caterpillar, the manufacturer of heavy earthmoving equipment, and by the Precision Metalforming Association, a small business group whose members process raw steel for industrial users such as the automobile industry.

As in the case of semiconductors, the VRAs were allowed to expire in 1991 in part because CASUM posed an extremely difficult question to government officials: How are Caterpillar, John Deere, and other

[31] Hart 1993.
[32] Irwin 1996b.

domestic steel-using firms supposed to compete at home and abroad against such foreign competitors as Komatsu when they are forced to pay a hefty premium for the steel they must purchase?[33] If Caterpillar laid off workers because higher domestic steel costs led to sales being lost to foreign producers, those workers could justifiably ask whether the government believed that jobs in the steel industry were more important to the economy than jobs in the equipment-manufacturing industry.

The protectionist steel industry used to get its own way when lobbying Washington for import relief. Now it has to battle steel-consuming industries for political influence. When the steel industry filed massive antidumping suits in 1998–99, steel-using groups formed the "40-to-1" coalition, referring to the fact that the fewer than two hundred thousand steelworkers are outnumbered by 8 million employees in steel-using industries, particularly in construction, metal fabrication, heavy machinery, and transportation equipment. The jobs of workers in steel-using industries would be at risk if steel prices were artificially increased. General Motors, which purchases over seven million tons of steel annually, warned that imposing tariffs on imported steel would make GM's domestic operations "less competitive in the international marketplace to the extent that those operations are subjected to costs not incurred by offshore competition, and to the extent that U.S. import barriers impede access to new products and materials being developed offshore, or remove the competitive incentives to develop new products in the United States."[34]

In 2002, when the Bush administration was considering whether to impose special safeguard tariffs on imported steel, the steel-users coalition—the Consuming Industries Trade Action Coalition, or CITAC—responded once again. According to a study commissioned by CITAC, the proposed import relief would save between four thousand and eight

[33] As Moore (1996, 111–12) notes, "the overall strategy of CASUM was to turn the debate away from the actions of foreign firms and governments and away from an argument about free trade versus protection. Instead, CASUM tried to direct the discussion toward the VRA's effects on U.S. manufacturing interests, especially exporters and small businesses. This was a highly effective tactic since both have broad political support." Moore notes that "CASUM also appealed indirectly to protectionists elements in Congress by emphasizing that VRAs rewarded unfair traders through the transfer of quota rents." That is, foreign exporters reaped large profits by selling at higher prices in the U.S. market.

[34] Lindsey, Griswold, and Lukas 1999, 7.

thousand jobs in the steel industry. But, by increasing steel prices and imports of steel containing products, the import restrictions would reduce employment by thirty-six thousand to seventy-four thousand in other sectors of the economy. The higher prices would force stee. consumers to pay between two and four billion dollars in extra costs, would cost the economy eight jobs for every one steel job created, and thus cost consumers about $425,000 per job saved in the steel industry.[35]

A year after the Bush administration imposed tariffs of up to 30 percent on certain steel imports in March 2002, the International Trade Commission surveyed steel consumers about the impact of this action. About half of steel purchasers reported an increase in contract or spot prices after the tariffs were imposed. Based on the survey responses, about 8 percent of the decline in employment in steel-consuming firms between 2002 and 2003 was attributed to the safeguard measure.[36] Once again, in deciding whether to limit steel imports, the government faced the choice of protecting jobs in the steel industry or protecting jobs in automobiles, commercial building, wire products, electronic equipment, heavy machinery, oil and gas drilling, and other steel-using industries.

These examples demonstrate the first lesson of economics there is no such thing as a free lunch. Every government intervention involves a trade-off of some sort. Higher sugar prices increase employment in sugar production, but reduce employment in food-manufacturing industries. Higher semiconductor prices increase employment in the semiconductor industry, but decrease employment in the computer industry. Higher steel prices increase employment in the steel industry, but decrease employment in the steel-using industries. When a domestic industry asks the government to impose trade barriers that would ra.se the domestic price above the world price, the choice means trading off jobs in one sector of the economy for jobs in another sector, not creating or losing jobs overall.

Why do policymakers usually fail to see themselves as facing such a trade-off? For one thing, if downstream consumers do not organize politically, the indirect consequences of trade barriers may never get brought to legislators' attention. And the nature of the political process

[35] Francois and Baughman 2001.
[36] U.S. International Trade Commission 2003, 2–50.

gives members of Congress and officials in the executive agencies responsible for trade policy a strongly biased view of the effects of trade. Constituents who lose their jobs in import-sensitive industries, such as steel, invariably complaint to their representatives and government agencies about foreign competition. Legislators and bureaucrats cannot ignore these voters and it is hard to resist the temptation to help by "doing something" about the situation, even if that imposes hardship on others who are often silent. Meanwhile, those who owe their jobs and high wages to exports or to industries that depend upon inexpensive intermediate goods almost invariably fail to express their appreciation to policymakers for not interfering in the process of trade. As a result, those seeking to limit trade tend to be more vocal than those who benefit from open markets.

_____The Politics of Protection

If free trade is so beneficial and protectionism so costly, then what explains the attractiveness and persistence of high trade barriers? One reason why free trade is so controversial is that, in the short run, not everyone stands to benefit from the policy. Changes in trade flows and in trade policy have a ripple effect through the economy and alter the distribution of income. Because some groups are harmed by trade and benefit from trade barriers, it is not clear that free trade policies will be adopted. The actual policy will depend upon the relative political strength of those supporting and opposing trade restrictions, based on underlying economic interests or any other motivation.

Indeed, specific groups that benefit from protectionist barriers usually exert political influence beyond their numbers. Political influence tends to be skewed in favor of those seeking government assistance because those who stand to gain have more at stake than those who stand to lose. As Vilfredo Pareto pointed out long ago, "a protectionist measure provides large benefits to a small number of people, and causes a very great number of consumers a slight loss."[37] This circumstance makes it easier to enact such measures. Pareto's idea that the benefits of trade protection are highly concentrated, while the costs are widely diffused, has

[37] Pareto 1971, 379.

been a central point of departure for explaining the existence and persistence of import restrictions.

The U.S. sugar program, once again, illustrates this imbalance in costs and benefits. Import restrictions have kept domestic sugar prices at roughly twice the world price. The General Accounting Office estimated that domestic sugar producers reaped about $1 billion in 1998 as a result of this policy. However, 42 percent of the total benefits to sugarcane and sugar beet growers went to just 1 percent of all producers; indeed, just seventeen sugarcane farms collected over half of all the cane growers' benefits. Clearly, the owners of these few farms have a powerful incentive to maintain the import restrictions. Although the sugar policy imposes far larger costs on consumers of sweeteners ($1.9 billion according to the GAO) than are distributed to growers, consumers are far more numerous, and these costs are spread widely among them.

This combination of concentrated benefits and dispersed costs leads to an enormous imbalance in the relative size of the political forces opposing and favoring any change in the sugar policy. The incentive for household consumers to oppose the policy is virtually nonexistent: even though the total cost across all consumers is large, the cost to each individual consumer is small: only about seven dollars per person per year. On the other hand, the policy creates large, tangible benefits for a few producers, who are willing to devote substantial resources to defend the policy. In the 2002 election cycle (January 2001 to December 2002), the sugar and sugar beet political action committees spent $3.1 million in campaign contributions. Since 1990, the sugar industry has made campaign contributions totaling more than $20 million.[38] As a result, such special interests have an influence on policy that is disproportionate to their size.

Yet such imbalances are not the whole story. Many small groups could benefit from special government policies, but few actually succeed in organizing and obtaining it. Why are some special interests are able to form a political organization or interest group while others are not? And why do only some of those that organize succeed in influencing policy? The formation of interest groups is a critical element of the politics of trade policy. Unfortunately, economists and political scientists

[38] See data available at http://www.opensecrets.org.

have not been overwhelmingly successful in revealing much about the organization of economic interests.[39] However, several hypotheses are worth exploring.

One difficulty in forming a successful political interest group is the "free rider" problem. If a tariff benefits all firms in an industry regardless of whether they contributed to the political effort to get the tariff imposed, then some firms may choose not to contribute. They would prefer that others undertake the burden because, if protection is secured, the shirking firms cannot be excluded from the benefits of higher prices as imports are squeezed out of the market. But at the same time, the firms participating in seeking protection, the lower the probability of obtaining protection.

Industries that are relatively concentrated, either economically (a small number of firms) or geographically (the same regional location), are best positioned to overcome the costs of collective action. They can monitor the political contributions of others and attempt to punish or exclude free riders. The free-rider problem also explains the difficulty of mobilizing the dispersed opponents of programs. The numerous but widely dispersed consumers who pay higher prices for sugar have a collective interest in changing the current policy, but there is a strong incentive to shirk from any organized effort to do so.

For other economic interests, however, political organization is not even necessary. For example, wheat farmers in Kansas and Nebraska, tobacco farmers in North Carolina, and citrus producers in Florida do not require much political organization to ensure that their elected representatives take their interests to heart. Legislators represent the preferences of important unorganized constituents in order to raise the probability that they will be reelected. In addition, with the spread of antidumping and other bureaucratic mechanisms for obtaining protection, described in chapter 5, it is not even clear that political contributions by interest groups are the predominant means by which trade policy is affected. The free-rider problem is less of an obstacle in antidumping cases because the definition of an industry is often so narrow that even a single firm has the standing to file a petition.

[39] Rodrik (1995) surveys the economic literature on the political economy of trade policy.

Thus, because of the conflicting interests of specific groups, there is no reason to believe that free trade will necessarily be adopted as a country's trade policy. But what if citizens could actually vote on trade policy matters? An interesting benchmark to consider is the trade policy that would emerge in a democratic vote under majority rule. While trade policy is rarely determined in this way, this is a useful starting point for thinking about the policy that would arise in a competitive, representative political system.

In a direct democracy, trade policy would be determined by the preferences of the median voter.[40] If free trade raises aggregate income but reduces the income of the median voter, then free trade might not get a majority vote to pass in a referendum. For example, the distribution of workers' skills across the electorate is potentially an important determinant of the median voter's interests. Suppose workers with a high school education lose one dollar as a result of free trade, while those with a college education gain two dollars. If workers with a college degree constitute at least one-third of all voters, free trade would raise overall income. But if the less-educated workers comprise more than half of the electorate, the median voter would oppose the policy, unless guaranteed a compensatory income transfer.

As noted in chapter 1, educational attainment does appear to be an important factor in shaping the American public's views of trade policy. Several studies have shown that the more education a person receive, the more likely that person is to support open trade policies.[41] This is consistent with the view that economic interests are at stake: the United States exports goods and services that require a highly educated workforce, whereas it imports more labor-intensive goods where, in the competing domestic industry, few years of formal education are required. Because the fraction of the population receiving advanced education has risen in recent decades, support for freer trade might be expected to grow over time.[42]

---

[40] See the classic analysis by Mayer (1984). The median voter is the decisive marginal voter whose views determine which side will win under majority rule.

[41] Scheve and Slaughter 2001a, 2001b. Mayda and Rodrik (2004) examine how various factors (income, education, employment, political views) are correlated with individual trade policy views for many countries around the world.

[42] In 2002, for example, 32 percent of persons aged sixty-five to seventy-four had received at least some college education, while 58 percent of persons aged twenty-five to

Other factors affecting the median voter's views on trade include the manner in which voters perceive their economic interests to be related to trade policy. One such factor is the degree to which workers are potentially mobile between different sectors of the economy or different regions of the country. For example, a worker who over time has built up industry-specific skills (such as a steelworker) will probably view trade policy differently from someone whose skills are useful in several different industries (such as an accountant working in the steel industry). A coal miner in West Virginia who refuses to consider relocating to another part of the country is going to think about economic change differently from someone who is willing to move thousands of miles in search of a new opportunity.

In most developed countries, trade policy is determined by elected representatives in the legislature. In this case, the distribution of economic interests across electoral districts can interact with the rules of the political system (a winner-take-all versus a proportionate representative system) and shape the outcome. If a sizable minority of the electorate is opposed to free trade but is uniformly distributed across districts, then a winner-take-all system might result in the election of few opponents to free trade, whereas their political strength might be greater in a proportional system.

Politicians can be crafty in exploiting the geographic variation in trade interests by using selective promises of protection to win votes. To help get NAFTA passed by the House of Representatives, President Clinton negotiated a special safeguard agreement for citrus producers just to win the support of Florida's congressional delegation. During the 2000 election campaign, candidate George Bush promised to aid steelworkers in West Virginia, which helped swing the state to the Republicans for the first time in decades and helped him win the election. (The Bush administration followed through on its promise by imposing tariffs on imported steel in 2002.) In general, the states of North Carolina, Alabama, and Idaho have a high concentration of economic activity in commodities

---

thirty-four had reached this level of educational attainment (U.S. Bureau of the Census 2004, 154). There is also evidence that home ownership is a factor that shapes an individual's preferences on trade policy. Even highly educated individuals tend to express support for protectionist policies if they own a home in a region that is adversely affected by imports. Scheve and Slaughter 2001b.

that are protected by import restrictions. The state of Washington has a large stake, and many other states have a small stake, in open trade due to the export orientation of producers.[43]

Finally, trade policy also depends upon how the conflict between these competing groups is mediated by policymaking institutions in the government. These institutions may be biased in favor of one group over another, either because certain groups have better access to decision makers or because those decision makers are more sensitive to the interests of some groups. This can obviously affect the direction that trade policy takes. For example, antidumping policy (considered in chapter 5) is essentially nonpolitical and administered in a routine, bureaucratic way by government agencies. Small, narrowly defined industries tend to choose the antidumping route to trade protection, whereas larger industries may have the political clout to get protection directly from the president and Congress. Because of all these variables, generalizations about the politics of trade policy are difficult to make. So it should not be surprising that political economists have failed to answer basic questions about how firms achieve political influence.

But one generalization seems fairly robust: once policies are in place, they are difficult to change, particularly if change involves taking benefits away from any industry. During the Korean War, Congress introduced support measures for owners of mohair goats, whose wool was useful for making warm army uniforms. These subsidies persisted for forty years after the end of the war because farmers adamantly opposed their withdrawal and politicians did not want to fight them. Although the government program was abolished in 1994, saving $200 million, it was revived just a few years later. Other industries—such as steel, textiles and apparel, and semiconductors—have found that once the government gives you a special program, that program becomes institutionalized at various levels of government and becomes very difficult to take away.

It has been said that voting for freer trade is an unnatural act for a politician because they are taking away tangible benefits for some in exchange for uncertain benefits for others. When imports increase, some groups know with a high degree of certainty that their jobs and incomes are at stake. Yet there is uncertainty about which individuals and industries

---

[43] U.S. International Trade Commission 2004, 125.

stand to gain jobs and income when exports increase. Uncertainty about whether an individual will benefit from or be harmed by trade can lead to a status quo bias in favor of maintaining trade restrictions. Even if the entire electorate recognized that a clear majority would benefit from free trade, a reform in which most voters would benefit might not pass in a popular vote if the majority thinks that it is unlikely to gain from the reform. This uncertainty means that the expected value of reform could be negative for a majority of voters, in which case they would block it. This logic gives the political system a status quo bias.[44]

The status quo bias is simply reinforced if voters are risk averse (wherein they prefer a lower but certain return over a higher but less certain return) or loss averse (wherein they are more sensitive to losses than to equivalent-sized gains, and thus prefer to avoid any loss). These factors might help explain why countries with trade restrictions find it politically difficult to eliminate them. In such cases, tariffs may be viewed as a social welfare mechanism to prevent substantial reduction of real incomes in certain sections of the community. This function might explain why so many tariffs in the past seem to have had income maintenance as their goal and why they have continued, even when designed to be only temporary. For example, if the goal is to keep real incomes of certain farmers, steelworkers, or textile manufacturers higher than they would be otherwise, there is less of a motivation to reduce trade barriers, even though other income transfer policies would be more efficient than restricting trade.

Despite the forces that favor the imposition and maintenance of trade restrictions, political leaders in many countries have recognized the economy-wide benefits of free trade and have been able to overcome political inertia, throw off existing measures, and adopt more open trade policies. The United Kingdom eliminated virtually all protectionist policies in the mid–nineteenth century when export-oriented cotton textile interests grew powerful enough to defeat import-competing agricultural producers. The United States significantly reduced its tariffs in the mid–twentieth century as it came to dominate world trade in manufactured goods. As chapter 6 discusses, many developing countries—from Korea in the 1960s to Chile in the 1970s to China in the 1980s—have undertaken radical changes

---

[44] Fernandez and Rodrik 1991.

in economic policies in the direction of open markets.[45] Often these changes require creative political leaders who respond to a crisis or form new political coalitions in a way that breaks through the status quo.

_____Is Protection Ever Beneficial?

The theory and evidence reviewed thus far have failed to address the idea that, in certain instances, import restrictions might be economically beneficial.[46] In fact, economists have identified certain conditions under which trade protection can actually improve welfare. Broadly speaking, trade interventions can be beneficial when they are used to improve the terms of trade, to promote industries with positive externalities, or to capture rents in international markets.[47] Although these theoretical cases exist, daunting political problems remain in actually having government implement policies that can capture these benefits. Let us consider each case in turn.

When a country has the ability to influence the prices of its exports and imports on the world market, then trade restrictions can potentially raise national income by improving the ratio at which a country exchanges exports for imports, otherwise known as a country's terms of trade. An improvement in the terms of trade, either through higher export prices or lower import prices, increases the purchasing power of exports in terms of the imports they procure. This translates into higher income because the country can acquire more imports for the same amount of exports.

The power to influence the world market price is usually held by a country that dominates production of a certain good. For example, the United States produced 80 percent of the world's cotton prior to the Civil War. Southern cotton producers collectively had a significant impact on the world price, but each producer alone had no particular influence. The United States might have been better off if producers had formed a cartel to restrict exports or, barring that, if the government had imposed

[45] For a set of case studies on unilateral moves to free trade, see Bhagwati 2002.

[46] Adam Smith fully conceded that there are sound noneconomic rationales for restricting trade, such as protecting industries essential for national defense.

[47] Corden (1974) provides a good overview of the various cases in which protection might be economically justifiable. Irwin (1996a) explores the debate among economists about these cases.

an export tax to force up the world price of cotton. The Organization of Petroleum Exporting Countries (OPEC) has used limits on production to help increase the world price of oil, and its members have reaped billions of dollars in additional revenue as a result. (Of course, it is always difficult for such cartels to prevent smaller members from cheating and to prevent nonmembers from increasing production.)

Except in such special cases, the terms-of-trade motive for trade restrictions has little relevance for most countries' policies.[48] Few countries have the ability to manipulate their terms of trade, and most policymakers probably have little idea what the terms of trade are or what conditions would have to be met for tariffs to be set optimally.[49] Most governments are highly sensitive to domestic political concerns about trade and have not set up institutions that are insulated from politics and can search out commodities in which optimal tariffs might be employed.

To the extent that countries can influence the price of their exports, the appropriate response is an export tax, something that is unlikely to be popular. In addition, any gains from such a policy could evaporate if competing suppliers emerged or if other countries imposed retaliatory duties. Finally, such a trade restriction is not desirable from the standpoint of world welfare and global efficiency. An improvement in the exporting country's terms of trade implies a deterioration in the importing country's terms of trade and actually leaves the world as a whole worse off.

Another situation in which trade interventions can, in principle, yield economic benefits is when they serve as a second-best measure to promote industries that generate positive externalities. In the case of positive externalities, the private costs of production are higher than the social costs of production because producers do not take into account the benefits of their actions for other sectors of the economy. As a result, the domestic industry produces less of a good than is socially desirable. These benefits can be captured if the private and social costs of production

[48] See Panagariya, Shah, and Mishra (2001) for evidence that developing countries are price-takers on world markets and therefore cannot improve their terms of trade by restricting exports or imports.

[49] There is an "optimal" reduction in exports beyond which a country is worse off because the cost from reducing trade more than offsets the gain from a higher world price for its exports. If domestic producers are aware of their market power, they can appropriately determine the price of their exports with less need for government interference. See Rodrik 1989.

are properly aligned, which can sometimes be achieved through domestic subsidies. If subsidies cannot be used, there may be a second-best case for promoting the industry through protection. Recent theoretical cases have considered optimal trade policy for industries in which there are static or dynamic external economies, such as learning-by-doing or R&D spillovers, in which the production experience or research of one firm benefits others in the industry, as is alleged to be the case in certain high-technology industries. In theory, circumstances can arise in which some government promotion may be appropriate.

But as a practical matter, using trade policy to correct for such market failures is problematic. Correctly identifying these externalities is, by their very nature, extremely difficult.[50] Even if the externality can be identified, the first-best policy of a subsidy has to be ruled out. Using tariffs to promote a targeted industry has been likened to acupuncture with a fork: the relevant market failure may be corrected, but at the cost of introducing a by-product distortion, such as a higher price for domestic consumers. Finally, the relevant externality must be external to the firm and internal to the country. The R&D or learning benefits could spill over between countries, particularly if foreign firms maintain a presence in the domestic market or have an ownership stake in the domestic firms, or when the knowledge cannot be limited geographically. In this case, any promotion scheme benefits all firms around the world, not just domestic ones, significantly narrowing the cases in which intervention would produce purely a national advantage instead of simply providing an international public good.[51] It is particularly difficult for the United States, where policy is determined largely by lawyers who are responding

[50] Industrial policy advocates propose various criteria for determining which industries are better than others and therefore deserve promotion. One proposed criteria was industries with high value-added per worker, but as Krugman (1994) notes, these are really just capital-intensive industries. This would lead one to support the cigarette industry and the oil pipeline industry. Sometimes it is argued that the presence of external economies of scale is demonstrated by geographically concentrated industries. Just because most U.S.-made carpets come from one county in Georgia, to use a commonly cited example of this phenomenon, does not mean that the carpet industry deserved to be subsidized at its inception or deserves to be subsidized now.

[51] Irwin and Klenow (1994) studied memory chip production in the semiconductor industry and concluded that international learning-by-doing spillovers were about as substantial as within-country spillovers. In the case of R&D spillovers, Branstetter (2001) suggests that the domestic component is stronger than the international component.

to self-interested producers, to discern impartially which industries exhibit such dynamic externalities and which do not, let alone the degree to which the knowledge spills over to foreign firms.

Many industries that are expected to create positive externalities fail to do so. For example, in the late 1980s and early 1990s, high-definition television (HDTV) was widely believed to be a "technology driver" for the high-technology industry: if the United States failed to dominate the underlying technology, it would lose its competitive position in commercial applications and in related industries, such as semiconductors and workstations. Whichever country invested in the "right" technology first was expected to have a strategic advantage over latecomers in what was projected to be a lucrative new market. To this end, Europe and Japan moved quickly to subsidize their producers. Japan invested nearly $1.2 billion in HDTV research (much of it from the Ministry of International Trade and Industry and the state broadcaster, NHK), while taxpayers in the European Community spent about $1 billion on HDTV research through 1991.[52]

Fearing the United States would be left behind, in 1989 the American Electronics Association proposed that Congress appropriate $1.35 billion in direct subsidies and loan guarantees to support HDTV research. Congress authorized $30 million in research grants through the Defense Department and promised more, but the first Bush administration opposed the funding. The ensuing stalemate prevented any further spending. Yet gridlock not only saved American taxpayers millions of dollars, it proved to be the best policy. The European and Japanese technologies were developed first, but they settled on an analog standard that was soon viewed as obsolete. Meanwhile, frustrated by the impasse in Washington, American firms set to work themselves on HDTV research and, by entering the field somewhat later, were able to improve upon foreign research. Ultimately, American firms created a digital system that was later selected as the industry standard by the Federal Communications Commission. Moreover, HDTV has not yet become the driving or profitable technology that many influential commentators thought it would.

The final rationale for trade intervention is to capture rents or profits in the international market. To understand this process, consider

---

[52] Hart 1994; Dai, Cawson, and Holmes 1996.

a firm that is competing against a single foreign rival in an imperfectly competitive market (i.e., one in which there are above-normal profits) in a third country. In this case, a government export subsidy for the firm could induce the foreign rival to cut its output, thereby shifting profits from the foreign to the domestic firm. This practice is known as strategic trade policy, in which the government undertakes a precise, strategic intervention on behalf of domestic firms in a way that increases national welfare.[53] For example, European support for Airbus is commonly believed to be an attempt to shift profits away from Boeing in the lucrative market for wide-bodies aircraft.[54]

While there was much enthusiasm for this idea in the 1980s, numerous theoretical and practical objections have diminished its appeal. First, successful intervention depends crucially upon key parameters in the market's structure that make it difficult for governments to determine the best policy. For example, one study showed that if the firms competed by setting prices rather than quantities, then the optimal policy would switch from an export subsidy to an export tax. The introduction of asymmetric information between the firms and the government further increases the range of possible outcomes and makes clear-cut predictions even more difficult. Setting aside theoretical issues, calibrated simulation models of strategic trade policy reveal that the potential gains from implementing the optimal policy are exceedingly small. When the right policy is excruciatingly difficult to determine in the first place and depends upon getting parameters of industry structure and competitive interaction exactly right, the small potential payoff suggests that such interventions are not worthwhile, especially when the potential outlays are high.

Theoretical work on optimal trade interventions is usually developed in the context of an omniscient government that has full information and the capability of setting policy in an optimal manner. In the real world, governments are neither omniscient nor immune to external pressure. Do the theoretical results stand up when the government is confronted with political pressure to use policy on behalf of certain industries? Not surprisingly, the answer is no. Research has shown that the

[53] Brander (1995) provides a comprehensive survey of this literature.

[54] Irwin and Pavcnik (2004) examine the impact of Airbus's A-380 super jumbo on Boeing sales of the 747.

case for such interventions is substantially weakened when government policy is subject to strategic manipulation by politically active firms.[55] Thus, there are many reasons to be skeptical about whether a government can determine where strategic intervention will be worthwhile among the many industries competing for government assistance, especially in a representative democracy, where trade policy is often driven by the interests of politically active domestic producers.[56]

The three theoretical possibilities for trade intervention discussed here depend upon particular circumstances in special cases and require constant adjustment to changing market conditions. Free trade is a much simpler policy because it does not need changing when the underlying economic conditions change. Furthermore, any government that undertakes large, systematic sectoral interventions creates a great deal of concentrated political and economic power, not just to do good but also to make costly mistakes.

---

[55] Grossman and Maggi (1998) examine whether a welfare-maximizing government should pursue a program of strategic trade intervention or instead commit itself to free trade when domestic firms have the opportunity to manipulate the government's choice of the level of intervention. Domestic firms, for example, may overinvest in physical and knowledge capital in a regime of strategic intervention in order to influence the government's choice of subsidy. They find that this manipulation can make a commitment to free trade desirable even in settings where profit-shifting opportunities are available.

[56] Krueger (1990, 21) argues that "in the real world of scarce information, uncertainty, and pervasive rent-seeking, policy makers will inevitably miss the crucial and subtle distinctions between profits that are high because of rents and those that are high because of risk; between wages that are high because of rents, and those that are high because of skills; and between sectors that provide inputs, and those that result in spillover externalities."

4

Trade, Jobs, and Displaced Workers

The argument against free trade that resonates most strongly with the public and with politicians is that imports destroy jobs. Indeed, the greatest fear about international trade in general, and imports in particular, is that it can harm workers, reduce wages, and lead to unemployment. But is this an accurate view of trade as a whole? And if so, are import restrictions the remedy? This chapter addresses the relationship between trade and employment and examines government policies to assist displaced workers. The chapter also considers the underlying causes of trade deficits to see if a country is harmed when it imports more than it exports.

_____*Does Free Trade Affect Employment?*

The claim that trade should be limited because imports destroy jobs has been around at least since the sixteenth century.[1] And imports do indeed destroy jobs in certain industries: for example, employment in the Maine shoe industry and in the South Carolina apparel industry is lower to the extent that both industries face competition from imports. So we can understand why the plant owners and workers and the politicians who represent them would like to change this situation by imposing trade barriers.

But just because imports destroy some jobs does not mean that trade reduces overall employment or harms the economy. As we saw in chapter 3, blocking imports may protect jobs in industries that compete against imports, but it also diminishes employment in other industries by reducing exports and raising costs for import-using industries. Therefore,

---

[1] See Irwin 1996a, 36ff.

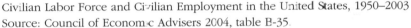

Figure 4.1

Civilian Labor Force and Civilian Employment in the United States, 1950–2003
Source: Council of Economic Advisers 2004, table B-35.

the statement that imports destroy jobs is incomplete because it fails to mention that trade creates jobs in export industries and import-using industries.

Since trade both creates and destroys jobs, a frequently asked question is whether trade has any effect on overall employment. Unfortunately, attempts to quantify the overall employment effect of trade are exercises in futility. This is because the impact of trade on the total number of jobs in an economy is best approximated as zero. Total employment is not a function of international trade, but the number of people in the labor force. As figure 4.1 shows, employment in the United States since 1950 has closely tracked the number of people in the labor force. For this reason, the longtime chairman of the Federal Reserve Board, Alan Greenspan, remarked, "Over the long sweep of American generations and waves of economic change, we simply have not experienced a net drain of jobs to advancing technology or to other nations."[2]

And while there is always some unemployment, represented by the gap between the two series in figure 4.1, this is determined more

[2] Greenspan 2004.

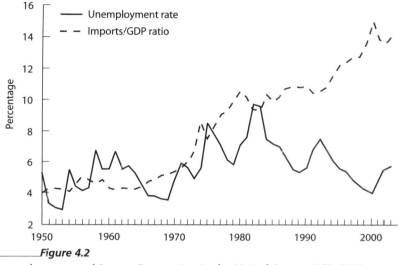

Figure 4.2

Unemployment and Import Penetration in the United States, 1950–2003
Source: Council of Economic Advisers 2004, tables B-42, B-103, B-1.

by the business cycle than by changes in trade flows or trade policy. Indeed, the business cycle has a rhythm of its own, largely independent of factors relating to trade. To show this more directly, figure 4.2 compares the unemployment rate with the ratio of imports of goods and services to GDP since 1950. Except for the period from 1970 to 1975, higher unemployment rates are not associated with an increase in imports as a share of GDP. Since the early 1980s, the unemployment rate has moved lower even as the imports-to-GDP ratio has increased. When unemployment rose in the early 1980s, the early 1990s, and the early 2000s because of the economic recessions in each of those periods, imports were not surging but actually falling off because of declining demand.

As figure 4.1 demonstrates, overall job creation has exceeded job destruction over time. Even though the net change in employment is relatively small in any given year, a striking feature of the U.S. labor market is that gross rates of job creation and destruction are very high. In a dynamic and rapidly changing economy, jobs are continuously created and eliminated, at a rate of about 4 million per month. In 2003, for example, there were 47 million job separations (40 percent of which were layoffs and discharges, the remainder being quits) and 48.4 million

_____Table 4.1
Number of Workers Affected by Extended Mass Layoffs, 1996–2003

Year	Total Number of Workers, All Reasons	Due to Import Competition	Due to Overseas Relocation	Percentage of Total Due to Imports and Relocation
1996	948,122	13,476	4,326	1.9
1997	947,843	12,019	10,439	2.4
1998	991,245	18,473	8,797	2.8
1999	901,451	26,234	5,683	3.5
2000	915,962	13,416	9,054	2.5
2001	1,524,832	27,946	15,693	2.9
2002	1,272,331	15,350	17,075	2.5
2003	1,216,434	23,734	13,205	3.0

Source: Bureau of Labor Statistics (www.bls.gov).

Note: Displaced workers are those who face involuntary separations due to plant closings, mass layoffs, etc., and does not include those who lose their jobs due to temporary layoffs or voluntary separations.

hires. National employment rose by about 1 million between January and December of that year, but clearly the net change in jobs was a small fraction of the gross flows of workers in and out of the labor force and between jobs.[3]

How much are imports to blame for the job losses experienced in any given year? Not much. Changes in consumers tastes, domestic competition, productivity growth, and technological innovation, in addition to international trade, all contribute to the churning of the labor market. It is virtually impossible to disentangle all of the reasons for job displacement because they are interdependent; for example, technological change may be stimulated by domestic or foreign competition. Yet to the extent that such attributions are made by the Bureau of Labor Statistics, trade is a tiny factor in the displacement of labor. As table 4.1 shows, import competition and overseas plant relocations accounted for about 3 percent of all employment separations due to mass layoffs in recent years. (This conclusion should not come as a total surprise because, as noted in chapter 1, merchandise trade directly affects only the 15 percent of the labor force that is employed in agriculture, mining, and manufacturing.)

[3] Calculated from data at Bureau of Labor Statistics' website at www.bls.gov.

Indeed, study after study has confirmed that the trade-induced turnover in U.S. labor markets is small in comparison with the overall turnover.[4] Trade is only slightly related to cross-industry variation in worker displacement rates. Although industries with high displacement rates are often import-sensitive, not all import-sensitive industries have high displacement rates. One respected study concludes finds that there is "no systematic relationship between the magnitude of gross job flows and exposure to international trade. . . . On balance, the evidence is highly unfavorable to the view that international trade exposure systematically reduces job security."[5]

But how can we be sure that the number of jobs destroyed by imports will be matched by the number of jobs created elsewhere in the economy? One reason is that macroeconomic policy can be adjusted to offset any imbalance in the forces that drive job creation and destruction. If imports begin rolling in and trigger widespread layoffs, for example, the unemployment rate may begin to rise. If the unemployment rate rises, and with it the risks of a recession, the Federal Reserve Board is likely to ease monetary policy and reduce interest rates, other things being equal. This action not only stimulates the economy in the short run, but also leads to a depreciation of the dollar on foreign exchange markets, which in turn makes U.S. exports less expensive to foreign consumers and imports more expensive to U.S. consumers. As a result, employment goes back up and returns to its long-run relationship with the labor force. (The trade deficit will be discussed at the end of this chapter.)

Yet the effect of trade on jobs is such a politically sensitive issue that it is prone to exaggeration in political discourse. For example, the debate over NAFTA in the early 1990s largely consisted of claims and

---

[4] See Addison, Fox, and Ruhm 1995. Kletzer (1998b, 455) also concludes that "increasing foreign competition across industries accounts for a small share of job displacement" across industries because there are "high rates of job loss for industries with little trade."

[5] Davis, Haltiwanger, and Schuh 1995, 48–49. They find that there is a higher rate of gross job destruction in sectors with very high penetration by imports, but that this differential disappears after controlling for industry wages. "This is evidence that import-intensive industries exhibit greater gross job flows because their workers have relatively low levels of specific human capital—not because foreign competition subjects these industries to unusually large and volatile disturbances" (49). To put it simply, workers who lack industry-specific skills are more apt to switch jobs and are less apt to remain in any given industry than workers who have industry-specific skills.

counterclaims about whether the agreement would add to or subtract from total employment. NAFTA opponents claimed that free trade with Mexico would destroy jobs: the Economic Policy Institute put the number at 480,000 workers. NAFTA proponents countered with the claim that it would create jobs: the Institute for International Economics suggested that 170,000 jobs would be created.[6] Those stressing the job losses gave the impression that there would be a permanent reduction in the number of people employed in the economy. Those stressing the positive employment effects gave the impression that more trade would lead to a higher level of employment and that this should be the motivation for pursuing more open trade policies. (As we saw in chapter 2, however, the reason for pursuing more open trade policies is not to increase employment but to facilitate the more productive employment that comes with mutually beneficial exchanges that raise aggregate income.)

Both of these impressions were false because at the end of the day it is virtually impossible to know the precise effect of the trade agreement on employment changes. These estimates of the medium-term (i.e., several-year) impact of NAFTA on employment are also a fraction of the monthly turnover in U.S. labor markets.[7] And as demonstrated by the experience after 1995, when NAFTA went into effect, the fears of massive job losses in the United States as a result of free trade with Mexico proved to be unwarranted. The "giant sucking sound" of jobs being lost to Mexico, as famously predicted by Ross Perot, the Texas billionaire who ran for president in 1992, was never heard. As several analysts noted in 1998, four years after NAFTA went into effect:

> By any reasonable measure, even the gross job turnover induced by the agreement has been slight. According to the Department of Labor, over the nearly four years from January 1994 through mid-August 1997, 220,000 workers had petitioned for adjustment assistance (cash and training allowances) under the legislation enacted when the trade deal was signed. Of this

[6] Orme 1996, 107. See Hufbauer and Schott 1993 and Scott 1999.

[7] One study estimated that the total employment loss in the United States from 1990 to 1997 due to imports from Mexico would average 37,000 workers per year, and due to imports from Canada 57,000 workers per year. They note that this is exceedingly small in an economy in which 400,000 workers separate from their jobs every *month* and that created over 200,000 jobs per *month* during this period. See Hinojosa-Ojeda et al. 2000.

total, 136,000—an average of about 40,000 workers per year—
were certified as eligible for assistance (under both the more
general trade adjustment assistance program and that created as
part of NAFTA). Even this figure overstates NAFTA's true
impact, because to be eligible under both programs workers
only need to show that "imports" have contributed to their
losses, but not specifically as a result of NAFTA. By way of
comparison, the gross monthly turnover of jobs in the United
States exceeds 2 million. Since NAFTA, overall employment in
the United States has risen by more than 10 million.[8]

Even when judged by the liberal standards of the NAFTA assistance program, only 2.4 percent of displaced workers on permanent layoff required assistance for being harmed by the agreement.[9]

The claims of large employment gains were equally flawed. Analysts at several Washington think tanks (both favorable and unfavorable
to NAFTA) settled upon the rule of thumb that every $1 billion in exports
generates or supports 13,000 jobs (implying conversely that every $1 billion
in imports eliminates the same number of jobs) as a way of evaluating
the employment effects of trade agreements. Some NAFTA proponents
argued that, because Mexico was to eliminate relatively high tariffs against
U.S. goods while U.S. tariffs against Mexican goods were already very
low, the agreement would generate more exports to, than imports from,
Mexico. Using the rule of thumb, it was therefore reasoned that NAFTA
would result in net job creation. For example, President Clinton's trade
representative, Mickey Kantor, claimed that the agreement would create
200,000 new jobs within two years.

Such formulaic calculations and predictions were made to fight
the dire forecasts that thousands of jobs would be lost as a result of NAFTA,
but there was never any reason to believe these figures. Even if tariff reductions are asymmetric, exports may not grow more rapidly than imports.[10] And it is a further mistake to think that changes in the trade balance
translate into predictable changes in employment; a booming economy

---

[8] Burtless et al. 1998, 57.

[9] Schoepfle 2000, 115.

[10] Trade agreements themselves have little effect on bilateral trade balances or the
overall trade balance, as we will see later.

with low unemployment may be accompanied by a growing trade deficit because people have more money to spend on imports. In this case, the claims for the job-creation benefits of NAFTA soon boomeranged. When the peso collapsed in late 1994, for reasons that had nothing to do with NAFTA, imports from Mexico surged and the U.S. trade surplus evaporated.[11]

Despite the fact that trade and trade policy have little relationship to a country's overall level of employment, trade policy debates in Washington and elsewhere are often framed through the lens jobs, jobs, jobs. Yet trade does have important implications for employment in different sectors of the economy and even the wages paid to workers. We now turn to each of these concerns.

_____Trade and the Manufacturing Sector

Even those who may agree that the effect of trade on total employment is essentially zero may oppose free trade because they believe that it shifts jobs into less desirable sectors. One of the greatest concerns in recent decades has been that trade has led to the "deindustrialization" of the U.S. economy in which good jobs in manufacturing have been sacrificed for bad jobs in services.

It is certainly true that the number of jobs in manufacturing has declined in recent decades. U.S. employment in manufacturing fell from 17.9 million workers in 1970 to 14.5 million in 2003. Manufacturing's share of total employment fell even more sharply, from 25 percent of the nonfarm workforce in 1970 to 11 percent in 2003. At the same time, real manufacturing output has increased significantly, by nearly 40 percent in the 1990s alone, and has declined only slightly as a share of GDP when measured at constant prices. This contrast is shown in figure 4.3, which illustrates the vast increase in domestic manufacturing output while the manufacturing workforce has been unchanged or declining. How is this possible? By rapid increases in labor productivity. Just as U.S.

---

[11] NAFTA opponents then argued, using the rule-of-thumb formula endorsed by NAFTA proponents, that thousands of jobs had been lost as a result of trade with Mexico because the trade surplus had become a trade deficit. An analyst at the Economic Policy Institute, for example, claimed that the trade deficit with Mexico and Canada destroyed 440,172 American jobs between 1994 and 1998.

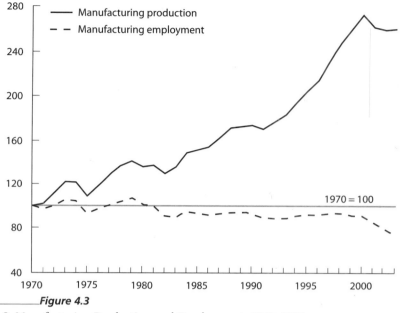

————*Figure 4.3*

U.S. Manufacturing Production and Employment, 1970–2003
Source: Council of Economic Advisers 2004, B-51, B-46.

agricultural output has increased steadily as the number of farmers has fallen, manufacturing has been a victim of its own success in increasing labor productivity.

The flip side to these developments is that an increasing share of the labor force is employed in the service sector. As consumers have shifted their spending to such services as health care, education, recreation, and personal finance, the economy has responded by devoting more resources to those sectors. Because of the relatively poor performance of productivity in these service sectors, a greater share of the labor force has been devoted to these occupations in order to increase output and meet consumer demands.[12]

Has trade contributed to the shift of employment away from manufacturing? A little, but the strong growth in labor productivity is overwhelmingly responsible for the fact that the number of workers in manufacturing has fallen even as output has increased. The problem with

[12] This is not a uniquely American phenomenon, but one that has taken place (sometimes to an even greater extent) in most developed countries. See Burtless et al. 1998, 54.

blaming trade for the relative decline in manufacturing employment is that the United States is both a big exporter and a big importer of manufactured goods, as table 1.1 showed. The trade deficit in manufactured goods is smaller than the overall trade deficit, because the United States is a large net importer of mineral fuels (petroleum). The trade deficit in manufactured goods is also a small percentage of GDP. Thus, even if the United States had balanced trade in manufactured goods after 1970, the effect on output and employment in manufacturing would have been modest.

A simple thought experiment illustrates this point. Between 1970 and 2000, the share of nonfarm employment in manufacturing fell twelve percentage points, from 25 percent to 13 percent. If manufacturing productivity remained fixed at its 1970 level, manufacturing's share of employment would have to have risen eight percentage points in order for output to have matched its 2000 level. Alternatively, if the United States had balanced trade after 1970 but labor productivity grew as rapidly as it did, manufacturing's employment share would have been only one percentage point higher than it actually had been—14 percent, instead of 13 percent. Accordingly, "the effect of long-term productivity improvements on the shift to service-providing jobs is far more important than increased manufactured imports."[13]

But if imports of manufactured goods were lower, wouldn't domestic production of manufactured goods be higher? Not necessarily, as imports and domestic production may be complements rather than substitutes. As figure 4.4 indicates, annual changes in domestic manufacturing output and in real manufactured imports are positively correlated: an increase in imports is positively related to an increase in domestic production. This is because a strong and growing economy brings about more production and more imports, whereas a weak economy tends to see a falloff in both.

Even in labor-intensive industries highly affected by trade, job losses come as much from technological change—the substitution of

---

[13] Council of Economic Advisers 2004, 70–71. The rise in subcontracting of services formerly done within manufacturing firms may explain part of the decline in measured manufacturing employment. If a worker paints a car in a car factory, that job counts as part of manufacturing. If the assembled car is sent out to a paint company for the work, that job counts as a service job.

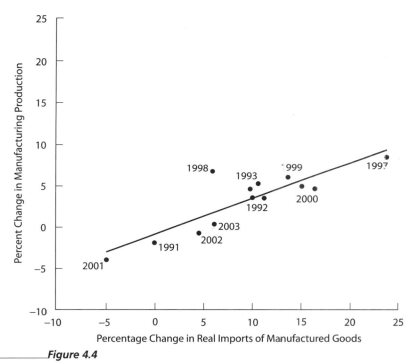

_____Figure 4.4
Change in Production and Imports of Manufactured Goods, 1991–2003
Source: Federal Reserve Board (manufacturing industrial production) and
Bureau of Economic Analysis (real imports).

capital for labor and the introduction of new technology—as from imports. Trade protection cannot arrest this process of change. For example, the apparel industry has experienced a secular decline in the number of workers that the trade barriers of the Multi-Fiber Arrangement (MFA) have been powerless to stop.

Still, some people justify import restrictions as a way of slowing the movement of workers out of manufacturing industries. Here, two points should be recognized: jobs are "saved" in the industry only by destroying jobs elsewhere, as we have already seen, and protection is a costly and inefficient jobs program. The consumer cost per job saved as a result of trade restrictions can be calculated by dividing the total cost of protection to the consumer (due to the higher prices that they pay) by the number of jobs that protection maintains in the industry. In the textile and apparel industry, for example, trade restrictions cost consumers about

$24 billion annually and prevent the loss of roughly 170,000 jobs in the industry. To preserve one job in the textile and apparel industry, therefore, consumers pay $140,000 a year. This is a stiff price for society to pay merely to keep workers employed in relatively low-wage occupations. The cost per job saved is even higher in the industries typically associated with high-paying manufacturing jobs, such as the machine tool industry ($350,000 per job) or the sugar industry ($600,000 per job).[14]

Many of the fears about trade and manufacturing employment are now being echoed with respect to the service sector. In the past, most workers in services were insulated from foreign competition. But now, as discussed in chapter 1, many services are tradable. A growing concern is that service workers will see their jobs "outsourced" to low-wage countries such as India. Although many of the outsourced jobs involve relatively low-skill work, such as call centers, even highly paid professionals, such as radiologists and software programmers, have found that their work can be shifted to much lower paid but technically qualified English-speaking workers in India.

Many of the outsourceable jobs have already been lost. Still, the fears about a "service sector sucking sound" have been exaggerated. One widely cited estimate is that 3.3 million white-collar jobs will be outsourced between 2000 and 2015, amounting to about 55,000 per quarter, on average. In contrast to this high figure, the actual number of service sectors jobs lost appears to be small. The Bureau of Labor Statistics began asking about the overseas transfer of jobs in collecting data on mass layoffs in the first quarter of 2004. In that quarter, 8.7 percent of all layoffs were due to the movement of work and 2.5 percent (a total of 4,633 jobs) related to the movement of work to another country.[15]

In addition, there are natural limits to how much work will be outsourced. Wages in India's software industry, a major center of outsourced work from the United States, have been rising at a rate of close to 15 percent per year. While Indian wages remain much lower than American wages, higher demand for skilled Indian workers has put upward pressure on costs that will diminish the advantage of outsourcing.[16]

[14] Hufbauer and Elliott 1994.
[15] Bureau of Labor Statistics 2004.
[16] Scheiber 2004.

Finally, it should be remembered that international trade—in services, as in goods—is not a one-way flow but a two-way street. The BLS does not collect statistics on the number of jobs created by work that is "outsourced" to the United States. The estimate of jobs lost due to outsourcing mentioned above does not take into account the projected increase in demand for skilled information technology workers in the United States. But as chapter 1 noted, the United States is a major net exporter of services to other countries. In 2003, the value of U.S. exports of legal work, computer programming, engineering, management consulting, and other private services was $131 billion. U.S. imports of such services, including call centers and data entry to developing countries, among other things, was $77 billion.

This is true even in the narrower category of "computer and data base processing service" in which the United States exported over $5 billion and imported just over $1 billion in 2002.[17] For example, in late March of 2004, IBM won a ten-year $750 million outsourcing contract from an Indian company. Bharti Tele-Ventures, India's largest private telecommunications company, will transfer some jobs from Asia to the United States and France. IBM will service Bharti's hardware and software requirements and take over its customer billing and relations operations.

_____Trade and Wages

Another concern is that trade puts downward pressure on U.S. wages as firms strive to match lower wages in developing countries, unleashing a "race to the bottom" in cutting labor costs. Such fears are misguided because high American wages are based on the high productivity of U.S. workers. And the growth in a country's average wages is determined by the growth of a country's productivity. As figure 4.5 shows, the growth of worker compensation (deflated by the producer price index) tracks growth in productivity remarkably well.[18] Foreign competition does not suppress

[17] Lindsey 2004.

[18] Thus, workers have been compensated for the growth in output per worker in terms of the revenue received by firms. When compensation is deflated by the consumer price index, however, the growth in real wages is lower because consumer prices (which include items such as the cost of housing) have risen more rapidly than producer prices. However, it is well known that the consumer price index is biased upward and overstates the rise in the cost of living.

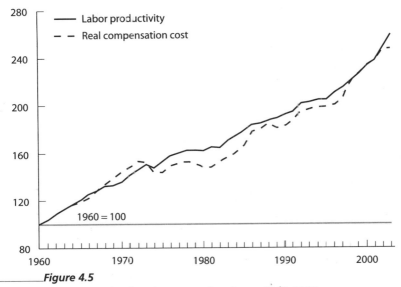

_____**Figure 4.5**

Labor Productivity and Labor Compensation Costs, 1960–2003
Source: Council of Economic Advisers 2004, table B-49. Productivity is output per
hour of all persons in the business sector. Real compensation is compensation
per hour divided by producer price index of total finished goods from table B-65.

this growth. Rather, as chapter 2 described, trade can foster growth in productivity through several channels. Foreign competition cannot take away
the advantages that give rise to this high productivity, namely, the use of
sophisticated technology, a substantial investment in education and human
capital, and the many other advantages of operating in the U.S. market.

Furthermore, firms that compete against imports tend not to cut
wages because they do not determine what those wages will be. Those
firms must pay the prevailing market wage as determined by the alternative employment opportunities of their workers. Research has shown
that domestic industries do not adjust to an intensification of import competition by reducing wages, but by reducing employment.[19] That is, import competition does not drive down wages in the competing domestic

[19] In a careful study, Revenga (1992) examined the impact of changes in import
prices (a good measure of import competition) on industry wages and employment. The
positive relationship between import prices and industry employment indicates that a fall in
import prices would reduce domestic employment. The relationship between import prices
and industry wages was also positive, but the magnitude miniscule. This evidence suggests
that industries adjust to import competition primarily by altering employment, not wages.

industry, but rather drives down the number of workers. This makes sense: if a firm tried to cut wages, the best workers would leave because they have skills that give them opportunities elsewhere in the economy. The least desirable workers would stay because they have no attractive alternatives. Rather than cut wages, firms usually adjust to competition by reducing employment. Then they can choose which workers to keep and which to lay off in an attempt to raise productivity and position the company to survive.

Although average wages are determined by the underlying attributes that make American workers productive, trade can affect the *distribution* of wages in an economy. And here, a very basic point must be stressed: the perception that imports destroy good, high-wage jobs in manufacturing is almost completely erroneous. It is closer to the truth to say that imports destroy bad, low-wage jobs in manufacturing. This is because wages in industries that compete against imports are well below average, whereas wages in exporting industries are well above average. The United States tends to import labor-intensive products, such as apparel, footwear, leather, and goods assembled from components. Comparable domestic industries in these labor-intensive sectors tends to employ workers who have a lower than average educational attainment, and who therefore earn a relatively low wage. For example, in 2003 average hourly earnings of Americans working in the apparel industry were 40 percent lower than in manufacturing as a whole. Average hourly earnings were 28 percent lower in the leather industry and 23 percent lower in textile mills than in the average manufacturing industry.[20]

By contrast, the United States tends to export more skill-intensive manufactured products, such as aircraft, construction machinery, engines and turbines, and industrial chemicals. Workers in these industries earn relatively high wages. For example, in 2003 average hourly earnings in the aircraft and aerospace industry were 44 percent above the average in manufacturing, 4 percent higher in industrial machinery, and 19 percent higher in pharmaceuticals. One study reports that even "after being adjusted for skill differences, wages in export-intensive industries are 11 percent

[20] U.S. Bureau of the Census 2004, 413.

above average, whereas wages in import-intensive industries are 15 percent below average."[21]

Because exports increase the number of workers in relatively more productive, high-wage industries, and imports reduce the number of workers in relatively less productive, low-wage industries, the overall impact of trade in the United States is to raise average wages. Conversely, any policy that limits overall trade and reduces both exports and imports tends to increase employment in low-wage industries and reduce employment in high-wage industries. Restricting trade would shift American workers away from things that they produce relatively well (and hence export and earn relatively high wages in producing) and toward things that they do not produce so well (and hence import and earn relatively low wages in producing) in comparison with other countries. Employment gains for the low-wage textile machine operators in the factory mills would be offset by employment losses for the high-wage engineers in aircraft and pharmaceutical plants.

This general finding—industries that compete against imports tend to be low-wage—has two important exceptions: steel and automobiles. Wages are high in these two industries, and yet they confront competition from imports and are relatively unsuccessful in exporting.[22] Not coincidentally, they also have strong labor unions. Could protecting these unionized manufacturing industries be justified on the basis of preserving high-wages jobs? Some researchers suggest yes, arguing that the existence of wage premiums in such industries justifies government support.[23]

---

[21] Katz and Summers 1989, 264. Similarly, plants that export pay a wage premium of 7 to 11 percent above nonexporting plants after controlling for various other factors (Bernard and Jensen 1995, 71). Labor economists use educational attainment as a proxy for skill level because education is observable, whereas skill is not. This is not quite satisfactory because one can be a very skilled artisan in the textile and apparel industry, for example, without a formal education and yet still receive a relatively low wage.

[22] As Katz and Summers (1989, 264) note, "the widely cited examples of automobiles and steel, where very high wage industries face substantial import penetration and are almost completely unable to export, appear to be atypical. As a rule export-intensive industries are the ones that have substantial wage premiums."

[23] Katz and Summers (1989, 264) argue that this generally would imply export promotion schemes, since "as a rule export-intensive industries are the ones that have

But the case for protecting these industries to preserve the wage premium is extremely dubious. First, it not even clear that these wage premiums, which are the large unexplained variation in the interindustry wage structure and which some economists attribute to labor market rents, should be explained on that basis.[24] If the variation is unexplained, we cannot be certain of what it represents, which makes it a questionable target for intervention. Second, even if workers in certain industries earn a wage premium, the case for promoting those industries depends on those premiums being taken as given. If instead the wage premium is determined by the behavior of labor unions, then using protection to promote the industry might enhance the union's ability to raise wages above the competitive level and exacerbate the wage premium without significantly increasing employment.

Unions strive to attain a combination of higher wages and greater employment for their members. If imports are restricted and the demand for steelworkers increases as domestic firms expand their production, the union can focus more on obtaining higher wages and less on increasing employment. Several studies show that this response, in which unions increase their pressure to raise wages, can ultimately undermine the policy's aim of increasing employment and capturing wage premiums.[25] In this case, protectionist policies exacerbate rather than ameliorate the underlying distortion, namely, the union's ability to raise wages above the competitive level. In this way, the policy

---

substantial wage premiums," but the automobiles and steel industries are the atypical import-competing sectors in which wages are above average. They argue that the abnormally high wages reflect the high marginal product of workers, which they take to be indicative of an economic distortion that results in too few workers being employed in such industries. In principle, therefore, policies to increase employment in these industries would capture these rents for the economy, offset the underlying distortion, and thereby improve national welfare.

[24] The unexplained variation could reflect unobserved worker characteristics such as productivity. In an incisive comment published along with the Katz and Summers (1989) article, Robert Topel notes that the sorting of individuals based on their productivity (e.g., people who work in the communications industry may be more productive than private household workers) and certain job characteristics (e.g. miners earn more than restaurant waiters) cannot be captured by statistical data and yet provides an alternative explanation for the high wages. There remains much debate about this point. See, for example, Gibbons and Katz 1992.

[25] See de Melo and Tarr 1992 and 1993 and Swagel 2000.

negates the benefits that it aimed to capture and imposes costs on other industries.[26]

Finally, the structure of the automobile and steel industries has changed significantly over the past twenty years. A large share of output in both industries is now produced in the United States by nonunionized workers. Japanese and European automakers in the United States and the domestic minimills of the steel industry hire workers who are not part of the United Auto Workers or the United Steelworkers of America. Thus, the large wage premiums earned by unionized workers in these industries have been compressed because of greater domestic competition coming from firms using nonunion workers.

Yet another concern is that trade leads to increasing income inequality in the United States. Over the past three decades, the wage premium for college-educated workers relative to workers with less education (high school degree or dropout) has risen substantially and then leveled off. There is evidence of an absolute decline in the real wages of workers with very little education. In theory, trade can have sharply different effects on the wages of different types of workers.[27] This is implicit in what we have discussed: trade creates jobs in high-wage industries in which the United States exports (aircraft, machinery), and reduces jobs in low-wage industries in which the United States imports (apparel, footwear).

Has international trade contributed to increasing wage inequality in the United States? The consensus of researchers seems to be that

[26] Dickens (1995) also points out that workers who will fill the high-wage vacancies are themselves likely to come from fairly high-wage jobs. This undercuts the ability of activist policies to capture labor rents. There is also the issue of equity. By restricting imports, the government is implicitly forcing workers in other industries earning average wages or below to pay more for automobiles and steel products so that already highly paid workers in those industries can earn even more.

[27] In a classic article published in 1941, economists Wolfgang Stolper and Paul Samuelson connected the distribution of wages in an economy to the prices of various goods, prices that in turn are affected by the international market. They reached the unambiguous conclusion that some factors of production will receive an absolute gain as a result of free trade, while other factors will suffer an absolute loss. For example, if we consider only skilled and unskilled labor, a rise in the relative price of skill-intensive goods increases the real wage of skilled workers and decreases the real wage of unskilled workers. While the precise relationship between product prices and factor rewards depends upon many other factors, such as the degree to which labor can move between sectors, the key conclusion is that trade can have sharp consequences for income distribution.

increased demand for educated workers due to technological changes is mostly responsible for the rising wage premium. By contrast, the role of trade in generating wage inequality appears to be modest. How has this conclusion been reached? If trade had been driving the changes in relative wages in the United States during the 1980s, then theory suggests that the price of unskilled labor-intensive goods should have fallen relative to the price of skilled labor-intensive goods. But after closely examining the data, economists failed to detect any such decline. In addition, they found that manufacturing firms were consistently choosing to employ more skilled labor relative to unskilled labor, despite the rising cost of hiring those skilled workers. This evidence is consistent with an increase in the demand for educated workers.[28]

Another way of looking at the question examines the quantities of imports of labor-intensive goods as a factor that may cause the displacement of less educated workers and reduce their wages. In this case, the volumes of traded goods, rather than their prices, is the focus. This approach yields essentially the same conclusion. Examining the period from 1980 to 1995, one study finds that the wages of college graduates rose 21 percent relative to high school graduates. At the same time, trade and immigration accounted for only about two percentage points (or 10 percent) of this change.[29] The relatively small contribution of trade is related to the fact that imports of manufactured goods from developing countries, presumably the primary source of unskilled labor-intensive goods, rose from just 1.0 percent of GDP in 1970 to 3.2 percent in 1990, hardly a dramatic increase in light of the spectacular increase in the labor market return to education during this period.

Trade, then, does not appear to be primarily responsible for increased wage inequality. Evidence instead points to technological change as having raised the demand for more highly educated workers. For

[28] The pioneering work here was done by Lawrence and Slaughter (1993). These findings stimulated an enormous amount of research on the impact of trade on wages, but subsequent work has not fundamentally altered this basic conclusion. See the papers in Collins (1998) and Feenstra (2000) for an overview. Some economists have dissented from this general verdict. Feenstra and Hanson (2003), for example, link outsourcing to lower relative wages for production workers.

[29] Borjas, Freeman, and Katz 1997. However, they found that these factors are somewhat more important in explaining the wage gap between high school graduates and high school dropouts.

example, the advent of ATM machines and personal computers reduced the demand for bank tellers and secretaries and increased the demand for skilled technicians and highly educated personnel. Whereas international trade would shift the demand for skills between sectors of the economy, skill-biased technical change would increase the demand for skilled workers in all sectors. One study found that nearly three-quarters of the overall shift in labor demand (for nonproduction workers) was a change in demand within industries rather than between industries.[30] Furthermore, the relative wage of educated workers in many developing countries has been increasing as well, a pattern that can be explained by skill-biased technical change but not by international trade.

But if trade has contributed even modestly to increased wage inequality, we can understand why adversely affected workers would oppose free trade. Survey evidence indicates that workers with less educational attainment, those whose wages have lagged the most in recent decades, are also the most skeptical of the benefits of free trade.[31] Although these workers may have a legitimate economic interest in preventing trade, it does not make sense to deal with their concerns by harming the overall economy. It is no more reasonable to help them by imposing barriers to trade than it would be to ban ATM machines or word processing so as to increase the demand for bank tellers and secretaries. This might help them in the short run, but would also reduce economic opportunities for others now and for their children in the future. The more constructive response is to encourage workers to make investments in education and, where possible, cushion the blow for those who are adversely affected by trade. One reason the debate over trade policy is never-ending, however, is that policies to cushion the blow are often viewed as inadequate.

Displaced Workers and Trade Adjustment Assistance

Although free trade is good for the economy as a whole, some workers in import-competing industries will be displaced from their jobs as a result of foreign competition. Without some policy to help these workers, opposition to free trade will always be politically potent. What government

[30] Berman, Bound, and Griliches 1994.
[31] Scheve and Slaughter 2001a.

programs exist to help workers displaced from their jobs as a result of imports? Do these programs work well, and should trade-displaced workers get better treatment than workers displaced for other reasons?

As discussed earlier in this chapter, import competition accounts for only a small fraction of workers who lose their job every year. Even so, who are the displaced workers in import-competing industries and what is being done to help them? Workers in import-sensitive industries "are similar to other displaced manufacturing workers—slightly older, with virtually no difference in educational attainment or job tenure"—but are more likely to be women.[32] And even among import-sensitive industries, workers in very high import-share industries tend to have less education, have shorter job tenure, and are more likely to be female than workers in medium and low import-share industries.[33] The two most salient of these characteristics are gender and relatively low levels of education. These underlying characteristics tend to determine the labor market experiences of these workers, not the fact that they are employed in industries that compete against imports.

For example, workers displaced from high import-share industries are less likely to find new employment within a certain time period. This fact could be interpreted as indicating that the reemployment prospects of workers who have been laid off from industries that compete against imports are worse than average. But this correlation disappears once one controls for the higher proportion of female workers in those industries. In other words, women in general tend to have lower reemployment rates after being laid off any job. They may opt to leave the labor force, for example, or take more time off between jobs than men do. It is this characteristic, rather than anything special about import-competing industries per se, that accounts for the lower reemployment rate of workers displaced from high import-share industries. As one researcher concludes, "Trade-displaced workers may have more difficult labor market

[32] "The most striking difference between import-competing displaced workers and other displaced manufacturing workers is the degree to which import-competing industries employ and displace women. Women account for 45 percent of import-sensitive displaced workers, relative to 37 percent of the overall manufacturing displaced. Some industries stand out: Women account for 80 percent of those displaced from apparel, 66 percent from footwear, and 76 percent from knitting mills (part of the textile industry)." Kletzer 2001, 3.

[33] Kletzer 1998b, 450.

_____Table 4.2
Labor Market Outcomes for Displaced Workers in North Carolina, 1986–1992

	Textiles	Apparel	Other Manufacturing
Percentage reemployed	90.6	86.4	93.9
Duration of unemployment (quarters)	2.1	2.3	1.9
Ratio of new to old wage	0.99	1.22	0.90

Source: Field and Graham 1997.

adjustments, but the source of the difficulty is their otherwise disadvantaged characteristics, not the characteristics of their displacement industry."[34]

What about the wage losses suffered by workers thrown out of work as a result of imports? As it turns out, workers displaced from industries in which import penetration was increasing rapidly had lower earnings losses than other displaced workers.[35] In general, the size of the earnings losses depends largely on how long the workers had been employed in the jobs from which they were displaced (the longer they were employed, the greater the earnings loss) and whether the workers found reemployment in the same industry or in a different industry (if reemployed in a different industry, then the earnings losses are greater). Because workers in import-sensitive sectors tend to be low-wage workers with shorter job tenures, workers displaced from industries that compete with imports generally have lower earnings losses than the average displaced worker.

This phenomenon is illustrated by the textile and apparel industry. Between 1990 and 2004, employment in this industry declined by more than 50 percent, with more than 800,000 jobs lost, due to technological change as well as imports. As shown in tables 4.2 and 4.3, about 90 percent of textile and 86 percent of apparel workers in North Carolina who lost their job as a result of layoffs or plant closings between 1986 and 1991 were reemployed by 1992, a slightly lower percentage than those in other manufacturing industries. But in contrast to displaced workers in other manufacturing industries, who experienced an average 10 percent drop in wages after finding new employment, displaced apparel workers who found new jobs actually received higher wages, while textile

[34] Kletzer 2000, 375.
[35] Addison, Fox, and Ruhm 1995.

_____Table 4.3
Reemployment within Same or Another Industry, Displaced Workers in North Carolina, 1986–1992

	Reemployed in Same Industry		Reemployed in Another Industry	
	Proportion	New/Old Wage Ratio	Proportion	New/Old Wage Ratio
Textiles	50%	1.003	50%	0.969
Apparel	38%	1.049	62%	1.336
Other Manufacturing	64%	0.972	36%	0.761
All Other Sectors	83%	1.026	17%	0.967

Source: Field and Graham 1997.

workers experienced little change in their wages. The explanation is that apparel workers receive very low wages in the first place and that over 60 percent of laid-off apparel workers found reemployment in another manufacturing industry.

Table 4.4 presents more recent data for the entire United States. Although a majority of workers displaced between January 2001 and December 2003 were reemployed by January 2004, a sizable fraction remained unemployed or left the labor force. Particularly in the apparel industry, displaced workers tend to be older women who never earned a high school diploma, and therefore are more likely to have difficulty finding new employment or to leave seek employment. Of the manufacturing workers who found employment, the new jobs paid about 15 percent less than their old jobs. But because workers in the textile and apparel industry

_____Table 4.4
Status of Workers Displaced from Full-Time Jobs between January 2001 and December 2003 (as of January 2004)

	Labor Market Outcome (percentage distribution)			Of Those Re-employed full time			
	Reemployed	Unemployed	Not in Labor Force	At Lower Wage	At Same or Higher Wage	Ratio of New/ Old Wage	Median Weekly Earnings in Lost Job
Textiles and Apparel	71	14	15	72%	28%	0.99	$355
Manufacturing	60	23	17	64%	36%	0.84	$622

Source: Displaced Workers Survey Bureau of Labor Statistics, July 30, 2004 press release available at http://www.bls.gov/bls/newsrels.htm, and unpublished data from the Displaced Worker Survey.
Note: For workers over age of twenty with job tenure of at least three years.

are paid much less than the average worker in manufacturing, those that were reemployed were likely to earn about the same wage as they originally had.

While most workers displaced from industries that compete against imports eventually find employment in the same industry, in related manufacturing industries, or in the nontraded service sector, they almost never find employment in export-oriented industries. A worker laid off from the apparel industry, for example, is extremely unlikely to find employment in the aircraft industry, because a different skill mix is required. This pattern creates a problem for policymakers: workers harmed by imports will not reap the benefits of new employment opportunities in export-oriented industries. Telling these workers that rising employment in export industries will offset the decline in their current industry of employment is not likely to persuade them that free trade is a good thing.

The plight of displaced workers should not be trivialized; numerous studies have shown that their earnings losses are generally sizable and persistent.[36] There is no debate about whether unemployed workers should receive government assistance. The question is whether trade-displaced workers should benefit from a special government program beyond that given to the far more numerous workers who are displaced for other reasons. Special adjustment assistance for workers laid off as a result of imports has been justified on efficiency, equity, and political grounds, but unfortunately all three rationales are open to question.

The efficiency rationale is that government assistance can speed up the process of adjusting to trade and thereby make it more efficient. This is doubtful on both theoretical and empirical grounds. In theory, the government should intervene to accelerate adjustment only if some market failure is associated with that process. The simple fact that the adjustment process sometimes operates slowly and with friction is insufficient grounds for intervention.[37] In addition, the empirical studies of displaced workers alluded to earlier generally suggest that the labor market experiences of those displaced from trade-sensitive industries are not much different from workers with similar characteristics who have been displaced from industries not sensitive to trade. Therefore, efficiency considerations

[36] Kletzer 1998a.
[37] Mussa 1982.

do not seem to justify singling out trade-affected workers for more generous treatment than that extended to other displaced workers.

The equity rationale—fairness dictates that workers displaced
by imports should be given special treatment—is also questionable.
Workers may lose their jobs for any number of reasons: increasing domestic competition, fluctuations in the weather, substitution of capital
for labor, changes in technology, shifts in consumer tastes, and so on.
Even if it were possible to single out workers who have been dislo-
cated for trade-related reasons, there is no compelling case for treating
them differently from those who have lost their job for other reasons.
In fact, it seems grossly unfair to provide a comfortable cushion for the
workers displaced because of imports and not to those laid off because,
say, higher interest rates cut into the demand for housing or automobiles. What is the reason for providing more generous compensation to
the apparel worker in Georgia who loses a job to imports than to the
typewriter assembler at Smith-Corona displaced because of computers
or the Kellogg's worker laid off because General Mills begins producing tastier cereals?

The political argument for trade adjustment assistance is that the
public does view these various causes of job loss as different. Trade
displacement is much more politically sensitive than job loss due to domestic competition or technological change. Therefore, trade adjustment
assistance can mitigate the opposition to trade legislation by reducing the
concentrated losses from liberalization. Still, there is little direct evidence
that trade adjustment assistance (TAA) has proven important in obtaining
negotiating authority, in securing the passage of legislation, or in maintaining support for the system of open trade. The ability of TAA to buy
the political support of labor groups has weakened due to the well-
known shortcomings of the program.[38]

Yet ever since the Trade Expansion Act of 1962, Congress has
ensured that trade adjustment assistance has been a component of trade
legislation. The original purpose of TAA was to compensate workers for
loss of income, but since then, the goal has shifted toward other assistance, such as training and reemployment services.

[38] TAA may have facilitated the passage of trade bills in 1962 and 1974, when
Congress presumably included it in exchange for labor's support for (or muted opposition
to) the trade legislation. Destler 1998.

TAA was revamped in 2002 and currently works in the following way.[39] Unemployed workers can typically receive up to twenty-six weeks of unemployment insurance. If they exhaust this benefit and are declared eligible for TAA by the Department of Labor, they can then receive financial support under the trade readjustment allowance (TRA) for an additional fifty-two weeks, bringing total support to seventy-eight weeks (about a year and a half).[40] Eligible workers are those where increased imports have "contributed importantly" to declining production and layoffs in their industry. In addition, workers in firms whose upstream suppliers or downstream customers have been adversely affected are also eligible for assistance, as are those whose firms shifted production to another country with a free trade agreement with the United States or that receives preferential access. In recent years, about two-thirds of all petitions have been certified, affecting somewhat over 100,000 workers, but this could rise by another 50,000 due to the expanded certification criteria in the 2002 revision.[41]

A special NAFTA assistance program was set up in 1994, relating only to those affected by trade with Canada and Mexico. Under this program, workers could receive benefits even as a result of trade diversion. In other words, if NAFTA diverts trade to Mexico in such a way that higher imports from Mexico substitute for lower imports from another country, workers may be eligible for assistance. As long as Mexican imports have increased, no causal link from NAFTA to the job loss is required. For example, when a sawmill in the state of Washington shut down because federal forest lands were declared off limits to save the spotted owl, the 135 workers affected were declared eligible for NAFTA-TAA because of timber imports from Canada subsequently increased.[42] A unique feature of the NAFTA program is that assistance is available not just to workers who lose their jobs as a result of imports, but also for those who lose their jobs if their employer shifts production to Canada or

---

[39] Baicker and Rehavi 2004.

[40] In the past, when the financial benefits of unemployment insurance were more generous, workers receiving TRA were apparently quite happy to take the benefits and wait for their old jobs to reappear, rather than seek retraining in an effort to adjust to the import competition. In 1988, therefore, Congress shifted the program's focus away from financial compensation and toward adjustment assistance by making enrollment in a government-certified training course a requirement for receiving TRA allowances.

[41] U.S. House of Representatives 2003, chap. 6.

[42] Richards 1997.

Mexico. Once again, participation in a government-approved training program is required for those receiving benefits.

In fiscal year 2002, the Labor Department spent about $95 million in TAA benefits (mainly training) and about $200 million in TRA assistance (extended unemployment insurance payments). These expenditures are a fraction of total spending on unemployment insurance. The program is inexpensive because few workers are actually involved in it; workers declared eligible for TRA do not necessarily collect benefits. In fact, only about 20 percent of workers who are declared eligible for some form of trade adjustment assistance actually take advantage of it. This is because workers either get rehired or reemployed in the interim, receive union compensation, or do not wish to enroll in a training program. Although it is too soon to determine the effects of the 2002 program changes, the take-up rate is expected to increase to 30 percent because of the more generous provision of assistance.[43]

While the budgetary outlays are relatively small, the TAA program is not perfect. Workers provided with benefits over a longer period of time do not have an incentive to find a new job quickly. And prolonging the period of unemployment—as the TAA does—does not usually result in better labor market matches for those workers. The mandatory training programs have not addressed this problem because they are not very successful. As one study found, although TAA was well targeted in serving workers who were permanently displaced from their jobs and who experienced significant earnings losses, there was no evidence that training had a substantial positive impact on the earnings of the trainees. Those who went through the training program did not find better-paying jobs than those who did not attend the program.[44] This bleak assessment is not unique to TAA: there is little evidence that any government training program works well. After studying many such training programs, the OECD reached the sober conclusion that "broad training programs aimed at large groups of the unemployed have seldom proved a good investment, whether for society or for the program participants."[45]

[43] Baicker and Rehavi 2004.

[44] Decker and Corson 1995.

[45] Organization for Economic Cooperation and Development 1994, 37. Heckman (1999, 106) is more blunt about government-sponsored job-training programs: "the evidence strongly suggests that investing in low skilled, disadvantaged adult workers makes

Thus, as currently designed, TAA is not ideal. To the extent that the program merely provides an incentive for trade-displaced workers to remain unemployed for a longer period of time than other displaced workers, it fails to help workers or improve economic efficiency. So how should the system be changed? The training requirement should clearly be dumped: workers do not like it anyway, and it provides no economic value. The benefits should not be tied to time out of work because doing so only prolongs the period of unemployment. Since it is not the case that a longer search leads to a better job match for workers, assistance programs should encourage quick reemployment.

The 2002 legislation revising the trade adjustment assistance programs contains an interesting pilot program that deserves careful study. Because the current TAA discourages work and fails to compensate for income losses, since payments cease when a worker takes a lower-paying job, time-limited earnings insurance was introduced to provide compensation while preserving the incentive to find work. This Alternative Trade Adjustment Assistance (ATAA) gives selected workers over fifty years old cash benefits equal to 50 percent of the difference between their old pay and their new pay (capped at $10,000) if they are reemployed at a lower wage within twenty-six weeks of being laid off and earn less than $50,000 in their new job.[46] Under this scheme, workers would receive these special payments only when they became reemployed.

Any proposal that seeks to provide compensation while preserving the incentive of workers to find employment is worth exploring. It is too soon to say how well the wage insurance and other new provisions of the 2002 reauthorization of TAA will work. Although the costs of the program are also unknown, even something running a few billion dollars—a large expansion in benefits—would be relatively inexpensive in comparison to the gains from keeping markets open to trade. Such a scheme, however, would force a reexamination of the entire concept of unemployment insurance. A potential problem with earnings insurance is that it could be costly, although it could replace existing programs

---

no economic sense." There is some evidence that programs targeted at specific groups, such as youths and women, may work better than others, but even here those who enter such programs seldom experience labor market outcomes that are much different from those who do not enter such programs.

[46] Baicker and Rehavi 2004.

rather than be added to them. One researcher estimates that a two-year earnings insurance program would cost $1 billion.[47] This is only about 5 percent of the cost of unemployment insurance during a recession and is just a fraction of the gains from trade. But a more expansive program is thought to cost as much as $9 billion.

Another potential problem with trade-related assistance is the inefficiency of any government program that attempts to redistribute income to a targeted group. The costs of administering a compensation program might well be much higher than the losses incurred by displaced workers.[48] Aside from the high costs of such a program, basing a compensation program on past earnings runs the risk of trying to create a riskless society. Should the government insure against all losses that individuals incur in the labor market, particularly when the individuals themselves do not seem interested in purchasing such insurance?[49]

Still, public policies should be geared toward helping workers manage their best in this period of rapid economic change. This includes such things as ensuring the portability of health and pension benefits in order to reduce the adverse impact of changing jobs, which must inevitably happen in an ever-changing economy.

The lamentable conclusion is that there is no easy solution and no obvious government policy that can address all of the concerns. Trade adjustment assistance has not worked as promised, and may even be an impediment to economic efficiency. A broader government program to help displaced workers should be examined and might be a small price to pay to reduce anxieties about international trade and maintain political support for open markets. But even if such a program is affordable and gets the incentives right, there is absolutely no guarantee that demands for import barriers by labor groups in import-competing sectors (such as the steelworkers union) will diminish. Even if fully compensated

---

[47] Jacobson 1998, 515–16.

[48] Jacobson (1998, 476) suggests that the "transaction costs associated with [compensation] are likely to be many times larger than the costs imposed on those adversely affected by change."

[49] As Jacobson (1998, 475) notes, "Neither society at large nor members of the risk pool potentially affected by costly job loss appear willing to pay for such (earnings) insurance . . . individuals adversely threatened by trade and other factors appear to lack the willingness to pay actuarially fair insurance," although this may be due in part to the existence of government compensation programs.

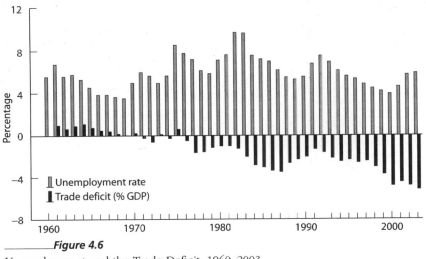

_____*Figure 4.6*

Unemployment and the Trade Deficit, 1960–2003
Source: Council of Economic Advisers 2004, tables B-1, B-35, and B-103.

for losing their job, these workers simply may not want to move to a different job in a different location when there is a chance they can stay employed where they are by stopping imports.

_____### What about the Trade Deficit?

In every year since 1976, the value of goods and services imported into the United States has exceeded the value of goods and services exported. Does the trade deficit injure domestic industries and have adverse effects on employment? Should the trade deficit be a matter of concern and reversing it an objective for trade policy?[50]

    The connection between the trade deficit and employment is much more complex than the simple view that jobs are lost because imports exceed exports. As figure 4.6 shows, the correlation between the merchandise trade deficit and the unemployment rate is actually negative: most

[50] To investigate the causes and consequences of the trade deficit, Congress set up the Trade Deficit Review Commission, which issued its report in November 2000. Unfortunately, the commission split along partisan lines: Democrats viewed the deficit as malign (a serious threat to employment in trade-affected industries), while Republicans viewed the deficit as benign (as reflecting the good state of the economy). The commission's report is available at http://govinfo.library.unt.edu/tdrc/index.html.

of the time, the trade deficit has risen during periods of falling unemployment and has fallen during periods of rising unemployment. As noted earlier, the business cycle may be driving this relationship: a booming economy in which many people are finding employment is also an economy that sucks in many imports, whereas a sluggish economy is one in which spending on imports slacken.

Yet these imports are not free: in order to acquire them, a country must sell something in return. Imports are usually paid for in one of two ways: the sale of goods and services or the sale of assets to foreign countries. In other words, all of the dollars that U.S. consumers hand over to other countries in purchasing imports do not accumulate there, but eventually return to purchase either U.S. goods (exports) or U.S. assets (foreign investment). Both exports and foreign investment create new jobs: employment in export-oriented sectors such as farming and aircraft production is higher because of those foreign sales, and foreign investment either contributes directly to the national capital stock with new plants and equipment or facilitates domestic capital accumulation by reducing the cost of capital.

A deeper understanding of the trade deficit, however, requires some familiarity with balance-of-payments accounting. Balance-of-payments accounting may be a dry subject, but it helps lift the fog that surrounds the trade deficit. This accounting also suggests which remedies are likely to be effective in reducing the deficit, should that be considered desirable.

The balance of payments is simply an accounting of a country's international transactions. All sales of U.S. goods or assets to nonresidents constitute a receipt to the United States and are recorded in the balance of payments as a positive entry (credit); all purchases of foreign goods or assets by U.S. residents constitute a payment by the United States and are recorded as a negative entry (debit). The balance of payments is divided into two broad categories of transactions: the current account, which includes all trade in goods and services, plus a few smaller categories; and the capital account, which includes all trade in assets, mainly portfolio and direct investments.

The first accounting lesson is that the balance of payments always balances. By accounting identity, which is to say by definition, the balance of payments sums to zero. This implies that

current account + capital account = 0.

Because the overall balance of payments always balances, a country with a current account deficit must have a offsetting capital account surplus. In other words, if a country is buying more goods and services from the rest of the world than it is selling, then the country must also be selling more assets to the rest of the world than it is purchasing.[51]

To make the link clearer, consider the case of an individual. Each of us as individuals exports our labor services to others in the economy. For this work, we receive an income that can be used to import goods and services produced by others. If an individual's expenditures exactly match his or her income in a given year, that person has "balanced trade" with the rest of the economy: the value of exports (income) equals the value of imports (expenditures). Can individuals spend more in a given year than they earn in income, in other words, can a person import more than he or she exports? Of course, by one of two ways: either by receiving a loan (borrowing) or by selling existing financial assets to make up the difference. Either method generates a financial inflow— a capital account surplus—that can be used to finance the trade deficit while also reducing the individual's net assets. Can an individual spend less in a given year than that person earns in income? Of course, and that individual exports more than he or she imports, thereby running a trade surplus with the rest of the economy. The surplus earnings are saved, generating a financial outflow—a capital account deficit—due to the purchase of financial investments.

What does this mean in the context of the United States? In 2003, the United States had a merchandise trade deficit of about $550 billion and a services trade surplus of $60 billion. The balance on goods and services was therefore a deficit of about $490 billion, but owing to other factors (net income payments and net unilateral transfers) the current account deficit was nearly $540 billion, or 4.9 percent of that year's GDP. This implies that there must have been a capital account surplus of roughly the same magnitude. Sure enough, in that year U.S. residents (corporations and households) increased their ownership of foreign assets by just under $280 billion while foreigners increased their ownership

[51] A country therefore cannot experience a "balance of payments deficit" unless one is using the old nomenclature that considers official reserve transactions (an important component of the balance of payments under fixed exchange rate regimes) as a separate part of the international accounts.

of U.S. assets by over $855 billion. Therefore the capital account surplus was approximately $575 billion. In other words, foreigners increased their ownership stake in U.S. assets more than U.S. residents increased their holdings of foreign assets, thus forming the mirror image of the current account deficit.[52]

The balance of payments "balances" in the sense that every dollar we spend on imported goods must end up somewhere. Here's another way of thinking about it: in 2003, the United States imported almost $1,770 billion in goods and services from the rest of the world, but the rest of the world only purchased $1,300 billion of U.S. goods and services. What did the other countries do with the rest of our money? They invested most of it in the United States. In essence, for every dollar Americans handed over to foreigners in buying their goods (our imports), foreigners used seventy-three cents to purchase U.S. goods (our exports) and the remaining twenty-seven cents to purchase U.S. assets. What assets are foreign residents purchasing? Some are short-term financial assets (such as stocks and bonds) for portfolio reasons; some are direct investments (such as mergers and acquisitions) to acquire ownership rights; and some are real assets (such as buildings and land) for the same reasons.

Is the current account deficit sustainable? As long as foreign investors are willing to continue purchasing U.S. assets, the deficit can be sustained. Once foreign investors decide to stop buying U.S. assets or to sell them, then the dollar will tend to depreciate on foreign exchange markets, increasing exports and decreasing imports and thus tending to reduce the trade deficit. This process can be slow and orderly and does not require a "hard landing" or sudden collapse in the dollar.[53]

In running a current account deficit, the United States is selling assets to the rest of the world.[54] These foreign purchases of domestic

[52] Council of Economic Advisers 2004, table B-103.

[53] In the mid-1980s, many commentators feared that the current account deficit was unsustainable and that the economy would face a "hard landing" once foreign capital stopped flowing into the United States. These fears proved to be misplaced: the economy did not suffer a hard landing when capital inflows slowed in the late 1980s, the dollar depreciated in an orderly way, and the current account deficits fell as a share of GDP.

[54] Sometimes the United States is likened to a developing country that has become a debtor nation. The United States is a "debtor" country in the sense that the stock of

assets allow the United States to finance more investment than it could through domestic savings alone. In essence, the United States is supplementing its domestic savings with foreign investment and thus is able to undertake more investment than if it had relied solely on domestic savings. The equation that expresses this relationship is

current account = savings − investment.

Once again, this equation is an identity, meaning that it holds by definition. A current account deficit (the capital account surplus) implies that domestic investment exceed domestic savings. Conversely, countries with current account surpluses have domestic savings in excess of domestic investment, the excess being used to purchase foreign assets via foreign investment (capital account deficit).

Figure 4.7 illustrates this point by presenting the U.S. current account as a percentage of GDP from 1960 to 2002, along with the evolution of savings and investment. The current account registered a slight surplus during the 1960s, indicating that the United States was making net foreign investments in the rest of the world. Since the early 1980s, however, domestic investment has been greater than domestic savings, meaning that the United States has been a net recipient of foreign investment.

That the U.S. current account was roughly balanced in the 1960s and 1970s is no coincidence. The ability of a country to run a current account surplus or deficit depends upon the degree to which capital is allowed to move between countries, which in turn is a function of the international monetary system and the exchange rate regime. In the absence of international capital mobility, domestic savings must equal domestic investment, and therefore the current account will be balanced. Under the Bretton Woods system of fixed exchange rates, which lasted from just after

---

foreigners own more U.S. assets than U.S. residents own foreign assets. But the U.S. situation is not really comparable to those of developing countries. In developing countries, foreign investment sometimes includes large amounts of short-term government debt, denominated in a foreign currency. It is misleading to compare these debts to the foreign purchase of U.S. assets by saying that the United States is borrowing from other countries. Borrowing implies a specific payback schedule, hence the repayment problems that developing countries sometimes encounter. In the U.S. case, foreign investors are simply choosing to purchase dollar-denominated assets from the owners of those assets. The investors often wish to take a direct, long-term ownership stake in the United States that they do not intend to reverse.

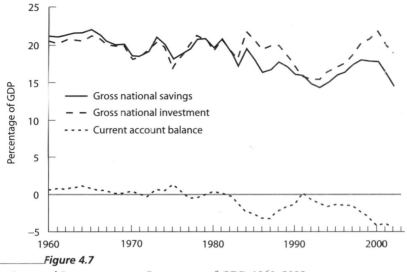

_____Figure 4.7

Savings and Investment as a Percentage of GDP, 1960–2002
Source: Council of Economic Advisers 2004, tables B-32, B-24, B-1.

World War II until 1971, governments maintained fixed exchange rates by imposing controls on capital movements. As a result, capital flows were minimal by present-day standards. When the international monetary system suppresses capital account transactions, the capital account balance must be close to zero, and therefore the current account balance must also be close to zero.

The Bretton Woods system collapsed in 1971, and since then international capital movements have been deregulated. With the return of international capital mobility, relatively large current account imbalances also began to emerge. The United States became a magnet for capital from the rest of the world, particularly after the early 1980s. For example, after Japan eased restrictions on the holding of foreign assets in 1980, Japanese investors took part of their large pool of capital (invested in its domestic market as a result of its high savings rate) and sought higher rates of return in foreign capital markets, particularly in the United States. Now that they were free to buy U.S. assets as well as U.S. goods, Japanese residents chose to allocate some of the dollars they earned in selling products in the United States to buying U.S. assets rather than U.S. goods.

Because the United States is a net recipient of foreign investment, it is difficult to say much about the impact of the trade deficit on the number of jobs in the economy. If the United States took action to reduce the trade deficit in an effort to reduce the number of jobs lost to trade, then net capital inflows from abroad would necessarily have to fall. Then domestic investment would have to be financed by domestic savings, implying higher interest rates, which would reduce the number of jobs created by business investment. In the end, a lower trade deficit's positive impact on employment would be offset by the negative impact of lower domestic investment and higher interest rates.

So what are the implications for trade policy? The current account is fundamentally determined by international capital mobility and the gap between domestic savings and investment. The main determinants of savings and investment are macroeconomic in nature. Current account imbalances have nothing to do with whether a country is open or closed to foreign goods, engages in unfair trade practices or not, or is more "competitive" than other countries. If net capital flows are zero, the current account will be balanced. Japan's $11 billion current account deficit in 1980 became a $87 billion current account surplus in 1987 not because it closed its market, or because the United States opened its market, or because Japanese manufacturers suddenly become more competitive. The surplus emerged because of financial and macroeconomic policy changes in Japan and the United States.[55]

Trade policy cannot directly affect the current account deficit because trade policy has little influence on domestic savings and investment, the ultimate determinants of the current account. If a country wishes to reduce its trade deficit, then it must undertake macroeconomic measures to reduce the gap between domestic savings and investment. Reducing the federal government's fiscal deficit, which acts to absorb domestic savings, could contribute to this result. Long ago it was believed that restrictions on imports would reduce the trade deficit. But that result would follow only

---

[55] Japanese exporters became more price competitive in the U.S. market due to the appreciation of the dollar in the early and mid-1980s, but this appreciation was driven by capital flows into the United States. While trade policy cannot directly affect the current account deficit, the deficit does affect trade policy. A large trade deficit resulting from an exchange rate appreciation puts a competitive squeeze on both exporting and import-competing industries and fuels protectionist sentiment.

if exports remained unaffected, an assumption that the Lerner symmetry theorem suggests, and experience demonstrates, is false. Adam Smith saw through such policies of restriction: "Nothing, however, can be more absurd than this whole doctrine of the balance of trade, upon which, not only these restraints, but almost all the other regulations of commerce are founded."[56]

To conclude, we have seen in the past two chapters that trade is a small part of the everyday shift of workers between various sectors of the economy, creating jobs in some industries but destroying jobs in others. While some workers are adversely affected by imports, government programs are in place to help them. Blocking imports may protect some jobs in industries that compete against imports, but harms employment in export-oriented and import-using industries. To fully understand trade policy, we must appreciate these oft-ignored indirect effects.

[56] Smith 1976, 488.

5

Relief from Foreign Competition: Antidumping and the Escape Clause

We have seen how trade policies aimed at reducing imports also reduce exports and employment elsewhere in the economy. Yet import restrictions are often justified as a way of providing relief to industries suffering from "unfair" foreign competition. Antidumping laws, which provide a means for tariffs on unfairly low-priced imports, have become the primary instrument for addressing such concerns. This chapter examines the U.S. antidumping laws and asks whether they provide a remedy for unfair trade, or are merely a convenient mechanism for protecting an industry from imports. We will also look at the escape clause procedure, which can provide industries with temporary relief from imports without the claim of unfair trade. Finally, we will examine whether trade protection really helps industries such as textiles and steel adjust to foreign competition and become more competitive.

Unfair Trade: Subsidies and Dumping

We are all familiar with the claim that imports cost jobs. But many people are also afraid that American industries are being harmed by unfair foreign trade practices. These include export subsidies and the dumping of goods at low prices that undermine the sales of U.S. firms. To counter such practices, the United States enforces several "fair trade" laws that allow import tariffs to be imposed. For example, when a foreign government subsidizes its exports to the United States, the subsidy is considered to be an actionable unfair trade practice if it injures domestic producers.

Of course, from a strictly economic point of view, an importing country might well benefit from receiving subsidized goods. Even if the subsidy harms domestic producers, the subsidy allows the importing country to purchase imports at a lower price, thanks to the generosity of foreign taxpayers. By improving the terms of trade, the foreign subsidy adds to the domestic gains from trade. For example, domestic oil producers would be understandably upset if the Organization of Petroleum Exporting Countries (OPEC) decided to subsidize oil exports to the United States, but the country as a whole would probably welcome the lower gas prices that would follow.

But such subsidies are not desirable from the standpoint of the world economy. For one thing, such subsidies cut into the exports of countries that have a natural comparative advantage in those products, and so distort the world's allocation of resources. Subsidies also generate political friction among trading partners, each viewing the other's government as putting its finger on the scales of international competition to tip the outcome toward its own favored producers.[1]

For these reasons, the United States led the effort to draw up an Agreement on Subsidies and Countervailing Measures in the Uruguay Round of multilateral trade negotiations in 1994. The subsidies agreement establishes rules on permissible types of subsidies and tries to ensure that such subsidies will not distort trade. Under the agreement, export subsidies and subsidies to industries that compete against imports are prohibited in principle, but subsides related to research and development, regional development, and environmental compliance purposes are permissible.

In the United States, domestic firms have legal recourse against subsidized imports. The remedy takes the form of tariffs known as countervailing duties (CVDs). Domestic firms initiate the legal process by filing a petition with the Department of Commerce and the U.S. International Trade Commission (ITC) alleging that imports have been subsidized by a foreign government. If Commerce determines that the imports have been subsidized and if the ITC decides that the domestic industry has been injured as a result of the imports, tariffs of the magnitude of the subsidy margin (as determined by Commerce) will be imposed.

---

[1] The United States, it should be noted, provides such export subsidies through the Export-Import Bank. In fiscal year 2003, the Export-Import Bank authorized $10.5 billion in support to U.S. exporters through loans, guarantees, and export credit insurance. Over $4.6 billion helped finance the sale of large commercial aircraft. Indeed, Boeing and General Electric receive the bulk of the funding support. World Trade Organization 2003, 69.

In recent years the CVD process has been rarely invoked by domestic firms. Are foreign countries subsidizing fewer of their exports to the United States? As a result of the multilateral subsidy agreement, perhaps so. But the more likely explanation is that domestic firms have found other ways to prevent such exports from entering the U.S. market. And in fact domestic firms find it much easier to obtain protection by accusing foreign firms of "dumping" in the U.S. market than by proving the existence of foreign subsidies.

From the standpoint of domestic firms seeking protection from imports, antidumping is where the action is. During the 1990s, five antidumping cases were initiated for every CVD case. This is true not just in the United States, but around the world. In the year ending June 2003, WTO members initiated thirteen countervailing duty investigations and 283 antidumping investigations.[2] The number of dumping cases swamps those of other trade remedies. What exactly is going on here?

Dumping has been deemed an unfair trade practice by country authorities and world trade agreements, and the antidumping law is intended to combat it. Yet the gap between the rhetoric and the reality of antidumping trade policy is simply enormous. Dumping sounds awful, as though foreign goods were being unloaded on America's docks and priced below cost to force domestic firms out of business. But under the law, dumping simply means that a foreign exporter charges a lower price in the U.S. market than it does in its home market. This is nothing more than price discrimination. If the foreign exporter is found guilty, the United States can impose import duties to offset the difference.

Figure 5.1 shows the annual number of U.S. antidumping investigations since 1970. Fluctuations in antidumping activity are related to such factors as the exchange rate and the unemployment rate (an appreciation of the dollar and a higher unemployment rate increase the number of cases) as well as the rise in the import-to-GDP ratio. In addition, the number of antidumping cases ratcheted up in the early 1980s after administrative authority over the antidumping laws was transferred from the Treasury Department (which was indifferent to such petitions) to the Commerce Department (which took them up with great enthusiasm) and a change in the antidumping law encouraged multiple petitions.[3]

[2] World Trade Organization 2004, 45–46.
[3] Irwin 2004.

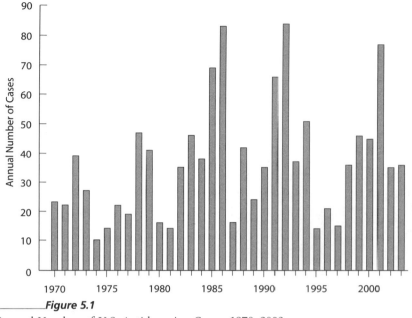

_____Figure 5.1
Annual Number of U.S. Antidumping Cases, 1970–2003
Source: Import Administration, U.S. Department of Commerce.

While the details of antidumping (AD) are quite complex, it is important to understand why these laws have become such a nuisance.[4] The AD process is activated when a domestic industry, represented by an industry association or in some cases just a single firm, files a petition with the Commerce Department and the ITC. The petitioners must have legal standing to file a petition. (In 1999, for example, Commerce rejected an antidumping case filed by a group of Texas oil producers against Saudi Arabia, Mexico, Venezuela, and Iraq on the grounds that the petitioners did not represent the entire industry.) The legal fees associated with filing an AD case typically amount to about a million dollars, although more complex cases can cost several million dollars.[5]

[4] There is now a voluminous literature that finds fault with the antidumping laws. For recent analyses, see Barfield (2003) and Lindsey and Ikenson (2003). Blonigen and Prusa (2003) provide an excellent survey of recent research on antidumping policy.

[5] In the early 1990s, the U.S. International Trade Commission (1995, 4-3) surveyed petitioners and found a simple petition would cost about $250,000. The price is much higher today, particularly if the petitioner wants the law firm to provide additional support for the petition.

The Commerce Department determines if dumping has occurred and, if so, calculates the dumping margin. Specifically, Commerce ascertains whether a foreign exporter made sales in the United States at prices that are at "less than fair value." Sales are less than fair value if the export price, the price charged in the U.S. market, is less than the so-called normal value. The normal value is determined one of three ways: by the price charged by the foreign exporter in home market sales, by the price it charged in third-country sales, or by constructed value, which is an estimate of what the price should have been based on the costs of production plus administrative expenses and a profit margin. The dumping margin is simply the difference between the export price and this determined normal value divided by the export price. For example, if a foreign firm charges $100 for a good in its own market and exports it to the United States for $80, then the dumping margin is 25 percent, or $(100-80)/80$.

After receiving a petition, Commerce almost always rules that dumping has occurred. From 1995 to 1998, Commerce ruled that dumping had occurred in 98 percent of all cases.[6] And the dumping margins were large: the average AD duty imposed during the same period was a whopping 58.8 percent.[7] However, the average dumping margin varies widely depending upon the method used to calculate the normal value. As table 5.1 shows, during the 1995 to 1998 period, the average margin on (affirmative) cases that compared the U.S. price to the exporter's home market price was just 7.36 percent. When Commerce compared the U.S. price to its constructed value, the average margin was 35.70 percent. In cases involving nonmarket economies, such as China and the former Soviet Union, the average margin was about 67 percent. In cases using "facts available," in which Commerce essentially accepted the data presented by the petitioner, the average margin was nearly 96 percent. Because of a greater reliance on the constructed value method over the price comparison method, the average dumping margin has steadily increased over time.[8]

---

[6] Lindsey and Ikenson 2003, 24–25. From 1980 to 1992, Commerce ruled that dumping had occurred in 93 percent of all cases. Congressional Budget Office 1994, 50.

[7] Lindsey and Ikenson 2003, 26. The average antidumping duty imposed has risen over time. The average duty was 22 percent in the period from 1981 to 1983 and 56.8 percent in the period from 1991 to 1995. Congressional Budget Office 1998, 25.

[8] See Blonigen 2003.

_____Table 5.1
Antidumping Margins by Calculation Method, 1995–1998

Calculation Method	Determinations (affirmative only)	Average Dumping Margin (affirmative only)
U.S. prices to home market prices	4	4.00%
	(2)	(7.36%)
Constructed value	20	25.07%
	(14)	(35.70%)
Nonmarket economy	47	40.03%
	(28)	(67.05%)
"Facts available"	36	95.58%
	(36)	(95.58%)
Total	141	44.68%
	(107)	(58.79%)

Source: Lindsey and Ikenson 2003, 26.
Note: Not all methods shown.

When U.S. prices are compared to actual foreign market prices, rather than to some constructed value, the dumping margins appear to be quite low. Yet even when a foreign firm charges exactly the same price in the U.S. market as in its home market, dumping can be found to exist. This is because Commerce compares the average of the foreign firm's home price to the prices charged on individual sales in the United States. If any *individual* U.S. price is below the *average* home market price, which must be the case if there is any movement in the prices over time, then dumping is found to occur. Instances in which the U.S. price exceeds the foreign price are ignored. This not only guarantees a finding of dumping, but artificially inflates the dumping margin.[9]

In contrast, something is clearly amiss when a method other than the price comparison approach is employed. When Commerce is unable to collect enough data on the exporter's home market prices, it may resort to the constructed value method. When Commerce undertakes a constructed value calculation, it attempts to estimate the foreign exporter's costs of production plus an allowance for administrative, selling, and general expenses and profits. Prior to 1995, U.S. antidumping practice was to augment the estimated costs of production by at least 10 percent for administrative expenses and at least 8 percent for profits.[10]

[9] Ikenson 2004.
[10] Congressional Budget Office 1994, 31.

Multilateral agreements reached under the Uruguay Round mandate that Commerce cannot tack on these arbitrary amounts to the estimated costs, but must use the actual administrative expenses and the actual profit, when available. However, there is still room for Commerce to use questionable numbers and thereby raise the dumping margin.

When dealing with nonmarket economies, such as China and the states of the former Soviet Union, where prices may not be market determined, Commerce estimates production costs using wage rates and other factor costs from a surrogate country of similar level of economic development. For example, in estimating China's costs of farming crawfish in 1997, Commerce used the cost of fish caught at sea in "comparable" economies with freer markets, such as India, Pakistan, Sri Lanka, and Indonesia, and took transport costs within China from a 1994 newspaper report on trucking costs in India. Not surprisingly, this method leads to unusually large dumping margins. In this case, Commerce announced dumping margins ranging from 85 to 201 percent, implying that Chinese crawfish farmers generously decided to sell their product for just one-third to two-thirds of production costs. In another case using the constructed value method, Commerce once determined (with apparent precision) that natural bristle paintbrushes from China were sold at less than fair value with a dumping margin of 351.9 percent, and imposed tariffs of the same amount.

The finding of such high dumping margins is not limited to nonmarket economies. In June 2003, in a case involving polyethylene retail carrier bags (PRCBs, otherwise known as the thin plastic shopping bags one finds at grocery stores), the Commerce Department found margins as high as 123 percent for Thailand, 102 percent for Malaysia, and 77 percent for China.

The International Trade Commission's role in an antidumping case is to determine if the domestic industry has suffered or is threatened with "material injury" as a result of the less-than-fair-value imports. The definition of material injury, according to the law, is "harm which is not inconsequential, immaterial, or unimportant."[11] Only the harm to the competing industry is considered, not the harm or injury to consumers or other domestic industries that result from the imposition of import duties.

[11] U.S. House of Representatives 2003, 553.

While Commerce almost always finds dumping, the injury determination is a more difficult hurdle for the domestic petitioner to clear because of the injury standard itself and because the ITC is a quasi-independent agency (as opposed to Commerce, which is typically an advocate of the domestic industry in the process). Still, the ITC ruled affirmatively in about 83 percent of final determinations during the period 1999 to 2002.[12] Economic factors, such as changes in the industry's output, employment, and capacity utilization, are the main determinants of a favorable injury finding. But political factors, such as whether the industry is a constituent of the chairman of the ITC's congressional oversight committee, also appear to matter.[13]

If dumping is found to exist and the domestic industry is deemed to have suffered material injury, then antidumping duties are imposed. As of June 30, 2003, the United States had 278 AD duty orders in effect on goods coming from nearly fifty countries (mainly the European Union, China, and Japan), with most of them on iron and steel products. By contrast, the EU had 204 antidumping orders in place, India had 210, South Africa had 96, Canada had 87, and Brazil had 56.[14]

In the United States, AD orders existed on such narrowly defined goods as frozen concentrated orange juice from Brazil, cotton shop towels from Bangladesh and China, oil country tubular goods from Canada, fresh salmon from Chile and Norway, paper clips from China, large newspaper printing presses from Germany, stainless steel wire rod from France and elsewhere, fresh kiwi fruit from New Zealand, pasta from Italy and Turkey, aspirin from Turkey, and a host of other products.[15]

What happens when AD duties are imposed? Not surprisingly, imports fall sharply. Looking at table 5.2, we can see that imports subject to AD duties of over 50 percent fell 73 percent in volume and rose 33 percent in price, on average, from the year before the petition to the year after the petition. Imports subject to AD duties in the 25 to 50 percent

[12] Lindsey and Ikenson 2003, 3. The ITC ruled affirmatively in 66 percent of final determinations during the period 1980 to 1992. Congressional Budget Office 1994, 50.

[13] See the research by Moore (1992), Baldwin and Steagall (1994), and Hansen and Prusa (1997).

[14] World Trade Organization 2004, 46. By contrast, there were only fifty-seven U.S. countervailing duty orders in effect.

[15] For updated statistics and information on the administration of U.S. antidumping laws, see http://www.ita.doc.gov.

_____Table 5.2
Trade Effects of Antidumping Duties (comparing year prior and following initiation of AD investigation)

AD Duties	Import Volume	Import Price (unit value)
Over 50 percent	−73%	33%
Between 20% and 50%	−22%	2%
Under 20%	−16%	−10%
Non-Affirmative Decision	−3%	3%

Source: U.S. International Trade Commission 1995, 3–9.
Note: Import price effect does not include the AD duties.

range fell 22 percent in volume and rose 2 percent in price. The ITC study on which the table is based also found that developing countries were disproportionally harmed by AD duties: the quantity of their imports tended to fall over twice as much as imports from developed countries.

To a large extent, however, imports from countries not subject to the AD duties fill the void left by those smacked with the AD duties. This is because AD duties are only imposed on imports from countries named in the petition, leaving the market open to others who can produce similar products. Table 5.3 indicates that while imports from countries affected by the AD duties fell by 32 percent, imports of the same product from countries not subject to the duties rose 24 percent. Because of this effect, antidumping petitions are often filed sequentially to squash the imports that arise from other sources as a result of the initial antidumping action.[16]

For example, Micron Technology, a producer of dynamic random access memory (DRAM) computer chips in Boise, Idaho, filed an AD petition against DRAM imports from Japan in 1985. After the imposition of restrictions on Japanese exports, foreign DRAM production shifted to South Korea, so Micron filed an AD petition against Korean producers in 1991. After Korean exports were similarly restricted, Taiwanese producers entered the market, so Micron filed an AD petition against DRAM exports from that country in 1998. The story is similar in the case of salmon. Antidumping duties were imposed against imports of fresh salmon from Norway in 1991. After Chile began to develop its fishing

[16] Prusa 1997.

_____Table 5.3
Evidence of Trade Diversion in Antidumping Actions

	Import Volume	Import Price (unit value)
Affirmative, subject country	−32%	5%
Affirmative, non–subject country	24%	−5%
Nonaffirmative, subject country	−24%	4%
Nonaffirmative, non–subject country	19%	−3%

Source: U.S. International Trade Commission 1995, 3–15.

Note: *Affirmative* denotes cases in which AD duties were imposed; *subject* indicates imports subject to the duties; and *non-subject* indicates imports from other countries or firms not subject to the duties.

industry and filled the void left by the Norwegians, they too were hit with AD duties in 1998.

The simplest way for domestic petitioners to avoid this problem is to file multiple petitions against several sources. When the Coalition for Fair Preserved Mushroom Trade filed an AD petition concerning imports of preserved mushrooms in 1998, for example, it targeted imports from Chile, China, India, and Indonesia all at the same time. During 1999 to 2001, when the steel industry filed numerous antidumping cases, they named twelve countries in cold-rolled steel products, twelve countries in steel concrete reinforcing bars, and twenty countries in cold-rolled carbon steel flat products. The countries ranged from the usual suspects of Japan and Korea to more obscure producers such as Latvia and Moldova.

Congress facilitated the move toward multiple filings by changing the law in 1984. Prior to that time, the injury determination was conducted on a country-by-country basis, even if multiple petitions were filed. After the 1984 change, the ITC had to consider the combined impact of imports from all named countries on the domestic industry. The cumulation provision is estimated to have raised the probability of an affirmative decision by 20 to 30 percent, thereby changing the ITC's determination from negative to positive in one-third of such cases.[17] This, in turn, has given petitioners an additional incentive to file petitions against multiple countries.

Sometimes petitioners exclude certain countries from petitions as a matter of corporate strategy. For example, in 1994, the Maui Pineapple Company in Hawaii filed an AD petition against imports of canned pineapples from Thailand, resulting in the imposition of AD duties up to

[17] Hansen and Prusa 1996.

51 percent, depending on the company. Thailand's canned pineapple exports to the United States fell from $101 million in 1993 to $51 million in 1997. Over the same period, imports of canned pineapple from Indonesia jumped from $9 million to $51 million because that country's exports were not subject to AD duties. But Maui did not file an AD petition against Indonesian imports because at that time it was forming a joint venture with one of the country's largest pineapple producers. Similarly, in 1994 Bic filed a petition alleging that disposable lighters from China and Thailand were being dumped in the U.S. market, but did not include Mexico in the petition because Bic had a factory there.[18]

It is important to note that trade diversion occurs even in cases where the final ITC injury decision is negative and no duties are imposed. Even when the domestic industry was found not to have suffered injury, imports from countries that had been the target of the case fell 24 percent on average, while imports from countries not targeted rose 19 percent. Thus, simply filing an antidumping petition can reduce imports from targeted sources even if duties are not imposed. According to one study, when a petition is ultimately rejected, imports from the sources named in the petition fall by about 15 to 20 percent, whereas if the petition is accepted, imports fall about 50 to 70 percent.[19]

A reason for this "chilling effect" on imports is the uncertainty surrounding the AD process: if dumping is found, domestic importers will be liable for the payment of dumping duties after Commerce issues its preliminary determination. To minimize their potential financial exposure, importers quickly stop purchasing from the foreign suppliers named in the petition. There is also an "investigation effect" on imports when an antidumping petition is filed: before Commerce has even made a preliminary determination about dumping, import volumes fall and prices rise by about one-half of the full effect of imposing duties.[20]

_____The Costs of Antidumping

Despite the apparent ease with which domestic firms can obtain some form of protection under the antidumping laws, only a tiny fraction of

[18] *Rushford Report*, September 1999, 3.
[19] Prusa 2001.
[20] See Blonigen and Prusa 2003.

total U.S. imports are covered by AD duties. AD and CVD orders covered just 0.5 percent of all imports in 2001.[21] In any given year, the value of imports targeted by antidumping petitions is sometimes less than one-tenth of 1 percent of imports. Given these relatively small figures, does the antidumping process really matter?

There are several reasons why antidumping continues to merit close scrutiny. First, these tariffs quickly add up. The net welfare cost of AD and CVD actions in the United States was a whopping $4 billion in 1993.[22] With the demise of the Multi-Fiber Arrangement in 2005, this makes them collectively the most costly of all U.S. import restrictions.

These costs are only going to mount over time as more cases are filed. This is because AD duties are hard to remove once they are imposed. The mean duration of AD measures terminated in the period from 1980 to 1994 was over nine years in the United States, as opposed to five years in the European Union.[23] One of the few reforms of AD actions in the Uruguay Round was to introduce a sunset rule starting in 1995. This required that all AD duties be terminated after five years unless a review finds that this would lead to a recurrence of dumping and injury. Yet Commerce is unlikely to revoke an antidumping order over the objections of the domestic industry. In 180 sunset cases considered between July 1998 and December 1999, the ITC revoked AD or CVD duties only 31 percent of the time.[24]

Second, the coverage figures understate the harm in antidumping actions. The very existence of the antidumping law allows it to be used as a tool to enforce collusive agreements. For example, in 1989 U.S. producers of ferrosilicon formed a cartel and reduced output. The lower output was used to prove injury and justify the imposition of antidumping duties against five foreign competitors. When Brazil started exporting ferrosilicon in place of the others, their producers were invited to join the U.S. cartel. When they refused, they too were hit with an antidumping case.[25]

---

[21] World Trade Organization 2003, 50. In 1991, the figure was 1.8 percent (U.S. International Trade Commission 1995, 4-1).

[22] Gallaway, Blonigen, and Flynn 1999.

[23] Congressional Budget Office 1998, 98.

[24] Moore 1999.

[25] Eventually, criminal and civil legal actions were taken against the cartel members. See Pierce 2000.

When an exporter is confronted with the prospect of potentially severe duties that exporters from other countries will not have to endure, the target has a powerful incentive to negotiate some sort of export restraint agreement that will allow the exporter to avoid the imposition of duties. In some cases, the foreign exporter tries to reach a suspension agreement with Commerce (and approved by the petitioner) that terminates the petition. The quantity of imports falls by the same margin in cases that are settled as those in which duties are imposed, although the import price does not rise as much in settled cases.[26] The Uruguay Round also allows "price undertakings," in which exporters can agree to minimum export prices in order to avoid the imposition of duties. Thus, even when no duties are imposed, antidumping can result in trade restrictions and even collusive outcomes.[27]

Finally, the antidumping process is so heavily biased against foreign firms that it is prone to abuse and manipulation by domestic firms. The problem is not that the process is overtly political and subject to political influence, although that problem can arise in some high-profile cases. Rather, AD rules are intentionally stacked in favor of the domestic petitioner, both in reaching a conclusion that dumping has occurred and in the size of the dumping margin. Even the Congressional Budget Office notes that the Commerce Department "effectively serves as investigator, prosecutor, judge, and jury in dumping and subsidy determinations." And although it should be neutral in these roles, Commerce is "actually an advocate of one of the parties to the case."[28]

The antidumping process is riddled with subtle tricks and arbitrary biases that invariably favor the domestic petitioner, making it ironic AD rules are a part of the "fair trade" laws. The application of AD measures often hinges on a narrow technicality, such as the definition of the relevant industry. In the case of cut flowers from Columbia, the ITC initially ruled that the domestic industry was not materially injured. After Commerce later accepted petitions maintaining that each individual flower species was a different "industry" (the rose "industry," the

---

[26] Withdrawn petitions used to be considered a signal of a collusive settlement, but Taylor (2004) shows this not to be the case. Only about 10 percent of all petitions were withdrawn in the 1990s.

[27] See Moore 2000.

[28] Congressional Budget Office 1994, 41.

chrysanthemum "industry," etc.), the ITC then made an affirmative injury ruling. In the case of frozen concentrated orange juice, Commerce ruled that fresh oranges and industrial concentrate orange juice are "like products" even though the markets and pricing for the two products are quite different.

Even the Commerce Department's Office of Inspector General was critical of the way that the Department's Office of Import Administration handled the eighty-four antidumping and countervailing duty petitions filed by the steel industry in June 1992. The office said that the agency "adopted several controversial and confusing policies that undermined the principles of transparency and consistency . . . [and were] not only inconsistent with past practice, but were also applied inconsistently from one case to the next." The report added that Import Administration "applied policies that made reporting more onerous for respondents, caused confusion among analysts, and made IA's decisions appear arbitrary, even to its own staff."[29]

And if there was not already sufficient incentive for firms to file antidumping petitions, Senator Robert Byrd (D-W.Va.) opened the door to more mischief in late 2000. Senator Byrd slipped into an agricultural appropriations bill a provision that hands over all the revenue from antidumping duties to the petitioning industry. Although the Clinton administration opposed the measure, the president signed the bill for its other provisions. Thus, petitioning firms will not only be able to charge domestic consumers higher prices for their products, but will receive a check from the government for a share of the tariff revenues. In fiscal year 2003, the government was expected to make disbursements of $280 million.[30]

This has led to a scramble for government cash, particularly because the legislation is retroactive. In 2001, companies put in requests for $1.2 trillion in back antidumping tariff revenue. The chief beneficiaries have been two ball bearing companies whose lawyers helped write the Byrd legislation. Torrington Company received $63 million in Byrd money in 2001 but has sought reimbursements of $23.4 billion (its sales in 2001 amounted to $1.1 billion).[31] The Byrd provision encourages domestic

[29] U.S. Department of Commerce 1993, 20.
[30] World Trade Organization 2003, 48. See also Congressional Budget Office 2004.
[31] King 2002.

firms to become bounty hunters and start filing AD petitions to receive tariff revenue payments from the government. In a dispute initiated by the EU and seven other countries, a WTO panel ruled in 2002 that the subsidy was inconsistent with the WTO rules. Because the United States has not changed the provision, the EU received permission from the WTO in September 2004 to impose up to $150 million in trade sanctions against the United States.

In other countries, antidumping is a widely criticized feature of U.S. trade policy. Yet the United States refused to put antidumping reform on the agenda for future trade negotiations until the WTO ministerial conference in Doha, Qatar, in November 2001. This change is partly because the antidumping genie is out of the bottle: the United States is increasingly becoming a target as well as a user of these actions. Whereas antidumping actions were once instituted mainly by the United States, European Union, Australia, and Canada, now developing countries (such as Mexico, Argentina, South Africa, and others in Asia) have copied them and have become aggressive users of these measures against exports from developed countries.[32]

While the Congressional Budget Office did not find systematic evidence prior to 1995 that other countries were singling out American firms for antidumping enforcement in retaliation for AD actions, evidence did "lend some credence to fears that U.S. policy may be starting to come back to haunt U.S. exporters as other countries follow its lead."[33] Growing anecdotal evidence points to this conclusion. For example, Micron Technology, previously mentioned as the DRAM producer who filed a series of petitions, was itself accused of dumping memory chips in Taiwan shortly after it succeeded in getting AD duties imposed on Taiwanese exports. And even though the ITC rejected a petition accusing Mexico of dumping emulsion styrenebutadine rubber, the U.S. petitioner soon faced charges by its Mexican competitor of dumping the same product in that country.[34] If antidumping actions remains unchecked, such retaliatory cases can only be expected to multiply in coming years.

[32] Prusa 2001.
[33] Congressional Budget Office 1998, xiv.
[34] *Rushford Report*, April 1999, 7.

_____*Is Antidumping Defensible?*

The antidumping process involves many arbitrary judgments and is subject to abuse. Can any economic rationale be mustered in favor of the AD laws? The problem is that price discrimination, charging different prices in different markets, is a normal business practice and an accepted feature of domestic competition. Exporters often find that competition is more intense in the international market than in their home market, where they have a more secure position with domestic consumers. Therefore, exporters have to offer price discounts in foreign markets.

On economic grounds, the fact that a firm charges different prices in different markets is neither unfair nor a problem unless it harms competition (such as through anticompetitive actions or predatory practices) or reflects a market-distorting policy. If geared toward preventing these actions, antidumping policy could have some merit as a means of preserving competition or correcting alleged market distortions. Unfortunately, the antidumping laws are not written to identify and respond to such situations. This leaves the impression that the laws exist only to protect domestic firms if they can jump through a few bureaucratic hoops.

For example, the antidumping laws might be worthwhile if they prevented predatory pricing by foreign exporters. Predatory pricing would occur when an exporter prices its goods below cost in an effort to eliminate American producers and achieve a monopoly position. Firms engaging in predatory pricing must be prepared to incur substantial losses initially and then recoup those losses through the future exercise of monopoly position. But this makes sense only if the firm can effectively knock out most of its competitors in the United States and in other countries. Were the Bangladesh shop towel producers trying to eliminate their foreign rivals and achieve a monopoly position? Were the flower growers from Colombia trying to do the same? Most foreign exporters want to receive as high a price as possible from their sales. Few companies entertain the delusion of driving all of their competitors out of business in the world market.

In fact, in the overwhelming majority of AD cases, such predatory motives can be ruled out as utterly implausible. One researcher examined the structural characteristics of every one of the 282 industries involved in every dumping case in the 1980s in which duties were imposed or in which the case was suspended or terminated.[35] To isolate the cases in which predatory pricing might be considered plausible, she first eliminated all cases in which the industry in the United States and in the challenged country was relatively unconcentrated. These were excluded on the grounds that barriers to entry in such industries are probably not substantial. And without barriers to entry, anticompetitive practices are unlikely to exist because even if the firm drives rivals out of business, it cannot raise prices to finance the losses sustained in the price war if other firms can simply reenter the market once prices go up.

The researcher also eliminated cases in which there were multiple exporters from a single country or from several countries, reasoning that successful collusion by such firms would be unlikely and that there are enough firms to preserve competition. Finally, she eliminated all cases in which the import penetration level was not significant, or in which import growth was not rapid, since the imports would be unlikely to create market power if they did not comprise a large share of the U.S. market. In the end, only thirty-nine cases were left, just 14 percent of all those considered, in which the industries were characterized by substantial domestic or foreign concentration. Of these remaining cases in which the preconditions for predation did exist, we cannot say for sure that predation was in fact a motive, only that it could not be ruled out.

The antidumping statue is not employed to prevent predatory conduct or preserve competition, but simply to protect the domestic industry from foreign competition—at the expense of domestic consumers, of course. One legal scholar concludes that while the antidumping laws were "originally marketed as anti-predation measures, they are now written in a way that compels the administering authorities to impose antidumping measures in a vastly broader class of cases—all instances in which dumping causes material harm to competing domestic firms."[36] A ITC commissioner once tried to shift the interpretation toward an anti-predation remedy. But petitioners appealed to the U.S. Court of International Trade, which ruled that focusing on competition effects "seems to assume that the purpose of the antidumping statute is merely to prevent

---

[35] Shin 1998.
[36] Sykes 1998, 29–30.

a particular type of 'injury to competition' rather than merely 'material injury' to industry."[37]

Some antidumping advocates claim that foreign firms have a protected home market in which they can earn high profits, and from which they can subsidize export sales. In this view, any price discrimination due to a sanctuary home market counts as a market-distorting practice that antidumping should attempt to remedy. But as one antidumping critic aptly notes, "the [antidumping] law lacks any mechanism for determining whether the prices practices it condemns as unfair have any connection to market-distorting policies abroad."[38] The law does not distinguish cases in which there may be a sanctuary market effect, or ask if dumping is at all related to market distortions. If antidumping advocates are sincere in their desire for an antipredation remedy that is not simply protectionism, they should be willing to amend the current law and include an explicit test for the protected sanctuary home market that is often alleged to exist.

The problem with antidumping is not just the way the law is administered. The fundamental problem is that antidumping laws are written with the presumption that price discrimination is a problem. But there is nothing inherently harmful or anticompetitive about price discrimination. Price discrimination is an accepted feature of domestic competition. It would be surprising if domestic prices were *exactly* the same as an exporter's home price.[39] As already noted, the government rarely undertakes direct price comparisons when making a dumping determination, but more frequently makes arbitrary calculations about production costs. The result is that "dumping is whatever you can get the government to act against under the dumping law."[40] It is hard to avoid the conclusion that the antidumping laws are simply a popular means by which domestic firms can stifle foreign competition under the pretense of "fair trade."

[37] Sykes 1998, 29–30.

[38] Lindsey 2001, 1.

[39] "In the typical antidumping investigation, the DOC compares home-market and U.S. prices of physically different goods, in different kinds of packaging, sold at different times, in different and fluctuating currencies, to different customers at different levels of trade, in different quantities, with different freight and other movement costs, different credit terms, and other differences directly associated selling expenses (e.g., commissions, warranties, royalties, and advertising). Is it any wonder that the prices aren't identical?" Lindsey and Ikenson 2003, 21.

[40] Finger 1993, viii.

Except in cases of gross abuse, antidumping is essentially a tool that firms can use to insulate themselves from falling import prices. Some industries will always be faced with import surges, such as the domestic steel industry in the aftermath of the Asian financial crisis of 1997–98, when a collapse in foreign demand sent world steel prices tumbling. After the domestic computer production outstripped demand in 1985, world prices of semiconductors fell through the floor, triggering a round of dumping complaints.

In such cases, the problem facing the petitioning industry is not any price differential between markets, that is, foreign firms charging a higher price in their domestic market than in the United States. The afflicted industry would find no consolation if the U.S. price were higher than the foreign price even as both were falling sharply. Rather, the basic problem for the industry is that prices everywhere are falling due to unforeseen circumstances. It may be reasonable to provide an industry facing such difficulties with temporary protection without any claim that trade is "unfair." And that is precisely what the escape clause is designed to do.

_____The Escape Clause

If a domestic industry is suffering as a result of import competition and yet does not allege that the imports are unfairly dumped or subsidized, the industry can still receive temporary protection. Ever since the passage of the Reciprocal Trade Agreements Act in 1934, when the United States embarked on its policy of negotiating tariff reductions with other countries, Congress recognized that trade liberalization might force difficult economic adjustments on particular sectors of the economy. Because of this, Congress insisted that if lower tariffs brought about serious injury to certain domestic industries, they should be provided with temporary relief to help them adjust to the new conditions of trade. To this end, the "escape clause" provides a mechanism for domestic industries to get a temporary exception to any negotiated tariff reduction.

Section 201 of the Trade Act of 1974 provides the current statutory basis for the escape clause.[41] It allows representatives of an industry (a trade association, firm, union, or group of workers) to file a petition

[41] The escape clause is also contained in Article 19 of the GATT and in the Agreement on Safeguards as part of the Uruguay Round negotiations.

with the International Trade Commission for temporary relief from import competition. The petition must include a specific plan that details how protection will be used to help the industry adjust. The ITC must then determine if the imports are, or threaten to be, "a substantial cause of serious injury," where "substantial cause" is defined as "a cause which is important and not less than any other cause."[42] Cutting through the legal verbiage, this simply means that imports must be the most important cause of injury. This legalistic language is nontrivial: The ITC rejected a Section 201 petition from the automobile industry in 1980 on the grounds that the most important source of the industry's difficulty was not imports, but the recession of that year.

If the ITC reaches an affirmative finding of injury, it must then recommend an appropriate remedy to the president. This remedy can include action on trade, such as higher tariffs, or other policies that would help facilitate the adjustment efforts of the domestic industry. The president then has wide discretion as to what action is taken. The import relief can take place over a period of four to eight years and must apply to imports from all sources (unlike antidumping, which, as we have seen, is selective).

Section 201 has been criticized as being merely a protectionist loophole that allows firms to obtain protection, with no allegation of unfair trade, and therefore permits a country to backslide away from open markets.[43] But such provisions function as essential safeguards that make trade liberalizing agreements possible. As other economists have noted, "Safeguard provisions are often critical to the existence and operation of trade-liberalizing agreements, as they function as both insurance mechanisms and safety-valves. They provide governments with the means to renege on specific liberalization commitments—subject to certain conditions—should the need for this arise (safety valve). Without them governments may refrain from signing an agreement that reduces

---

[42] U.S. House of Representatives 2003, 666.

[43] Expressing skepticism about the "safety valve" explanation for the escape clause, Sykes (2003) argues that the likelihood of direct protectionist legislation decreases if such legislation violates international obligations and results in international sanction. Therefore, "the ability of Congress to resist special interest pressures for protection . . . would likely be greater in the absence of Article XIX." Finger (1996) is equally skeptical about safeguards, dubbing them "legalized backsliding."

protection substantially (insurance motive)."[44] The presence of the escape clause, it can be argued, has encouraged cautious governments to liberalize trade more than might otherwise be the case.

Section 201 was invoked frequently in the 1970s, but has been used only sporadically in recent decades. Just nineteen cases were filed in the 1980s and only ten cases in the 1990s. This is partly because it has proven too difficult a way of getting protection: of the nineteen cases considered in the 1980s, for example, the ITC ruled affirmatively in only seven. Even then, there is no guarantee that the president will provide relief to the industry, and in practice presidents are often reluctant to grant it. This record is why Senator Ernest Hollings (D-S.C.) once made the dismissive quip that "Section 201 is for suckers."[45] The escape clause has been completely overshadowed by antidumping, where the injury standard is not as strict and presidential action is not required. In view of the ease with which antidumping actions can be initiated and affect trade, it comes as no surprise that firms have avoided Section 201.

The steel industry recently discovered another reason why escape clause actions are of limited value—administrative exemptions and WTO review. As a result of a campaign promise, President Bush initiated a large steel Section 201 case in 2001 and later imposed duties of up to 30 percent for three years on several types of steel products. But imports from countries having free trade agreements with the United States—Canada, Mexico, Israel, and Jordan—were exempt from the duties, and the Bush administration granted many additional product exclusions that allowed the import of specialized steel products. The European Union and seven additional countries also challenged the steel tariffs at the WTO, claiming they violated international agreements.[46] A WTO panel ruled that the safeguard decision was inconsistent with the Agreement on Safeguards, which allows tariffs to be imposed only when foreign products are being imported in a quantity sufficiently increased so as to cause serious injury. But the 2002 safeguard action was taken well after the Asian financial crisis of 1997–98 caused U.S. steel imports to swell, and imports generally declined

[44] Hoekman and Kostecki 2001, 303.

[45] Quoted in Low 1993, 57.

[46] Chapter 7 discusses the WTO's dispute settlement system in greater detail. For a discussion of how WTO agreements have created obstacles for the use of Section 201, see Irwin 2003.

from 1999 to 2001. In addition, the panel indicated that the U.S. recession rather than imports may have been the major cause of injury.

The Bush administration faced the decision of whether to maintain the safeguard duties and face possible foreign retaliation for violating the WTO agreement, or to rescind the duties and comply with the WTO finding. When the EU threatened to impose tariffs on $2.2 billion of U.S. exports, the government decided to lift the duties in December 2003, after just twenty-one months. The safeguard action proved to be much less valuable to the steel industry than it had hoped.

With the increasing abuse of antidumping measures, escape clause actions have come to be viewed in a more benign light. Section 201 is now seen as a potential solution to the problem of antidumping. Escape clause actions have several advantages over antidumping measures: there are no bogus claims of unfair trade, they provide greater flexibility in the scope and duration of nondiscriminatory protection, and the president is allowed to take into account the overall economic, security, and political interests of the United States in tailoring a relief package. Relaxing the high standards of the escape clause would make it a more attractive method of obtaining import relief and provide an opportunity to rein in the use of antidumping. The danger, of course, is that Congress might simply expand the use of the escape clause without constraining the use of antidumping.

Clearly, the challenge for policymakers operating in an era of greater economic integration is one of balance—making the escape clause available without compromising open markets: "if the standards for obtaining import-related remedies are too restrictive, the escape clause mechanism cannot serve as an effective shock absorber for protectionist pressures. On the other hand, if the eligibility criteria are too weak, any domestic industry that faces import competition may become eligible for temporary protection."[47] This trade-off is one of the most difficult challenges in trade policy.

_____Does Temporary Relief from Imports Work?

Some form of safeguards seems to be a political necessity. And we have seen that the escape clause can be a desirable alternative to antidumping

[47] Lawrence and Litan 1986, 79.

actions. But does temporary relief from imports actually provide a remedy for the ills afflicting the domestic industry? Although protection has been justified as a way of revitalizing certain industries, it may not be able to accomplish this objective.[48]

Ideally, such relief would offer temporary protection to industries that compete against imports, in exchange for assurances that the industry will undertake measures to adjust to the new competition. But in providing temporary relief, the government encounters a problem with time consistency. The industry would like to reap the benefits of protection without undertaking the costs of adjustment. When the government cannot credibly commit to eliminating protection in the future, an industry may find itself able to perpetuate the protection by not investing sufficiently in cost reductions. If the government bases its decision to renew protection on whether the industry has adjusted to the foreign competition, then the industry may have an incentive not to adjust in order to trigger a renewal of protection. Even making trade relief contingent on such investment does not eliminate the time consistency problem. Temporary, contingent protection may still become permanent protection.[49]

This pattern of repeated renewals of protection is sometimes seen in practice. Some industries have used temporary protection to adjust to competition from imports. The automobile, consumer electronics, and semiconductor industries have received temporary protection at one time or another, but adjusted to the new conditions of competition. This does not mean that protection helped promote the adjustment, just that protection was temporary. Indeed, blocking imports failed to solve the fundamental problem these industries faced, either because foreign competition was located in the United States through direct investments or because the industry depended heavily upon foreign export sales and the importation of components. Given the inability of trade policy to solve the underlying problems confronting these industries, domestic

[48] In addition to the discussion of certain industries below, Krueger (1996) presents a series of case studies on protection that examine whether import limits actually helped the domestic industry. Baldwin (1988) also discusses the inefficacy of protectionist measures in helping domestic industries.

[49] Tornell 1991.

firms adjusted by adopting new technology, moving to new market niches, and forming global alliances.[50]

Other industries have essentially received permanent protection over the past few decades by seeking and repeatedly receiving "temporary" protection. Two that stand out are the steel industry and the textile and apparel industry. Both face long-term structural adjustments to domestic and foreign competition and have stubbornly resisted pressures to adapt. The steel industry suffers from excess capacity worldwide, a strong union that has helped price domestic producers out of the world market, and growing domestic competition from smaller mills. The textiles and apparel industry, on the other hand, is struggling against the loss of comparative advantage in labor-intensive manufactures by becoming more capital-intensive, upgrading technology, and outsourcing.

The steel industry has received nearly continuous protection for over thirty years and is still seeking limits on imports. From 1969 to 1974, the large, integrated producers were protected from imports by a series of voluntary restraint agreements (VRAs). From 1978 to 1982, a Trigger Price Mechanism, consisting of minimum import prices, was in effect. From 1982 to 1992, a new round of VRAs was in place. When the industry failed to persuade the government to renew the VRAs, the industry filed a massive number of AD and CVD complaints in 1992–93. When the Asian financial crisis struck in 1997–98, sharply depressing world steel prices, the industry again filed many AD cases. As a result of the Section 201 escape clause case initiated by President Bush in 2001, the industry benefited from 30 percent tariffs on imports during 2002 and 2003.

Yet all this trade protection has never been enough for the steel industry. In fact, there are two steel industries in the United States—large integrated firms and smaller minimills. The big integrated firms—U.S. Steel, the former Bethlehem Steel, and others—use blast furnaces to create steel from raw inputs and then shape it into various products. Production is concentrated in Pennsylvania, Ohio, and West Virginia, and labor is represented

---

[50] Another way to adjust to import competition is simply to fade away, as has been the fate of the domestic footwear industry. Import penetration in the domestic footwear market rose from 13 percent in 1966 to 90 percent in 1996, while employment fell from 233,400 in 1966 to 46,100 in 1996. See Freeman and Kleiner (1998) on how the remaining firms in the domestic industry have adjusted their labor practices in order to survive.

by the United Steelworkers of America. The management and unions of Big Steel perpetually blame their problems on imports and are continually calling for import restraints to allow the industry to revitalize itself.

The smaller minimills take scrap steel and use electric-arc furnaces to produce various final products. Because they do not require iron ore and coal supplies, these firms are not geographically concentrated but spread around the country close to the markets they serve. Minimills have much lower costs than the big integrated steel firms, partly because their workers are not unionized. As a result, the minimills have grabbed U.S. market share away from the big integrated producers. The minimills accounted for about 10 percent of U.S. production in the late 1960s, but nearly 50 percent today. As the market share held by imports has remained steady at about 20 percent, almost all of the erosion in the market share held by the integrated producers is due to the minimills.

Thus, changes in market demand and competition from the minimills are mainly responsible for pushing several large steel producers into bankruptcy. Unlike imports, this domestic competition cannot be stopped at the border and is slowly forcing the integrated producers to adjust. But the process has been prolonged in part due to import restraints and the recalcitrant steelworkers union. The strength of the "steel triangle"—the Big Steel firms, the United Steelworkers union, and the their powerful representatives in the Congressional Steel Caucus—have ensured that the large producers continue to receive corporate welfare at the expense of taxpayers and consumers. In 2002, for example, the Pension Benefit Guaranty Corporation, a U.S. government agency, took over the pension plans of several steel firms whose unfunded pension liabilities exceed $8 billion.[51]

The textiles and apparel industry has also used its political influence to maintain an array of barriers designed to stop foreign competition. The United States negotiated export restrictions on cotton textile products with Japan in the 1950s. Although these trade restrictions were designed as a temporary measure to give the industry some breathing space to become more efficient, the industry always complained that the

---

[51] For an expose of steel's lobbying tactics and demands for corporate welfare, see Barringer and Pierce (2000).

protection was inadequate. Rather than being eliminated, the temporary restraints slowly spread to include other countries and products, gradually filling in the gaps from which imports were seeping in. The Short Term Arrangement on Cotton Textiles trade was signed in 1961, followed by the Long Term Arrangement on Cotton Textiles in 1962. Set to last for five years, the long-term arrangement was renewed for three years in 1967 and again in 1970. These trade restrictions were extended to wool and man-made textiles products in the first Multi-Fiber Arrangement in 1974. This was followed by the second MFA in 1978, the third MFA in 1982, and the fourth MFA in 1986, each of which continued to tighten the restrictions by expanding the country and product coverage. The MFA was finally abolished in 2005 (after a ten-year phaseout) over the strenuous objections of the industry, but its proponents have not given up the fight for more import restraints.

Unlike the large integrated steel producers, the textile and apparel industry has made some adjustments to compete against foreign imports. The textile industry has become less dependent upon unskilled labor-intensive production techniques by adopting advanced technology and more capital-intensive production methods (often using imported machinery). The consequent increase in productivity has sharply reduced industry employment. The apparel sector, which is less able to substitute capital for labor, has been harder hit and has turned instead to foreign outsourcing to remain competitive. Despite the plant closings and employment losses at the aggregate level, new firms have entered the industry, and within-plant productivity has increased in both textiles and apparel.[52]

Despite the inefficacy of import protection in solving an industry's problems, many industries still identify imports as the problem and protection as the cure. Some have even claimed that temporary protection "played a major role in revitalizing key American industries" in the 1980s. For example, the steel and auto industries faced many difficulties in the early 1980s, but received import relief and by the late 1980s had significantly improved their output, employment, and productivity.[53]

[52] Levinsohn and Petropoulos 2001.
[53] Tonelson 1994. His article is entitled "Beating Back Predatory Trade," but it is absurd to think that the woes of the steel, automobile, and textile industries were due to foreign predatory practices.

This view of protection completely misrepresents the experience of the 1980s. Revitalization was in fact the result of the economic recovery after the recession of 1981–82, which had been the worst economic downturn since the Great Depression. In addition, the appreciation of the dollar in the early 1980s squeezed import-competing and export industries, with relief coming when the dollar began to depreciation after 1985. To conclude from the 1980s that temporary protection is a proven method of boosting industrial competitiveness not only overlooks the more important macroeconomic context of that period, but ignores the fact that foreign competition is precisely what motivated American manufacturers to cut costs and improve their productivity. Diminishing competition through import restraints takes the pressure off domestic industries and dulls their incentive to improve efficiency.

For example, let us consider the celebrated Harley-Davidson motorcycle case. Even today, this is frequently heralded as a great success of "breathing space" protection. The story, as conventionally told, is that in the early 1980s Harley-Davidson was pushed to the wall by Japanese competition. After receiving temporary import relief in 1983 under the Section 201 escape clause, the company got its act together and came back stronger than ever.[54] In fact, Harley recovered so swiftly that it even requested that the final year of tariff protection be canceled.

The real story is different: import relief had nothing to do with Harley-Davidson's turnaround. At the time, Harley-Davidson produced only "heavyweight" motorcycles with piston displacements of over 1000 cc, while Japanese producers mainly exported medium-weight bikes (700 cc to 850 cc of piston displacement) to the United States. But in 1975 Kawasaki opened a production plant in Nebraska, and in 1979 Honda opened a plant in Ohio, both of which produced heavyweight motorcycles to compete directly with Harley-Davidson. They did not produce them in Japan because there was virtually no market for such large motorcycles in Asia.

The deep recession of 1981–82 particularly affected blue-collar workers, the main consumer base for Harley's products, and put the company under severe financial pressure. So they filed for import relief

[54] The company's management fully conceded that Harley's production process was far behind the cutting-edge Japanese manufacturing practices at the time the Section 201 petition was filed; see Reid 1990.

under Section 201 in September 1982, making no allegation of unfair dumping or subsidies. The ITC had problems determining that imports were the substantial cause of Harley's injury because imports were plummeting from the recession too. They finally decided that Harley had been injured because unsold inventories of imported medium-weight bikes (700–850 cc) were accumulating.[55] The ITC also ruled that Honda's Ohio plant and Kawasaki's Nebraska plant were part of the domestic industry that deserved protection.

The Reagan administration accepted the ITC's recommendation and adopted a tariff-rate quota on imports of motorcycles over 700 cc. A tariff-rate quota allows a certain quantity of imports to enter paying the usual tariff, but imports above that quantity have to pay the higher protective tariffs. These were initially set at 45 percent and then declined over five years. The protection had almost no impact on Harley-Davidson because Honda and Kawasaki were already producing heavyweight motorcycles in the United States, production that was not constrained. In fact, Honda and Kawasaki favored the Section 201 case because it could protect them from their Japan-based rivals Suzuki and Yamaha. But even Suzuki and Yamaha were able to evade the tariff-rate quota on imports of motorcycles over 700 cc: they simply produced a 699 cc version that was not subject to the quota.[56] Then Suzuki and Yamaha had room under the quota to export more larger (1000 cc) bikes before they had to pay the extra 45 percent duty.

Harley was deeply disappointed with the import relief. Because the final year of tariffs would have been very low and had virtually no effect on the motorcycle market, the company gave up the Section 201 relief a year before it was set to expire. Doing so gained Harley favorable publicity and helped convince President Reagan to visit a Harley plant in Pennsylvania, where he declared, amid a sea of red, white, and blue, that his administration was glad to lend Harley a helping hand.

[55] The inventory of medium bikes accounted for 80 percent of all unsold motorcycles, and the inventory buildup was much less for models larger than 1000 cc because of production cutbacks.

[56] Harley engineers purchased two imported motorcycles because they suspected that only the label on the engine had changed, but to their astonishment the engines were exactly 699 cc! Reid 1990, 89.

Harley saved itself from bankruptcy and turned itself around because a new management team, appalled at the lax inventory control system and antiquated production methods, dramatically improved the efficiency of the production process. Close attention to production detail, as well as the rebounding economy, helped rejuvenate Harley's economic prospects. Blocking imports contributed virtually nothing to Harley's recovery. As the chief economist of the ITC during this period later recalled, "if the case of heavyweight motorcycles is to be considered the only successful escape-clause case, it is because it caused little harm and it helped Harley-Davidson get a bank loan so it could diversify."[57]

Thus, one should not be overly optimistic about the ability of trade protection to help sectors with adjustment problems more severe than coping with a temporary surge of imports. Whether import restraints actually assist the domestic industry in its adjustment efforts is a debatable proposition. But even if protection contributes little to adjustment, the escape clause has been a political necessity and has helped maintain domestic support for the open world trading system.

[57] Suomela 1993, 135. In 1986, the company bought a mobile home producer, Holiday Rambler Corp.

_____6

Developing Countries
and Open Markets

Previous chapters have described the benefits of free trade and the costs of import protection, but many observers are skeptical that open trade policies can improve conditions in poor countries where a majority of the world's population live. This chapter examines whether the case for free trade is qualified by the special circumstances of developing countries. Recent experience suggests that developing countries can reap substantial benefits from adopting more open trade policies, but that such policies alone do not guarantee development, particularly when corruption, civil conflict, and other institutional failings prevent local entrepreneurs from taking advantage of world markets. This chapter also discusses developed country policies that are harmful to developing countries, such as agricultural subsidies, import barriers on labor-intensive manufactured goods, and requirements that labor standards be a condition for trade.

_____Trade Policy and Developing Countries

In past decades, developing countries were reluctant to participate in the world economy. Many people in poorer countries feared that rich countries would dominate and exploit them.[1] Powerful foreign multinationals, it was believed, would gain control of small economies unless governments restricted their activities. Furthermore, the prevailing view among

[1] "It is sometimes difficult for sophisticated economists and politicians to understand the deep historic and cultural problems some [developing] countries have with the idea of free trade. Some still equate it with oppression from colonial days." This comment comes from Mike Moore, the former director-general of the WTO. Moore 2003, 133.

economic experts in the 1950s and 1960s was that developing countries had limited opportunities to achieve growth through exports. International trade was expected to reinforce their comparative advantage in the production of simple primary commodities, thereby locking them into a pattern of specialization that would forever prevent their economic development.

Over the past two decades, these conclusions have been proven false. Countries that restricted foreign trade and investment may have avoided foreign exploitation, but remained desperately poor nonetheless. Meanwhile, international trade created opportunities that in fact promoted development and reduced poverty. Countries that encouraged trade did not remain stuck producing just raw materials, but began exporting an increasing array of labor-intensive manufactured goods.[2]

However, as a legacy of the past, many developing countries have had to overcome severe trade-related policy distortions, including quantitative restrictions on imports and exports, high tariffs, overvalued exchange rates, and administrative controls on foreign exchange allocation. Politically powerful interest groups, including state-owned enterprises that fear competition and government bureaucrats whose power is derived from their decision-making authority, have fiercely resisted trade liberalization and often have been able to block trade reforms. As a result, even after many developing countries have reduced tariffs and liberalized trade policies, they still have much higher tariffs than developed countries. As table 6.1 shows, import tariffs in developed countries are less than 5 percent, on average, while those in developing countries are substantially higher, in the range of 15 to 30 percent, on average. Although developing country tariffs are significantly lower than a decade ago, these tariffs are often just the tip of the iceberg, as many of these countries have in place significant nontariff barriers to trade. Thus, there is ample room for further reforms of trade policy in the developing world.

Of course, free trade is not the single most important factor behind economic development. For many countries, reforms in other areas may be of greater importance and hence a more urgent priority.

---

[2] Krueger (1997) provides an excellent analysis of how the old view of trade and development, based on erroneous assumptions and expectations, eventually gave way in the face of contrary evidence.

_____*Table 6.1*
Average Applied Tariff Rate on Industrial Products, 2001

	Percent
Developed countries	
United States	4.4
EU (15)	4.1
Japan	3.9
Australia	4.7
Canada	4.2
Developing countries	
Mexico	15.6
Brazil	13.8
Argentina	13.4
Bangladesh	21.9
India	31.0
Pakistan	20.1
South Africa	10.9
Cameroon	17.6
Gabon	17.5

Source: World Trade Organization 2003, 13.

These include ensuring the security of property, providing legal institutions that support market transactions (enforcing contracts, etc.), and encouraging the development of financial markets. In many instances, these goals can be achieved not by proactive government policies, but by eliminating poor policies and counterproductive practices: the government should not arbitrarily confiscate or expropriate goods or property, should not protect monopolies and create obstacles to new business formation, should not suppress financial markets with heavy-handed regulations, and so forth. Other nontrade reforms may require proactive government policies, such as improving public health and access to schools.

Still, trade policy reforms can play an important contributing role in promoting development. Recent experience has demonstrated that a shift toward more liberal trade policies can bring about striking improvements in economic performance. This in turn leads to improved socioeconomic outcomes, including the reduction of poverty, malnutrition, and infant mortality.

Consider the following extended quotation:

> History makes a mockery of the claim that trade cannot work for the poor. Participation in world trade has figured prominently in many of the most successful cases of poverty reduction—and, compared with aid, it has far more potential to benefit the poor. . . . Apart from financial benefits, export growth can be a more efficient engine of poverty reduction than aid. Export production can concentrate income directly in the hands of the poor, creating new opportunities for employment and investment in the process. . . . Experience from East Asia illustrates what is possible when export growth is broad-based. Since the mid-1970s, rapid growth in exports has contributed to a wider process of economic growth which has lifted more than 400 million people out of poverty. In countries such as Vietnam and Uganda, production for export markets has helped to generate unprecedented declines in the levels of rural poverty. Where export growth is based on labour intensive manufactured goods, as in Bangladesh, it can generate large income gains for women. . . . The benefits of trade are not automatic—and rapid export growth is no guarantee of accelerated poverty reduction. Yet when the potential of trade is harnessed to effective strategies for achieving equitable growth, it can provide a powerful impetus to the achievement of human development targets.

Which globalization cheerleader wrote this passage? The World Bank? The World Trade Organization? None of the above. This statement is from Oxfam, the British charitable organization that is also very critical of the current system of world trade.[3] Oxfam is among the growing number of nongovernmental development organizations recognizing that open trade policies enable countries to benefit from the growth of world trade.

[3] Oxfam 2002, 8–9.

The conclusions expressed in Oxfam's statement are supported by empirical analyses of the relationship between trade and growth focusing specifically on developing countries. One recent study by David Dollar and Aart Kraay examined the top one-third of all developing countries in terms of the increase in their trade-to-GDP ratio since 1980. These countries—the "globalizers"—experienced a 5 percent annual increase in real per capita income, whereas the other developing countries—the "nonglobalizers"— saw only a 1.4 percent annual increase in real per capita income.[4] The globalizers also cut import tariffs by twice the margin of nonglobalizers.

Individual country case studies reinforce the conclusions of the cross-country studies. As Dollar and Kraay note, "There are many interesting pair-wise comparisons between the globalising group and the nonglobalising group: Vietnam versus Burma, Bangladesh versus Pakistan, Costa Rica versus Honduras. In each of these cases, the economy that has opened up more has had better economic performance."[5]

It is sometimes believed that globalization has been imposed on countries. Yet globalization is also a choice. Through their trade and foreign investment policies, countries can choose the degree to which they want to be a part of the world economy. Many parts of the world have chosen not to participate in the world economy, and they have succeeded in being marginalized. For example, Egypt, once one of the great trading nations of the world, currently has an export (or import) to GDP ratio of less 10 percent, a fraction of what it is for many export-oriented developing countries. Egypt's own policies have stifled trade and kept this ratio artificially low.

Table 6.2 lists several small, poor developing countries that have experienced large changes in their trade-to-GDP ratio over the past decade. Cambodia, Vietnam, and Uganda have embraced the world market and have seen their trade-to-GDP ratios soar. Meanwhile, trade has shrunk as a part of the economies of Egypt, Nigeria, and the Dominican Republic. Some of these declines may be due to domestic disorder, macroeconomic mismanagement, or reduction in demand for country-specific goods (such as Zambia's copper), but some also represent government policies that deliberately hinder the ability of citizens to participate in the world economy.

[4] Dollar and Kraay 2004.

[5] Dollar and Kraay 2004, F24. Indeed, greater trade openness, measured by rising trade or declining trade barriers, has been a feature of virtually all rapid-growth developing country experiences in the last fifty years. Panagariya 2004a.

_____**Table 6.2**
Trade-to-GDP Ratio in Selected Developing Countries, 2002

	Trade-to-GDP Ratio, 2002	Percentage Point Change in Trade Share, 1990–2002
Cambodia	48	+36
Uganda	18	+13
Vietnam	51	+11
Bangladesh	15	+6
Egypt	9	−9
Nigeria	26	−8
Zambia	30	−8
Dominican Republic	33	−4

Source: World Bank 2004b, 306–9.

The greatest example of a country turning its back on the world economy is China in the fourteenth century. The imperial court prohibited any foreign trade (without official permission) for about two centuries after 1371, even going so far as to forbid the construction of new seagoing ships in 1436. While these efforts did not completely eliminate trade, they severely curtailed it at a time when Chinese merchants were very active in the Indian Ocean and Africa. China's action did not stop globalization. But China lost its technological leadership and fell very far behind the rest of the world in military and commercial strength. Eventually it fell prey to political domination by the West in the nineteenth century.

That lesson still holds true today: countries that deliberately seek to isolate themselves from the world will only find their living standards falling behind those of other countries. The failed, autarkic state of Burma is a sad reminder of this fate. In the Middle East, too many countries have resisted joining the world economy. At the time of the September 11, 2001, attack on the World Trade Center and Pentagon, Saudi Arabia, Iran, Iraq, Syria, Afghanistan, Algeria, and other countries in the region had one thing in common: they were not members of the WTO. With over 140 members, the WTO is not an exclusive club that shunned them. Instead, these countries did not (until recently) feel compelled to become part of the club, a symptom of their disengagement with the rest of the world.[6] According to the UN's Arab Human Development Report,

[6] Lindsey 2001.

many societies in the Middle East are closed, their economies stifled, their peoples repressed. They do not encourage business formation or welcome foreign investment, the exchange of goods across borders, or even international trade in ideas. According to the report, the Arab world translates about 330 foreign books annually, one-fifth of the number that Greece alone translates. Perhaps not surprisingly, the report found that one in two Arab youths is dissatisfied with the prospect of living in a closed society and has expressed a desire to emigrate.[7]

_____Two Billion People: China and India

Perhaps the most compelling examples of how more open trade policies can facilitate economic growth and development come from the two most populous countries in the world—China and India. Over the past quarter century, both countries have shifted from economic isolation to economic integration with the rest of the world. Both countries are now growing rapidly and have made remarkable strides in reducing poverty and raising the standards of living of their citizens.

Before 1979, China was virtually closed to world trade. China's trade operated under a strict system of state trading in which about a dozen foreign trade corporations monopolized all international trade. China followed a Soviet-style system of central planning that suppressed foreign trade and made import-substitution industrialization its overriding objective. Imports were minimized and exports were authorized only to the extent required to pay for imports.[8] The policy succeeded in building up domestic manufacturing, but investments in heavy industry failed to improve the welfare of China's citizens.

In December 1978, China began to end its policy of economic isolation. Under the leadership of Deng Xiaoping, the government decollectivized agriculture, freed foreign exchange transactions, allowed private entities to trade, and permitted foreign investment. Although reforms

[7] United Nations Development Program 2002, 30.

[8] "To achieve the goal of a self-reliant industrial economy, domestic industry was protected from foreign competition by direct controls on imports and investment and administrative allocation of foreign exchange combined with an overvalued currency. These policies, enforced by central planners and a central foreign trade monopoly, built an airtight wall between the domestic economy and the world economy." Shirk 1994, 8.

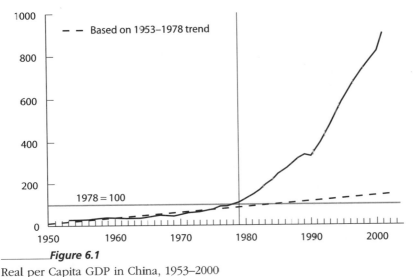

_____**Figure 6.1**
Real per Capita GDP in China, 1953–2000
Major reforms were initiated in 1979. Data from Penn World Tables, available
at http://www.nber.org.

were gradually introduced over the 1980s and 1990s and went well beyond trade policy alone, the opening of China's economy to the world
was a critical component of these changes. In 1992, the weighted average
tariff on manufactured goods was over 45 percent. China having joined
the WTO, its average tariff will eventually be less than 7 percent.[9]

The results have been stunning. China's exports and imports
have soared, as figure 3.1 illustrated. China's share of world trade rose
from about 1 percent in 1980 to more than 5 percent in 2002. Foreign investment in China has grown from virtually nothing in 1979 to about
$500 billion in 2003. As figure 6.1 shows, China's real per capita income
has grown at near double digit rates since the 1980s, making it one of the
fastest-growing countries in the world. As a result, the official rate of
poverty has fallen from 28 percent in 1978 to 9 percent in 1998.[10]

Of course, China did not just open up to trade, it fundamentally
changed the way its economy was organized. Yet the decision to open to
the world was not inevitable; it had a large internal market and could
have pursued import substitution or industrial policies. But its trade

[9] Ianchovichina and Martin 2003, 9.
[10] Bhagwati and Srinivasan 2002.

policy reforms were a vital component of its broader reforms and have played a critical role in its economic success.

India is another example of a country that dramatically improved its economic performance after moving to freer trade policies. For about four decades after becoming independent in 1947, India pursued a policy of self-sufficiency and industrial planning that required elaborate and complex import restrictions. Importing anything that was not explicitly on a government list of approved items was forbidden. Imports of "nonessential" consumer goods were banned, and those deemed "essential" (food, pharmaceuticals, etc.) were imported and sold only by state agencies. A labyrinth of government requirements—permissions, licenses, and certifications—had to be met before intermediate and capital goods could be imported.

Bureaucrats and politicians justified these draconian policies on several grounds. Government control over industry and trade was deemed essential to conserve resources and eliminate wasteful competition. The scarcity of capital was held to justify government approval for investment projects. The shortage of foreign exchange, it was believed, mean that hard currency should be allocated by government officials rather than by the market to ensure its use for projects in the "national interest." The fear of foreign domination lurked behind many of these policies and created resistance to market-based solutions, in favor of government-directed ones.

Unfortunately, the outcome was not good—sluggish growth, persistent poverty, inefficient industry, and lagging modernization. According to one quip, India suffered from 400 years of British imperialism and 50 years of the London School of Economics—and it is not clear which did more damage.[11]

However, an economic crisis in 1991 gave policymakers the opportunity to undertake a radical shift in policy.[12] India abandoned parts of its central planning system and abolished the requirement of government permission for all industrial investment expenditures, with some

[11] In the early and middle twentieth century, the London School of Economics was home to Fabian socialist ideas that influenced generations of Indian policymakers. Moore 2003, 132.

[12] The collapse of Communism and China's success in opening up its economy also helped convince Indian policymakers that state planning was a failure.

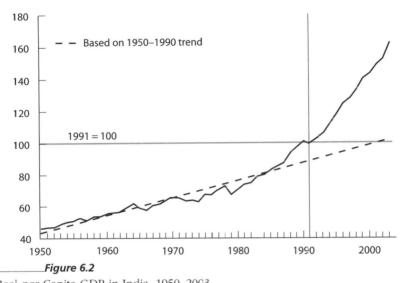

_____**Figure 6.2**

Real per Capita GDP in India, 1950–2003
Major trade reform was initiated in 1991. Data from International Monetary
Fund, International Financial Statistics database.

exceptions. Indian firms were permitted to borrow on international capital markets, the rupee was devalued and made convertible, quantitative
restrictions on imports were abolished, export subsidies were eliminated, and import duties were cut from an average of 87 percent in 1990
to 33 percent in 1994. Nontariff barriers covered 95 percent of all imports in 1988 but just 24 percent in 1999.[13] The "license raj"—the rigid
and complex system of import controls and foreign investment restrictions administered by government bureaucrats—was dismantled, unleashing the private sector from red tape but also exposing it to international competition.

　　The outcome has been astonishing. As figure 6.2 shows, growth
in real per capita income in India began to pick up in the mid-1980s,
when some tentative steps toward reducing import barriers and investment controls were taken, and accelerated after 1991.[14] The reduction in
trade barriers has also been linked to higher productivity; by one estimate,

　　[13] Srinivasan and Tendulkar 2003, 33–39.
　　[14] There is some controversy about the timing of the acceleration in growth and
what triggered it. Srinivasan and Tendulkar (2003, 23) argue that "growth performance was

India experienced a 20 percent increase in aggregate productivity growth and a 30 to 35 percent increase in intraplant productivity following tariff liberalization.[15] Most importantly, the poverty rate has fallen from 45 percent in 1983 to 26 percent in 2000, improving the lives of tens of millions of Indians.[16]

China and India provide dramatic illustrations of the improvement in economic circumstances that can result when poor economic policies are replaced with better ones, particularly with respect to international trade. Higher incomes translate into tangible improvements in the well-being of millions of people. This improvement in well-being cannot be measured in terms of dollars and cents alone, but in the lives that are saved as a result of moving people away from the knife edge of poverty, where a bad harvest or the loss of a job can spell malnourishment or even death. Hunger and malnutrition, illiteracy, and infant mortality persisted for decades after China adopted central planning in 1949 and India received political independence in 1947. Because of the economic opportunities opened up after the 1978 and 1991 reforms in China and India, respectively, tens if not hundreds of millions of people have a chance to join the middle class.

Thus, the higher income that comes with freer trade is important not just for crass material reasons, but because it can lead to a better life. With higher incomes, families can pay for more and better food, get access to medicines and better health care, and afford schooling for their children. One study examined the direct connections between trade openness and a society's health outcomes, specifically infant mortality and life expectancy. Even after controlling for a country's per capita income, average years of schooling, number of doctors per capita, and other factors, people in countries with lower tariffs had

---

distinctly better in the 1980s than in the earlier period" because of a real exchange rate depreciation rather than trade liberalization. "This surge in growth, however, was supported on the demand side by unsustainable fiscal policies, and it ended with an economic crisis in 1991." Rodrik and Subramanian (2004) argue that an attitudinal shift toward a more probusiness stance on the part of the government accounts for the pickup in growth after 1980, prior to economic liberalization, the importance of which they downplay. Panagariya (2004b) argues that liberalization in the late 1980s played a crucial role in increasing growth rates, which solidified after the 1991 economic reforms.

[15] Sivadasan 2003.
[16] World Bank 2003b, 7.

longer life expectancy and lower infant mortality. For example, an eleven-percentage-point reduction in the tariff rate—a change of about one standard deviation in the sample—is associated with between three and six fewer infants dying per thousand live births.[17] Such findings are a powerful reminder of the life-and-death stakes of good and bad economic policies.

The tragedy of India is that, by delaying economic reforms for so many decades, it contributed to the impoverishment of its people for so long. One Indian businessman writes with dismay:

> Most people remember the Emergency [suspension of democracy between 1975 and 1977] because it represented a generalized loss of liberty. They do not understand that by suppressing economic liberty for forty years, we destroyed growth and the future of two generations. For the average citizen it was a great betrayal. Lest we forget, we lived under a system where a third of the people went hungry and malnourished, half were illiterate while the elite enjoyed a vast system of higher education, and one of ten infants died at childbirth. Our controls and red tape stifled the entrepreneur and the farmer, and the command mentality of the bureaucrat, which fed the evil system, continues till today to frustrate every effort at reform.[18]

India has paid a very heavy price in human lives for delaying its reforms. But what China and India have accomplished is stunning. Though both countries still have a long way to go, the improvement in human well-being achieved over the past generation is mind boggling.

Of course, not all of the improved economic performance of China and India can be attributed to more liberal trade policies. China moved away from a system of central planning and collective agriculture, while India freed up bureaucratic obstacles to domestic investment. Nonetheless, trade reforms were a key component of the overall economic reforms. Both countries deliberately shifted from closed economies to ones more open to international trade.

[17] Wei and Wu 2003. For a survey of recent research on trade and poverty, see Winters, McCulloch, and McKay (2004).

[18] Das 2001, 175.

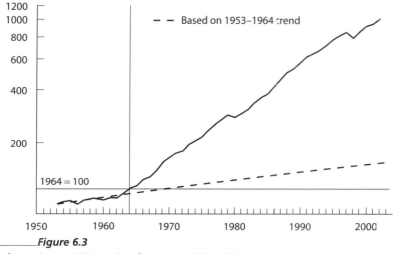

- - Based on 1953–1964 trend

_____Figure 6.3

Real per Capita GDP in South Korea, 1953–2002
Major trade reforms were initiated between 1963 and 1965. Data from International Monetary Fund, International Financial Statistics database.

_____Trade Policy Reform: Successes and Failures

China and India are dramatic examples of the tangible benefits of economic reform and international trade. On a smaller but no less dramatic scale, other developing countries have changed their economic orientation to the world and have seen improvements in economic performance.

In the mid-1960s, Korea changed its trade strategy sharply. The proportion of items automatically approved for import went from zero in June 1964 to 63 percent by December 1965. Korea's currency (the won) was devalued by nearly 50 percent, and a unified exchange rate was adopted. In 1967, many import quotas were abolished and tariffs were sharply reduced. The effective tax on imports fell from nearly 40 percent in 1960 to 8 percent by 1967.[19] Figure 6.3 shows the marked acceleration in Korea's growth of per capita income from around the time of these changes.

In the mid-1970s, Chile also sharply changed its trade policy. Between 1975 and 1979, Chile eliminated all quantitative restrictions and

[19] Frank, Kim, and Westphal 1975, 75.

exchange controls and reduced import tariffs from over 100 percent to a uniform 10 percent. After suffering a severe economic recession due to a banking crisis in the early 1980s, Chile continued trade liberalization. The payoff materialized in a 7 percent average annual growth rate for more than a decade after 1986.[20]

In the middle and late 1980s, Vietnam adopted economic reforms that helped increase economic growth to an average of more than 7 percent in the late 1990s and early 2000s. As in China, agricultural land reform helped jump-start the growth process. But trade and foreign investment have been important components of Vietnam's success. The poverty rate has been slashed in an astonishingly short time. The share of the population living in absolute poverty fell from 75 percent in 1988 to 58 percent in 1993 to 37 percent in 1998 to 29 percent in 2002. The opening of trade contributed directly to this process since exports of rice and labor-intensive manufactured goods are produced by poor households. After the implementation of a U.S.-Vietnamese trade agreement in 2001, Vietnam's exports to the United States doubled in 2002 and again in 2003.[21]

Unfortunately, not all countries that have liberalized their trade policies have enjoyed such dramatic successes. For example, Mexico significantly reduced tariffs and other trade barriers when it joined the GATT in 1985 and signed free trade agreements with the United States and Canada (NAFTA) in 1994 and the European Union in 2000. As a result, Mexico's trade and foreign investment increased significantly. The share of trade (average of exports and imports) in GDP rose from 13 percent in 1985 to 32 percent in 2002. These reforms improved productivity in industries exposed to international competition, as described in chapter 2.

However, Mexico's overall macroeconomic performance has been disappointing since NAFTA. Economic growth has been lackluster, employment is only slightly higher than before the agreement took effect, and real wages are actually lower. NAFTA opponents blame open trade for Mexico's problems. These critics say that NAFTA has harmed farmers and is responsible for the lack of improvement in the standard of living of workers.

[20] Edwards and Lederman 2002.
[21] Dollar and Ljunggren 1997.

The real source of Mexico's malaise is macroeconomic. In December 1994, about a year after NAFTA went into effect, and for reasons not related to the trade agreement, Mexico faced a speculative attack on the peso and was forced to devalue its currency. The peso crisis stemmed from an inconsistency between Mexico's monetary policy and its commitment to maintain a fixed exchange rate. The peso devaluation was a severe setback that slashed real wages overnight and sent the economy into a deep recession.

By keeping trade flows moving, NAFTA helped the Mexican economy through a difficult period. The continued expansion of trade promoted the country's recovery from this traumatic shock. Yet since the initial rebound, the Mexican economy has been weak. The reason for this disappointing performance is not trade related, but a persistent and severe credit crunch, including a deterioration in contract enforceability and an increase in nonperforming bank loans. Indeed, Mexico's credit-to-GDP ratio fell from 49 percent in 1994 to 17 percent in 2002, preventing any broad-based economic recovery.[22]

A decade after NAFTA went into effect, a Carnegie Endowment for International Peace study concluded: "Put simply, NAFTA has been neither the disaster is opponents predicted nor the savior hailed by its supporters." But the report also noted that "NAFTA has accelerated Mexico's transition to a liberalized economy without creating the necessary conditions for the public and private sectors to respond to the economic, social, and environmental shocks of trading with the two of the biggest economies in the world."[23] This suggests that other complementary policies are required if trade liberalization is to succeed in improving welfare, a point that will be discussed below.

Unfortunately, Mexico is not alone. Other developing countries significantly reduced tariffs in the 1990s but also have not performed well. In Latin America, Colombia cut its tariffs by more than half in 1991, while Argentina and Nicaragua reduced them from over 100 percent to just 15 percent in one stroke in 1992. In Africa, Kenya reduced its import duties from over 40 percent in the early 1980s to under 15 percent by the

---

[22] Tornell, Westerman, and Martinez 2004. See also Kose, Meredith, and Towe, forthcoming.

[23] Audley et al. 2003, 6.

_____Table 6.3
Growth in Real per Capita GDP, 1980s and 1990s

	1980–89	1990–98
Industrial countries	2.1	2.2
Developing countries	0.3	0.7
Europe and Central Asia	2.6	−1.1
Countries in conflict	−1.1	−1.3
Others	0.4	1.5

Source: World Bank 2001, 55.

late 1990s.[24] Yet the people of these countries have not seen much improvement in their standard of living.

This disappointing performance is sometimes interpreted as indicating that trade liberalization and increased integration with the world have failed to help developing countries and that therefore the strategy should be abandoned. This is the wrong conclusion to draw. In the case of Argentina, for example, monetary and macroeconomic instability—arising from excessive borrowing abroad and the resulting buildup of foreign debt—have had devastating effects far beyond any good that open trade could bring. Colombia and other countries have had to endure "shock therapy" to end hyperinflations and hemorrhaging budget deficits, forcing the economy through wrenching adjustments that overwhelmed the impact of trade liberalization. Until the mid-1990s, the overvaluation of West African currencies tied to the French franc severely constrained the ability of West African countries to stimulate growth through exports.

Indeed, the dismal performance of many developing countries can be attributed to macroeconomic mismanagement, ethnic and civil conflicts, and the difficulties of countries in transition from the economic policies of the former Soviet Union, not the failures of trade reform. The reforms of the 1990s have paid off for the countries that undertook them. In the 1990s, as table 6.3 reveals, growth accelerated in the 1990s for developing countries that did not suffer from civil conflict or painful transitions from communism. As the World Bank concluded: "With the exception of the countries in transition and conflict, there is little evidence

[24] World Bank 2001, 51.

that developing countries engaged in rapid trade liberalization and companion reforms saw a deterioration in performance."[25]

The right conclusion to draw is that the case for free trade requires a caution: other policies in developing countries can prevent the full benefits of trade liberalization from being realized. For example, a poor domestic business environment and excessive regulation may prevent trade liberalization from stimulating growth. One study reports that increased openness to trade is positively correlated with higher incomes, but that greater openness is associated with lower incomes in very heavily regulated economies.[26] If excessive regulations prevent resources from moving to the economy's most productive sectors and firms, then trade liberalization will fail to improve incomes. A sound domestic environment for business is required for countries to take full advantage of policy reforms that encourage global trade. Highly regulated economies are likely to perform better if they sweep away domestic impediments to economic activity before embarking upon trade reforms.[27]

Indeed, in some developing countries, administrative controls and poor infrastructure may be more important obstacles to trade than tariffs alone.[28] Inefficient customs and tax administration have hampered exporters who require imported components and materials for production. Chopping import tariffs does not in itself solve this problem. High transport costs and poor infrastructure have also prevented trade liberalization from boosting trade in low-income developing countries. As formal barriers fall, the quality and reliability of transport infrastructure (including roads, railways, airports, and seaports) and related services (including telecommunications and business services such as finance and insurance) are increasingly critical to trade.

[25] World Bank 2001, 55.

[26] Bolaky and Freund 2004.

[27] The World Bank has started to examine the high costs of business regulation in developing countries. "It takes two days to start a business in Australia, but 203 days in Haiti and 215 days in the Democratic Republic of Congo. . . . A simple commercial contract is enforced in 7 days in Tunisia and 39 days in the Netherlands, but takes almost 1,500 days in Guatemala. The cost of enforcement is less than 1 percent of the disputed amount in Austria, Canada, and the United Kingdom, but more than 100 percent in Burkina Faso, the Dominican Republic, Indonesia, the Kyrgyz Republic, Madagascar, Malawi, and the Philippines." World Bank 2004a, xiii.

[28] For example, Dollar and Kraay (2004) find that changes in average tariff rates are not highly correlated with change in trade volumes.

Landlocked countries are at a particular disadvantage in world trade since land transport charges have been estimated to be seven times greater than sea transport costs. Studies have found that higher transport costs and weak infrastructure explain much of Africa's poor trade performance.[29] For example, in sub-Saharan Africa, transport costs are five times greater than tariff charges. If goods are stranded for weeks at port, or roads are impassable due to the rainy season, cutting tariffs from 20 percent to 10 percent will not make much difference.

For this reason, trade facilitation has become a priority in international forums such as the World Trade Organization. Trade facilitation is simply the logistics of moving goods through customs and includes such mundane things as port efficiency, inspections and documentation, transparency of government regulations, and so on. Some policy changes can make a difference. For example, in the early 1990s Argentina began allowing private firms to operate public ports and invest in their infrastructure. As a result, cargo handling increased 50 percent between 1990 and 1995 and labor productivity surged, making Argentine ports among the cheapest in Latin America.[30]

In sum, trade liberalization is not a magic bullet guaranteed to bring about rapid growth in trade and higher incomes. Many other factors—political conflicts, macroeconomic instability, a poor domestic business environment—can stand in the way of the beneficial effects of trade and can prevent freer trade from yielding the ultimate payoff of higher living standards.

Industrial Policy and the East Asian Miracle

Despite the success that many countries have had with economic liberalization, developing countries still fear the consequences of opening their markets to the world. The old concerns about foreign domination and imports destroying important domestic industries continue to exist. Many people still cling to the view that import substitution and protecting infant industries is the right approach to trade and development.

[29] Limão and Venables 2001.
[30] World Trade Organization 2004, box IIB.5.

Import substitution refers to a deliberate policy of encouraging domestic production of manufactured goods in place of imports. Such policies were common in the 1950s and 1960s when industrialization was viewed as the key to economic development. Such policies often succeeded in building up capital-intensive industries and sometimes led to high rates of output growth. But they often failed to improve standards of living because the high investment rates required to maintain growth in the capital stock detracted from growth in consumption. In the case of Communist China, about a third of national income had to be reinvested to maintain growth in the capital stock, leaving little left over for consumers.[31]

These policies often turned out to be self-inflicted wounds. In many instances, capital-intensive industries were unsuited for developing economies that had a comparative advantage in labor-intensive industries. These industries required ongoing government support to function profitably. By sheltering firms from import competition, protectionist policies inhibited export growth and firms became inward looking, focusing on the domestic rather than the world market. This resulted in small and inefficient firms, since the domestic market was not large enough or competitive enough to promote firms that would be successful on the world market. India is the classic example of a country that built up many manufacturing industries by sheltering them from foreign competition, but failed to deliver a high standard of living to its people.

Although import substitution is widely acknowledged to have failed in comparison to export-promoting policies, export promotion may mean something more than free trade. Many observers point to the stunning growth of several East Asian countries and point to government industrial policies as the key to their success. The economic achievements of Japan in the 1960s and the "four tigers"—South Korea, Taiwan, Singapore, and Hong Kong—in the 1970s have raised new questions about free trade.

[31] "One consequence of this rising capital intensity of production was that gains in per capita consumption were very modest for a country in which per capita output grew relatively rapidly. Between 1957 and 1977 per capita national income rose at an average annual compound rate of 3.4 percent in real terms. Yet, because the share of output that had to be reinvested to sustain that rate of growth rose by fully one third (from 25 percent in 1957 to an average of 33 percent in the 1970s), improvements in real living standards were quite modest." Lardy 1992, 34.

Many contend that, with the exception of Hong Kong, these countries grew rich not because of free trade, but through wise government use of selective protection and targeted industrial policies.[32]

These countries did many things right—they enjoyed peace and political stability, encouraged high savings and investment rates, emphasized the importance of education and human capital accumulation, provided stable macroeconomic and exchange rate policies, and so on. Korea and Taiwan also pursued important land reforms early in their transition that led to rapid productivity growth in agriculture. In other words, these East Asian countries enjoyed many favorable conditions noticeably absent elsewhere, particularly in Latin America and Africa.

With the exception of Hong Kong, however, these countries did not pursue policies of nonintervention with respect to industry. To varying degrees, governments were involved in the allocation of capital and other resources to promote industrialization, and even employed the tools of trade protectionism. Some observers have concluded that, because the Japanese and Korean governments intervened in their economies to promote certain industries, their economic performance can be attributed to these interventions. In this view, the East Asian experience illustrates how careful industrial policy and protectionism, not free trade, promote economic development.

Yet there are reasons to be skeptical about this conclusion. It is always tempting to reach a conclusion about causality on the basis of correlation: because Japan or Korea intervened in its economy or used protectionist trade measures, the success of the economy is due to that policy. But assessing the contribution of industrial policy to economic growth is a difficult challenge. In a 1993 report on the East Asian miracle, the World Bank noted that

> their interventions did not significantly inhibit growth. But it is very difficult to establish statistical links between growth and a specific intervention and even more difficult to establish causality. Because we cannot know what would have happened in the absence of a specific policy, it is difficult to test whether interventions increased growth rates.[33]

[32] Wade 2004.
[33] World Bank 1993, 6.

Thus, when several factors promoting a good outcome exist simultaneously—a stable political environment, a good educational system, high savings and literacy rates, and so on—it becomes difficult to determine the precise contribution of any one specific factor, such as industrial policy, to the outcome. One cannot rule out the possibility that government intervention actually detracted from the economic success of the county but was more than offset by the other good forces.[34]

In the case of Japan, the country's success after World War II is sometimes attributed to the selective interventions by the Ministry of International Trade and Industry (MITI). MITI used "administrative guidance" to promote investment in and acquire technology for selected industries. Some argue that MITI was involved not just in "picking" winners by diverting resources to selected high-growth industries, but in "making" winners by ensuring their success on international markets.

But the actual evidence on MITI's contributions to Japan's success is weak. The two industries that achieved the most notable success on world markets—automobiles and consumer electronics—did not benefit from extensive government support, unlike some other heavy industries such as chemicals and steel. MITI also had notable failures in promoting its biotechnology and computer industries. In fact, one statistical study of Japanese industrial targeting found that a disproportionate amount of support went to low-growth sectors and sectors with decreasing returns to scale. This study failed to find evidence that productivity was enhanced as a result of industrial policy measures.[35]

Qualitative studies of Japan's policies lend support to this skeptical view. The consulting firm McKinsey concluded that robust domestic competition was a source of Japan's success. In many instances, MITI did not foster but actually tried to reduce competition by forming domestic cartels. (In the case of automobiles, for example, it discouraged Honda

---

[34] As Adam Smith once opined, "The uniform, constant, and uninterrupted effort of every man to better his condition, the principle from which public and national, as well as private opulence is originally derived, is frequently powerful enough to maintain the natural progress of things towards improvement, in spite both of the extravagance of government and of the greatest errors of administration. . . . But though the profusion of government must, undoubtedly, have retarded the natural progress of England toward wealth and improvement, it has not been able to stop it." Smith 1976, 343, 345.

[35] Beason and Weinstein 1996.

from entering the market in the 1950s, thinking that there were already too many firms in the industry.) However, in the case of machine tools, MITI helped standardize tolerances used in machines, thereby allowing large-scale assembly of machine tools and applied electronics technology. As one McKinsey analyst reported, "In all our studies of Japan, this is the only action by MITI that we found to have had a significant beneficial impact on the Japanese economy."[36] If this is MITI's one success, the importance of MITI has been vastly overrated.

South Korea may provide a better example of government industrial policy. Under the military dictatorship of Chung Hee Park, the Korean government employed competent technocrats who were directly involved in economic planning and investment allocation. These bureaucrats were insulated from political decisions and thus did not fall prey to corruption. The principal tool at their disposal was directed credit, which they used to promote capital-intensive industries such as chemicals, steel, and shipbuilding. While the government was involved in strategic decisions about the economy, it did not implement these decisions through state-owned firms or nationalized industries. Rather, once the government and private sector negotiated economic goals and the means to carry them out, the private firms were responsible for executing them. Furthermore, these firms were not insulated from competition; instead, they were encouraged to export and face the full brunt of international competition.

Still, as described earlier in this chapter, what jump-started the Korean economy in the mid-1960s was not industrial policy, but other reforms, including trade and exchange rate policy. One can also question the contribution of the technocrats to Korea's rapid growth since that time. Despite the government's emphasis on building up heavy capital-intensive industries, light labor-intensive industries increased productivity at a more rapid rate during the 1960s and 1970s. Indeed, during the 1970s, the most rapid growth in sectoral shares of value added occurred in lower-wage or low value-added per worker sectors.[37] Furthermore, as in the statistical study of Japan already mentioned, measures of industrial policy (such as tax incentives and subsidized credit) are not correlated with productivity

[36] Lewis 2004, 40.
[37] Dollar and Sokoloff 1990; World Bank 1993, 314.

growth at the industry level.[38] Korea's use of directed credit to promote industrial growth has also led to problems. Korean industry suffers from gross overinvestment and is far too reliant on capital-intensive production methods. Nonperforming loans and weakness in the banking and financial system are related to major economic crises in 1979–81 and 1997–98.

Several points stand out from the Korean experience. First, private firms were not shielded from competition but rather exposed to it and forced to meet the test of international markets. The reforms that put Korea on the path of export-led industrialization "did not achieve this result by the conventionally prescribed approach, which is to reduce greatly (if not eliminate) the domestic market's insulation from import competition."[39] Second, bureaucrats were insulated from political pressures to allocate resources to politically favored projects. The implementation of plans took place by relying on free market institutions and was negotiated with, not imposed on, private firms.

Because of the special historical, political, and cultural circumstances of Korea, even a leading proponent of the view that Korea's economy benefited from government industrial policy has concluded that "one has to be extremely skeptical about the prospects for replicating the Korean government's use of selective intervention."[40] Indeed, the political prerequisites for such judicious intervention are lacking in other Southeast Asian countries, such as Malaysia, Thailand, and Indonesia. The economies of these countries have performed well in recent decades, but corruption and rent seeking have given industrial policy there a bad name. In those countries, industrial policy is virtually synonymous with arbitrary interventions to help out political cronies. In Malaysia and Indonesia, there are "important recent instances of almost capricious selective industrial policy by the executive, with the technocracy having little say in its elaboration. . . . Such efforts did not attempt to achieve international competitiveness or to provide support for other industries seeking to achieve international competitiveness, even in the long run."[41] These

[38] Lee 1996.

[39] Rather, it established a "virtual free trade regime for export activity" that also "entailed tremendous openness to imports of raw materials, intermediate inputs, and capital goods." Westphal 1990, 44.

[40] Westphal 1990, 42.

[41] Jomo 2001, 473.

countries have welcomed foreign investment in labor-intensive export industries and have not sought to promote investment in heavy industry to the same degree as Japan or Korea.

Thus, there is no single East Asian model of economic development. Singapore and Hong Kong are small island states, the latter pursuing an almost pure free-market approach. Japan and Korea employed more activist industrial policies, but there is little evidence demonstrating their precise contribution (positive or negative) to the country's development. Malaysia and Indonesia have weaker political institutions that do not keep industrial policy free from corruption and rent seeking. Yet, for the most part, all of these East Asian countries have enjoyed macroeconomic stability, relied on private enterprise and market competition, stressed investment in human capital, and adopted outward-oriented policies rather than import substitution. These are the common elements cutting across the countries' vast differences.

A tentative conclusion regarding government's role in trade is that it should facilitate private sector development. Most developing countries that have shifted from the production of primary products to nontraditional activities have done so with the cooperation of the public sector. The government is not picking the sectors into which resources should move, but clearing obstacles and reducing uncertainties relating to investment—in general, facilitating private sector activities. Whether one considers Chile's diversification away from copper into fruits and salmon, Costa Rica and ecotourism, Bangladesh and garments, Colombia and cut flowers, governments have almost invariably played an important supporting role.[42]

Unfortunately, governments in many developing countries do not facilitate or support the private sector but instead create obstacles for its growth. Even worse, in many countries, particularly but by no means exclusively in Africa, economic success is best achieved by political power and connections rather than by commercial ability or effort.[43] Corrupt

---

[42] Hausmann and Rodrik 2003.

[43] The *Economist*'s Africa correspondent argues that personal advancement in Africa is easier to achieve through political success than commercial success. In his view, to become rich, or even minimally prosperous, one must either seek political power or cultivate and become a client of those in power. The more that African bureaucrats and politicians extort and expropriate, the less there is to extort and expropriate, which makes the competition for power even more desperate and violent. Guest 2004.

regimes that provide no security to economic transactions and throw obstacles in the way of business formation and commerce are perhaps the single greatest problem in promoting economic development.[44]

Recent experience has demonstrated that the economic status of developing countries is not immutably fixed by nature. Neither the geography nor the institutions of China or India or Korea changed when they embarked upon their policy reforms, and yet their economies have been utterly transformed by changes in government policy. Unfortunately, economic policies that stifle development are still pervasive around the world.

Developed Country Trade Policies

While developing countries have yet to reach their full potential in large part because of their own policies, trade barriers and subsidies in the developed world have not helped matters. Development nongovernmental organizations have excoriated the developed countries for keeping their markets closed to imports from developing countries. As an Oxfam report cries out, "the harsh reality is that [developed country] policies are inflicting enormous suffering on the world's poor. When rich countries lock poor people out of their markets, they close the door to an escape route from poverty."[45] This statement is exaggerated but contains some truth. Whether it is closed markets for agricultural goods, high barriers on the importation of labor-intensive manufactures, or efforts to require developing countries to adopt labor standards, many developed country policies are harmful to the interests of developing countries.

In terms of agriculture, the rich countries of the OECD maintain high trade barriers for agricultural products and heavily subsidize their farmers. For every dollar earned by OECD farmers, about 32 cents comes

---

[44] Adam Smith once stated that "[L]ittle else is requisite to carry a state to the highest degree of opulence from the lowest barbarism but peace, easy taxes, and a tolerable administration of justice: all the rest being brought about by the natural course of things. All governments which thwart this natural course, which force things into another channel, or which endeavour to arrest the progress of society at a particular point, are unnatural, and to support themselves are obliged to be oppressive and tyrannical." Unfortunately, all too many developing countries lack these three simple requirements. Smith 1980, 322.

[45] Oxfam 2002, 5.

_____Table 6.4
Agricultural Support in OECD Countries, 1999–2001 (billions of dollars)

	United States	European Union	Japan	Other OECD Countries
From domestic measures	$32.6	$38.5	$5.0	$6.3
From trade border measures	$18.7	$60.9	$47.0	$5.7
Total support to producers	$51.3	$99.3	$52.0	$12.3

Source: World Bank 2003a, 120.

from government policies. In 2003, the OECD subsidized domestic farm producers by $257 billion, of which $160 billion came from high prices resulting from tariffs and export subsidies and $97 billion was transferred by taxpayers through government payments to farmers.[46] As table 6.4 indicates, except in the case of the United States, most support comes through border measures rather than domestic subsidies.

The value of transfers to OECD farmers is greater than the entire GDPs of many developing countries. Because these domestic subsidies and trade barriers have a huge impact on world agricultural markets, they in turn affect developing countries, where agriculture is a very large sector, employing about 60 percent of the labor force and producing about 25 percent of GDP in low-income countries. Indeed, most of the rural poor in developing countries work in the agricultural sector.

Studies have shown that the reduction of agricultural tariffs and trade barriers by OECD and developing countries would produce substantial benefits for both sets of countries. If industrial countries alone opened their markets to imported agricultural goods, industrial country welfare would rise by almost $80 billion and developing country welfare by $12 billion (1997 dollars).[47] Most of the benefits of trade liberalization accrue to the developed countries because their consumers are footing most of the bill. (Similarly, if developing countries reduced their own agricultural trade barriers, which can be much higher than those in developed countries, they too would capture most of the benefits for themselves.)

However, the same mutual benefit does not hold true if industrial countries eliminated domestic and export subsidies to their agricultural

[46] Organization for Economic Cooperation and Development 2004, 17.
[47] International Monetary Fund 2002, 85.

producers. Many developing countries are net importers of agricultural goods and actually benefit from these subsidies. Because these subsidies reduce the prices of the goods that they buy on world markets, many developing countries would lose by their elimination. If industrial countries eliminated domestic and export subsidies without touching import barriers, then those countries would gain $14 billion in welfare, but developing countries as a whole would lose nearly $5 billion.[48] The gains from eliminating agricultural subsides accrue mainly to the country that eliminates the subsidy.

If industrial countries eliminated both import tariffs and production subsidies, developing countries would gain $8 billion overall. The greater market access in rich country markets would compensate the poorer countries for the higher food prices they would have to pay on some products. Indeed, research has shown that eliminating border measures such as tariffs will produce changes in world prices that are many times that from eliminating domestic agricultural subsidies.[49] Thus, from the standpoint of agricultural exporting developing countries, market access (lower import barriers) is much more valuable than domestic subsidy reduction. (Many of the poorest developing countries, which are net importers of agricultural goods, still stand to lose.)

Still, subsidies to specific crops can impose tremendous hardship on particular developing countries. Cotton is a prime—if exceptional—example. The United States and European Union heavily subsidize domestic cotton growers. In 2001–2, government subsidies to America's 25,000 cotton farmers amounted to nearly $4 billion, double the level a decade earlier. This is more than the entire GDP of the West African country of Burkina Faso. The European Union also subsidizes cotton producers by almost $1 billion per year.

Since the mid-1990s, world cotton prices have fallen by half. The United States accounts for about 20 percent of world cotton production, so any expansion of U.S. production tends to reduce the world price. These subsidies have inflicted great harm on cotton producers in Central

---

[48] Hoekman, Ng, and Olarreaga (2004) similarly find that a 50 percent cut in tariffs improves welfare for industrial, developing, and least developed countries alike, but a 50 percent cut in domestic subsidies helps industrial countries but harms developing and least developed countries.

[49] Hoekman, Ng, and Olarreaga 2004.

and West Africa and elsewhere, intensifying poverty in already very poor countries. Cotton exports accounts for 40 percent of exports in Burkina Faso and Benin and 30 percent of exports in Uzbekistan, Chad, and Mali. Cotton also accounts for over 5 percent of GDP in these countries.[50] Because cotton is such an important source of foreign exchange earnings for these countries, any decline in the world market price— due to subsidies or other reasons—has a tremendous negative ripple effect through their economies. The livelihood of more than 10 million poor farmers is at stake.

Several studies estimate that the elimination of U.S. cotton subsidies would reduce U.S. production by more than 25 percent, reduce U.S. exports by more than 40 percent, and increase world cotton prices by about 10 to 15 percent. This translates into a gain of $250 million in export revenues for twenty-two poor developing countries that export cotton. According to one study, U.S. cotton subsidies cost Burkina Faso 1 percent of GDP and 12 percent of its export earnings, Mali 1.7 percent of GDP and 8 percent of export earnings, and Benin 1.4 percent of GDP and 9 percent of export earnings.[51]

The case of cotton illustrates the stark impact of the concentrated harm that can be done by agricultural subsidies in the OECD. Now developing countries are beginning to use the WTO dispute settlement system to attack these large subsidies.[52]

In the case of manufactured goods, developed countries have low tariffs on average but much higher tariffs on labor-intensive manufactures, particularly textiles and apparel. These are precisely the goods in which developing countries have a comparative advantage. Developing countries have long complained about the Multi-Fiber Arrangement, but even with its abolition they still face very high tariffs. In the United

---

[50] Baffes 2004.

[51] Oxfam 2002.

[52] Brazil brought a case before the WTO dispute settlement process, arguing that U.S. cotton subsidies violated WTO rules. Most agricultural subsidies were given temporary immunity from legal challenge by the so-called peace clause in the Agreement on Agriculture in 1995, provided that the subsidies were capped at 1992 levels. In early 2004, the WTO panel ruled in Brazil's favor. The United States paid cotton producers $1.6 billion in 1992, but paid $2.3 billion in 1999 and $2.1 billion in 2001. The United States argued that these subsidies did not distort trade because they were not tied to production. For a general discussion of this issue, see Steinberg and Josling (2003).

States, for example, the exports of Mongolia, Bangladesh, and Cambodia, among the poorest countries in the world, faced an average tariff of about 15 percent. Meanwhile, the exports of Norway, France, and Singapore faced an average tariff of 1 percent. In 2001, Bangladesh paid $331 million in customs duties to get its goods into the United States; France paid $330 million. But Bangladesh exported just $2 billion, while France exported over $30 billion.[53]

U.S. policy does not deliberately attempt to stifle the trade of developing countries in favor of richer countries, but it implicitly does so by virtue of the tariffs it levies on different goods. Industrial products generally face very low import duties, whereas labor-intensive manufactured goods, such as clothing and consumer products, face much higher tariffs. The developing countries could have much better success in world trade if they did not confront these higher barriers in OECD markets. Yet this situation exists because developing countries opted out of multilateral trade liberalization agreements for many decades (receiving "special and differential treatment" under the GATT, as chapter 7 discusses), whereas developed countries reduced tariffs on the goods they traded.

Ironically, many in the developed world who are concerned about poverty and economic underdevelopment elsewhere do not focus on U.S. import tariffs as much as they do on working conditions provided by multinational firms in developing countries. This leads us to the controversial question of whether workers in developing countries are being exploited by foreign firms and, if so, what should be done about it.

Sweatshops and Labor Standards

Many multinational corporations have invested in low-wage developing countries to produce labor-intensive goods, such as clothing and shoes. This foreign investment has generated controversy, with companies such as Nike being accused of earning high profits by exploiting cheap labor in Asian sweatshops. Student activists, human rights groups, and other NGOs have decried the poor working conditions and treatment of labor in developing countries, and are sharply critical of multinational corporations for their failure to pay a "living" wage to workers there. Labor

[53] Gresser 2002.

unions in the developed countries have long maintained that countries with lower labor standards have an unfair competitive advantage in trade and that they attract jobs and investment at the expense of countries with higher standards.

These groups fault world trade negotiators for neglecting to include labor standards in trade agreements and thus failing to protect the interests of workers. Yet most developing countries strenuously object to any linking of trade policy and labor standards. They fear that if developed countries are allowed to restrict imports from countries deemed not to have adequate labor standards, they will have yet another excuse for denying low-wage countries access to their markets, thereby preventing developing countries from taking advantage of their comparative advantage in labor-intensive goods.

Before asking whether trade agreements should include provisions on labor standards, it is worth examining the perennial claim that low wages give a country an unfair advantage in trade. The key economic lesson is that low wages reflect low labor productivity. Workers in developed countries enjoy high wages and benefits because of their high productivity. Figure 6.4 illustrates the strong relationship between labor costs per worker (a measure of wages and benefits that firms must pay) and value added per worker (a measure of productivity) in manufacturing for sixty-three countries during 1995–99. The correlation is striking: the higher a country's average productivity, the higher the country's average wages. Econometric evidence has regularly shown that labor productivity alone explains about 70 to 80 percent of the cross-country variation in average wages in manufacturing. After also accounting for differences in per capita GDP and in price levels across countries, over 90 percent of the variation in wages between countries can be explained.[54]

Since average wages reflect average productivity, the cost advantage of low wages is generally offset by the cost disadvantage of low productivity. This implies that unit labor costs are roughly comparable across countries. Figure 6.5 depicts this relationship. In India and the Philippines, for example, average wages are less than 10 percent of those

[54] Even though these purely economic variables explain almost all of the differences in wage rates across countries, Rodrik (1999) finds that indicators of political freedom contribute some additional explanatory power.

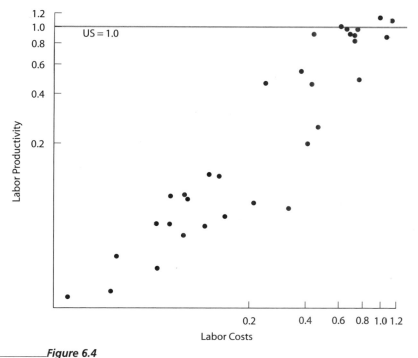

_____Figure 6.4
Labor Costs and Productivity in Manufacturing for 63 Countries, 1995–1999
(United States = 1.0)
Data from World Bank 2000, table 2.6.

in the United States. But the average productivity of workers is also less than 10 percent of that in the United States. Thus, the unit labor cost— the effective cost of hiring labor—is roughly comparable between the two countries. And, in fact, multinational corporations searching for cheap labor find that you get what you pay for: low wages imply a less productive workforce. Thus, multinationals generally find it profitable to turn to developing countries only for unskilled-labor-intensive activities, particularly those in which the productivity of workers is comparable to that in developed countries but the average wage is much less.[55]

[55] Of course, overall productivity depends not just on a worker's output, but the economy's infrastructure, the availability of technical and support personnel, and other factors. There are many examples of multinationals relocating production back in the United States because, despite the availability of inexpensive labor in other countries, the general environment for business made it difficult to make effective use of that labor.

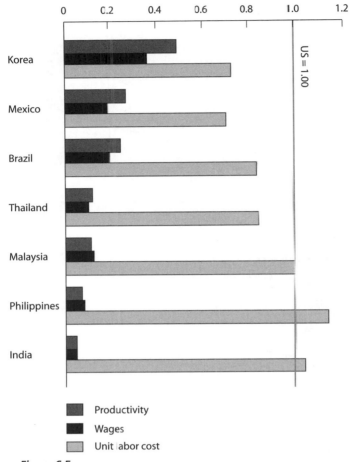

_____**Figure 6.5**
Labor Productivity, Wages, and Unit Labor Costs in Selected Developing Countries, 1990 (United States = 100)
Source: Golub 1999, 23.

As developing countries improve the productivity of their workers, through the acquisition of better technology or other mechanisms, competitive pressures bid up average wages. As a result, the growth in domestic wages tracks the growth in domestic productivity. Indeed, a country's average wage rate is determined almost exclusively by domestic productivity performance. As figure 6.6 shows, for example, the acceleration of productivity in South Korea in the 1980s was accompanied by a dramatic rise in labor compensation. By contrast, the Philippines has

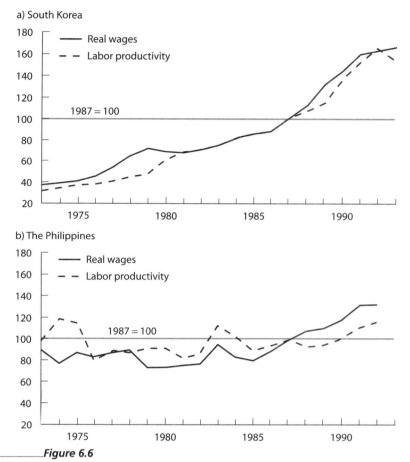

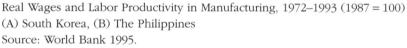

_____Figure 6.6
Real Wages and Labor Productivity in Manufacturing, 1972–1993 (1987 = 100)
(A) South Korea, (B) The Philippines
Source: World Bank 1995.

been much less successful at increasing productivity and therefore has not seen a comparable rise in wages. The evidence is clear: countries that successfully increase productivity experience a rise in wages, while countries whose productivity is stagnant see little change in wages.

Countries with low wages tend to specialize in unskilled-labor-intensive goods. Beyond this, there is little empirical evidence that low labor standards, in themselves, exert an important influence on trade flows. Several studies have failed to find a strong relationship between measures of labor standards and international trade flows (such as export performance in labor-intensive goods) or direct investment flows (such as whether countries with low standards attract more foreign investment).[56] The OECD has concluded that "empirical findings confirm the analytical result that core labor standards do not play a significant role in shaping trade performance. The view which argues that low-standard countries will enjoy gains in export market shares to the detriment of high-standard countries appears to lack solid empirical support."[57]

Low wages and poor working conditions in developing countries have sparked protests from concerned citizens in developed countries. The Worker Rights Consortium, established by students, unions, and human rights groups, has accused the athletic shoe manufacturer Nike and other multinationals of subjecting workers to sweatshop conditions and not paying a living wage. Working conditions in many developing countries are indeed horrible by the standards of developed countries, and everyone wants to see those standards of living improve. These activists have changed working conditions for the better by putting companies in the spotlight of bad publicity if their contractors treat their workers poorly.[58]

Still, the best and most direct way to raise wages and labor standards is to enhance the productivity of the workers through economic development. Trade and investment are important components of that development, and therefore efforts to limit international trade or to shut down the sweatshops are counterproductive. For example, most foreign-owned firms pay substantially higher wages than comparable domestic firms.[59] In Vietnam, for instance, while the general population (mainly employed in agriculture in rural areas) could afford per capita expenditures of $205 in 1998, people working in foreign-owned business

[56] See, for example, Rodrik 1996.

[57] Organization for Economic Cooperation and Development 1996, 33. The OECD (2000b, 33) concluded that "this finding has not been challenged by the literature appearing since the 1996 study was completed."

[58] Elliott, Kar, and Richardson (2004) examine the views of activists in developed countries that are pressing for better treatment of labor in developing countries. See also Harrison and Scorse 2004.

[59] See Aitken, Harrison, and Lipsey (1996) for a study of foreign firms in Mexico, Venezuela, and the United States. Lipsey and Sjöholm (2001) show that foreign-owned firms in Indonesia pay higher wages than locally owned firms.

spent $420 that year.[60] Poverty rates are much lower for those holding jobs with foreign-owned firms. While 37 percent of the Vietnamese workers were classified as poor in 1998, only 8 percent of those working in foreign-owned businesses were considered poor. And although 15 percent of all workers were classified as "very poor," none of the workers in foreign-owned textile and leather-goods businesses were in that category.

The fact that foreign-owned "sweatshops" in poorer countries pay above-average wages in the local labor market may explain the low turnover (or quit) rate of workers at such firms. It may also explain why these jobs are so desirable that, in some instances, workers must pay one month's salary as a bribe to employment officers at such firms in order to get hired. And even though the wages are low, the savings rates of factory workers is much higher than that of workers elsewhere in the economy— an interesting fact in light of the accusation that such firms are not paying a living wage. In fact, in Vietnam and elsewhere, workers often request overtime, as they are seeking to maximize their income. International codes and rules that limit hours of work may interfere with the desire of these individuals to earn more money.

Even if the wages and working conditions in developing countries are dismal by the standards of the present-day United States, these multinational firms are at least providing employment opportunities and incomes that might not otherwise exist, enabling the poor to support their families. Two reporters for the *New York Times* provide a vivid example. When they were first assigned to cover Asia, they, like most people, were outraged at the sweatshop conditions. They later changed their opinion: "In time, though, we came to accept the view supported by most Asians: that the campaign against sweatshops risks harming the very people it is intended to help. . . . Those sweatshops tended to generate the wealth to solve the problems they created . . . it may sound silly to say that sweatshops offer a route to prosperity, when wages in the poorest countries are sometimes less than $1 per day. Still, for an impoverished Indonesian or Bangladeshi woman with a handful of kids who would otherwise drop out of school and risk dying of mundane diseases like diarrhea, $1 or $2 a day can be a life-transforming wage."[61]

[60] Glewwe 2000.
[61] Kristof and WuDunn 2000, 70–71.

The fundamental problem facing workers in developing countries is not the existence of sweatshops, but the lack of good alternative employment opportunities. Efforts to stop exports from low-wage countries, to prevent investment there by multinationals, or to impose high minimum wages or benefits beyond the productivity level of the domestic workforce will simply diminish the demand for labor in those countries and take away one of the few opportunities that workers have to better themselves and their families. Opponents of sweatshops have failed to consider what alternative opportunities for employment can be created.

_____*Should Trade Agreements Have Labor Standards?*

Can including labor standards in trade agreements help improve labor conditions in developing countries? Almost alone, the United States has pressed for considering such standards in trade negotiations. And yet there is a great deal of ambiguity about which standards should be included, their precise definition, and how they should be enforced. Two categories of labor standards are typically discussed. "Core" standards are related to fundamental human rights and can be universal in their application, such as a prohibition on forced labor. "Economic" labor standards, by contrast, are tied more closely to a country's level of economic development and include minimum wages and working conditions.

Core labor standards have been defined by the International Labor Organization (ILO), an international body created in 1919 and composed of member governments, employers, and workers. In 1996, the ILO issued a Declaration on Fundamental Principles and Rights at Work stating that all countries, regardless of their level of economic development, have an obligation to promote the following principles and rights: freedom of association and the effective recognition of the right to collective bargaining; elimination of all forms of forced or compulsory labor; effective abolition of child labor; and elimination of discrimination in respect of employment and occupation.

Although such core labor standards are generally recognized and attract wide support, there is (with the exception of slavery) remarkably little international consensus on the precise definition of these standards and the method of implementing them. The ILO oversees over 180 conventions on various aspects of labor rights and practices, but very few of them have been ratified by all of the ILO members. As of early 2004, for example, the United States had ratified just 14 and had agreed to only two of the core conventions (on the abolition of forced labor and the prohibition of the worst forms of child labor). The United States has ratified few conventions partly because domestic labor law is largely the prerogative of state governments and partly because the language of the conventions may conflict with national policy. For example, convention number 111 seeks to abolish employment discrimination on the basis of sex and race, but has not been ratified by the United States because it might conflict with affirmative action.

Other countries have also failed to adopt ILO conventions because they are perceived to be inflexible or irrelevant to local circumstances. For example, conventions number 87 and 98 deal with the right to organize and collective bargaining. The United States has not ratified these conventions because many states allow the hiring of replacement workers, which under the ILO convention could be viewed as interfering with the right to strike. Many developing countries are simply indifferent to these conventions. As one economist has noted, "for an overwhelming majority of poor workers in developing countries whose dominant mode of employment is self-employment in rural agricultural activities or in the urban informal sector, unionization has little relevance. Even where relevant and where the freedom to form unions has been exercised to a significant extent, namely in the organized manufacturing and public sector in poor countries, labor unions have been promoting the interests of a small section of the labor force at the expense of many."[62]

Child labor has been a particularly controversial issue, and illustrates the limits of using ILO conventions and trade policy to reduce this practice. Convention number 182, signed by President Clinton at the WTO summit in Seattle in 1999, aims to eliminate the worst forms of child labor, such as slavery, the sale of children, forced labor, prostitution, and illicit activities. The United States prohibits imports of goods made with forced or indentured child labor, but does not have a generic ban on imported goods made with child labor. Indeed, dealing with non-exploitative child labor is a more difficult issue. The ILO charter establishing minimum ages of work has not been ratified by the United States,

---

[62] Srinivasan 1998, 76.

Canada, or other developed countries because of differing national views on the details. For example, Canada chooses not to prohibit work at night for children under thirteen.

Of course, child labor is a major issue in developing countries, and some activists have suggested that developed countries should refuse to import any goods made with child labor. But just as trade policy is an inefficient instrument for achieving environmental objectives, as chapter 2 suggested, it is also an inefficient instrument for raising labor standards. A import ban on goods made with child labor might stop the use of children to produce goods for the U.S. market, but it would not put an end to child labor. Only about 5 percent of working children are employed in the export sector in developing countries. An import ban might simply shift them to other sectors of the domestic economy (about 80 percent are employed in the primary agricultural sector). At worst, an import ban could push them into less desirable or more hazardous work, or even leave them without work and thereby condemn them to starvation.[63] Import bans fail to address the root cause of child labor or offer any resolution to the underlying conditions that create it.

The most effective way of eliminating child labor is to attack the fundamental causes, which are poverty and the lack of affordable or adequate educational opportunities. As figure 6.7 indicates, the incidence of child labor is strongly related to per capita GDP. In fact, about 80 percent of the international variation in child labor is explained by this variable alone. Child labor virtually disappears once a country's annual per capita income reaches $5,000. Developing countries can help reduce child labor by raising rural incomes through agricultural price liberalization. Evidence from Vietnam suggests that when the domestic price of rice rose after the government permitted more rice exports, farmers responded by reducing the use of child labor.[64] Developed countries can help developing countries raise their income by allowing them to sell their products more easily

---

[63] "Caroline Lequesne of Oxfam, a British charity, has just returned from Bangladesh, where she visited factories to determine the impact of American retailers' human-rights policies. She reckons that between 1993 and 1994 around 30,000 of the 50,000 children working in textile firms in Bangladesh were thrown out of factories because suppliers feared losing their business if they kept the children on. But the majority of these children have, because of penury, been forced to turn to prostitution or other industries like welding, where conditions pose far greater risks to them." *Economist*, June 3, 1995, 59.

[64] Edmonds and Pavcnik 2005a.

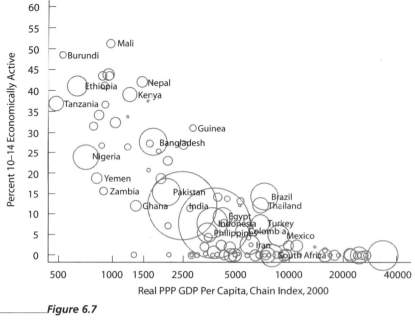

Percent 10–14 Economically Active

Real PPP GDP Per Capita, Chain Index, 2000

_____Figure 6.7

Child Labor and GDP per Capita, 2000
Source: Edmonds and Pavcnik 2005b.

in the markets of the richer economies. Compulsory education laws that mandate school attendance have also proven effective in reducing child labor and are more easily monitored than direct bans on imports.[65]

The WTO is not the proper forum for dealing with the issue of core labor standards because these standards are not directly related to international trade.[66] Even if a country did not engage in international trade but suppressed worker rights, labor standards should still be an issue because of the universality of core labor standards. To put it differently, if a country had a problem with the treatment of child labor but did not use that labor in exported goods, that practice should still be a source of global concern. Furthermore, the WTO lacks the institutional expertise

[65] Rising income and compulsory education accounted for the decline in the employment of children in the United States, and can do so in developing countries as well. The United States, it should be noted, did not ban child labor until the Fair Employment Act of 1938, a point when per capita income was well above that in many developing countries today.

[66] For a survey of work on whether trade policy should be used to improve labor standards, see Brown (2000).

and resources to deal with labor issues. As the WTO membership itself declared at the 1996 ministerial meeting in Singapore, the ILO is the competent body to set and administer labor standards. The effort to push labor standards onto the WTO's lap would undermine the ILO as well as burden the WTO with something it is not well equipped to handle.

The WTO has been tagged with the issue of labor standards primarily because trade sanctions are believed to be the most effective way of enforcing such standards. As we have seen, however, the threat of trade sanctions to enforce labor standards in developing countries risks harming the very workers we are trying to help. As Paul Krugman puts it, "even if we could assure the workers in Third World export industries of higher wages and better working conditions, this would do nothing for the peasants, day laborers, scavengers, and so on who make up the bulk of these countries' populations. At best, forcing developing countries to adhere to our labor standards would create a privileged labor aristocracy, leaving the poor majority no better off."[67] At worst, those export industries would be shut down, throwing those workers out of their jobs. Furthermore, the threat of using trade sanctions to enforce labor standards is precisely why developing countries are so afraid of including them in the WTO. Developing countries adamantly oppose efforts to link trade and labor standards, which is why pressing this issue is asking for a stalemate in the WTO.[68]

[67] Krugman 1998b, 84. Economic development is the only known way to increase wages. The alternatives—massive foreign aid, stronger demands for social justice—are unrealistic or ineffective. Krugman comments, "As long as you have no realistic alternative to industrialization based on low wages, to oppose [trade and industrialization] means that you are willing to deny desperately poor people the best chance they have of progress for the sake of what amounts to an aesthetic standard—that is, the fact that you don't like the idea of workers being paid a pittance to supply rich Westerners with fashion items."

[68] At the 1996 WTO ministerial meeting in Singapore, the United States pressed for the creation of a working group on labor standards. After sharp opposition by developing countries, the WTO membership agreed that the ILO instead was the appropriate venue for considering labor standards. Despite this agreement, the United States again called for an examination of labor standards in the WTO at the 1999 Seattle ministerial meeting. Developing countries were completely hostile, and even Canada failed to support the United States, while the European Union was willing to consider greater cooperation between the WTO and the ILO only if any linkage between labor standards and market access was ruled out. When President Clinton let slip the idea that labor standards should be included in trade agreements and enforced with trade sanctions, developing countries accused the United States of bad faith (ignoring the Singapore declaration) and were galvanized to oppose any new trade round on this basis. The president's statement almost single-handedly ensured the failure of the Seattle meeting.

To the extent that international cooperation in the ILO is considered useful, how should ILO charters be enforced? The problem is that if countries lack the political will to adhere to international rules, then the enforcement of those rules is beside the point. "Bad" regimes are unlikely to be moved by trade sanctions. Furthermore, under ILO rules, a government can only bring a complaint against another government if both have ratified the relevant convention. Through its failure to ratify many of the ILO conventions, the United States has effectively forfeited its right to use that organization to enforce labor rights abroad. For those countries that have ratified ILO charters or agree to accords on labor standards, enforcement is best carried out by embedding the ILO commitments in domestic law and enforcing them through civil actions and punitive judgments (such as fines) in the domestic legal system. The ILO is an international organization that is open to the participation of governments, business groups, and labor representatives, and so its charters have implications for private businesses (unlike the WTO, which is a government-to-government agency that sets rules only on government trade policies, not the practices of private firms).

If dealing with "core" labor standards is difficult enough, there are political pressures in developed countries to go beyond core standards and into the realm of "economic" standards. Labor unions and other NGOs have pressed for standards that include minimum wages, employment hours, occupational health and safety regulations, minimum age of employment, and so on. Without these economic standards, it is argued, developing countries will attract investment and gain jobs at the expense of developed countries, which will then face pressures to reduce labor standards. Such economic standards, however, have no place in a trade agreement because they are a function of economic development.[69] Labor unions' role in this push is worrisome from the standpoint of developing countries because all too often unions have simply sought to block trade.

As a result, while most advocates of higher labor standards are genuinely motivated by concerns about workers in developing countries, the politics of labor standards are such that attempts will be made to use

---

[69] As Robert Reich (1994), the secretary of labor in the Clinton administration, stated, "it is inappropriate to dictate uniform levels of working hours, minimum wages, benefits, or health and safety standards. The developing countries' insistence that they must grow richer in order to afford American or European labor standards—that they must trade if they are to grow richer—is essentially correct."

them to limit the market access of low-wage developing countries. In January 1999, the United States signed an agreement with Cambodia that promised a 14 percent increase in Cambodia's annual quota for textile shipments if the country agreed to meet certain core labor standards. Although the Cambodian garment industry established high minimum wages and agreed to paid vacations, unionization rights, and a ban on child labor, the Union of Needletrades, Industrial and Textile Employees (UNITE) wrote to the U.S. Trade Representative (USTR) opposing any increase in the quota. Following this, and without consulting other views, USTR ruled in December 1999 that Cambodia was not in "substantial compliance" with the agreement and denied the quota increase. The Cambodian government and garment industry were shocked because they believed they had gone beyond the agreement in improving standards. Five months later, USTR agreed to a smaller 5 percent increase after Cambodia and the ILO established a program to monitor work conditions.[70]

Unions such as UNITE, the Teamsters and the AFL-CIO also opposed legislation that gave African countries the same tariff preferences that the United States had previously extended to Caribbean and other poor developing countries. The African Growth and Opportunity Act of 2000 aimed to help the continent by giving duty-free access to the U.S.-market in selected goods. Instead of being viewed as a small way of helping African countries improve their economies, labor-backed opponents dubbed the legislation as "NAFTA for Africa." The proposal to allow African textile producers duty-free access to the U.S. market proved to be quite controversial even though Africa's share of U.S. apparel consumption was only 0.45 percent. The U.S. International Trade Commission concluded that the impact of removing the quota on the U.S. apparel industry would be negligible and that, at most, only 676 U.S. jobs would be affected.[71] Other analysts have suggested that the preferences might have an even smaller domestic impact because it would simply improve the position of Africa at the expense of China. Their staunch opposition to free trade with Africa fuels suspicions that labor unions are not really interested in helping poor African workers deeply mired in poverty, but oppose any measure that promises to increase trade.

[70] Cooper 2000.
[71] U.S. International Trade Commission 1997, 3–12

Experience has shown that it is all too easy to mask an antitrade agenda with labor and environmental concerns, as is evident by many anticommercial NGOs and anti-import labor unions. This is regrettable because there are deep and legitimate questions about using trade measures to enforce labor and environmental standards, and therefore the possibility of common ground gets lost in the advocacy of extreme positions. Yet there are inherent flaws in giving the WTO a non-trade-related mission, such as enforcing environmental agreements or enforcing labor standards. The risk is that these poorly targeted and indirect instruments for improving environmental and labor conditions will fail to achieve their objective yet at the same time expand the allowable rationales for trade barriers, thus undermining the liberal trading system without generating compensating benefits.

In conclusion, expanding world trade presents great opportunities for the world's developing countries. While trade policies in developed countries often hinder the ability of developing countries to improve their condition, developing countries cannot blame all of their problems on foreign trade barriers. Trade restrictions and barriers are much more extensive in the developing world than elsewhere. Much of the blame for the lack of development falls not on the people of these countries, but on their governments and their poor policies that inhibit economic activity. As the examples of India and China dramatically demonstrate, not the rest of the world, but their own misguided policies, have been holding them back from achieving higher rates of economic growth and poverty reduction.

7

The World Trading System:
The WTO and New Battlegrounds

Over the past half century, the multilateral system of world trade rules has provided a stable environment in which international trade has flourished. The Uruguay Round of trade negotiations, concluded in 1994, resulted in sweeping agreements to liberalize trade in agriculture and textiles and apparel and to extend trade rules to new areas such as services, investment, and intellectual property. In addition, the World Trade Organization was established as a formal multilateral institution with stronger procedures for resolving disputes than its predecessor, the General Agreement on Tariffs and Trade (GATT). In contrast to the rather anonymous existence of the GATT, however, the WTO has proven to be very controversial. This chapter assesses the WTO as an institution and examines the controversies surrounding its dispute settlement rulings, particularly on environmental measures.

The Origins of the GATT System

The impetus for establishing a formal system of world trade rules arose from the searing experience of the Great Depression in the 1930s. The Great Depression was a worldwide economic disaster. Between 1929 and 1932, the volume of world trade fell 26 percent and world industrial production fell 32 percent. Unemployment in many countries topped 20 percent. As the economic downturn intensified, most countries reacted by raising tariffs and imposing import quotas in an attempt to insulate themselves from the worldwide economic collapse. Widespread protectionism—in the form of tariffs, quotas, foreign exchange restrictions, and the like—materialized overnight.

The United States bears some responsibility for these developments. In the 1928 election year, prior to the economic downturn, President Herbert Hoover called for increased tariffs on agricultural imports to
help U.S. farmers. Once Congress started considering higher duties, however, things began to spin out of control. Logrolling coalitions pushed
tariff rates higher and higher, resulting in the infamous Smoot-Hawley
tariff of 1930. Warning of the adverse economic consequences of the
high tariffs, more than one thousand American economists signed a petition urging President Hoover not to sign the bill. The warning was not
heeded, and the Smoot-Hawley tariff helped push up average duties to
nearly 50 percent.[1]

While economic historians do not believe that the Smoot-Hawley
tariff caused the Great Depression, the high tariffs certainly played a role
in the downward spiral of U.S. trade and the overall economic decline.
The act also exacerbated world trade tensions and contributed to the
worldwide rise in trade barriers. As the League of Nations noted at the
time, the Smoot-Hawley tariff was "the signal for an outburst of tariff-
making activity in other countries, partly at least by way of reprisals."[2]

Out of the ashes of the depression emerged a new approach to
U.S. trade policy. At the request of President Franklin Roosevelt, Congress enacted the Reciprocal Trade Agreements Act (RTAA) in 1934. The
RTAA fundamentally changed U.S. trade politics by shifting tariff authority from the Congress, which proved very responsive to domestic
import-competing interests, to the executive branch, which was more
apt to consider the national interest and use tariff negotiations in the service of foreign policy objectives. This tipped the political balance of
power in favor of lower tariffs and put trade policy on a new course.
Even today, with some modifications, the RTAA serves as the basis of
U.S. trade policy.

The initial RTAA authorized the president to enter into tariff
agreements with foreign countries and to reduce import duties by no
more than 50 percent. Although the president's authority was limited to
three years (but has been renewed regularly), an important element of
the RTAA was the prior approval by Congress of any trade agreement

[1] For a discussion of this period, see Irwin (1998a).
[2] League of Nations 1933, 193.

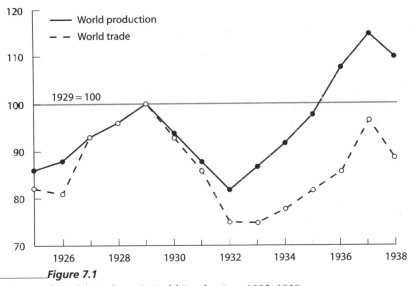

_____**Figure 7.1**
Volume of World Trade and World Production, 1925–1938
Source: General Agreement on Tariffs and Trade 1953, 110.

reached by the executive. Congress also endorsed the unconditional most-favored nation (MFN) clause, under which the lower U.S. tariffs negotiated with one country would be automatically extended to other countries.

By 1940, the United States had signed bilateral trade agreements with twenty-one nations that accounted for over 60 percent of U.S. trade. But the reduction in U.S. and foreign tariffs was modest and thus had only a limited impact on trade. The RTAA could not reverse the outbreak of protectionism around the world in the early 1930s. As figure 7.1 shows, world output grew again after 1932, but world trade failed to keep pace: if the depression led to the contraction of world trade, the protectionist policies of the 1930s constricted its recovery.

As an economic policy, the RTAA failed to live up to its expectations. But the RTAA had a lasting impact as a political innovation. The RTAA fundamentally changed American trade politics by tipping the political balance of power in favor of lower tariffs.[3]

[3] See the analysis of Bailey, Goldstein, and Weingast (1997) and Irwin and Kroszner (1999).

It did so in several ways. First, when Congress delegated tariff negotiating power to the chief executive, it effectively gave up the ability to legislate duties on specific goods. Congressional votes on trade now came to be framed in terms of whether or not, and under what circumstances, the RTAA should be continued. Vote trading among interests that favored various tariffs was no longer feasible. Thus, the RTAA reduced access to legislative mechanisms that supported redistributive bargains and logrolling coalitions that had led to high tariffs.

Second, the RTAA delegated authority and agenda-setting power to the president, who represented a broad-based constituency and was therefore more likely than to favor Congress lower tariffs. The national electoral base of the president is often thought to make the executive more apt to favor policies that benefit the nation as a whole, whereas the narrower geographic representative structure of Congress leads its members to have more parochial interests. Furthermore, the president is more likely than Congress to take into account trade policy's ramifications for foreign policy.

Third, the RTAA reduced the threshold of political support needed for members of Congress to approve negotiated agreements reducing tariffs. Prior to the RTAA, a minority could block foreign trade agreements because treaties had to be approved by a two-thirds majority in the Senate. Now, renewal of the RTAA required a simple majority in Congress. This shifted the threshold of political support needed to approve trade agreements and made them easier to enact. Whereas protectionist forces in the past had to muster only 34 percent of all senators to block a reciprocity agreement, now they needed 51 percent senators to kill a renewal of the RTAA.

Finally, the RTAA helped to bolster the bargaining and lobbying position of exporters in the political process. Previously, the main trade-related special interest groups on Capitol Hill were domestic producers facing import competition. Exporters were harmed by high tariffs on imports, but only indirectly. The cost to exporters of any particular import duty was minute, and therefore exporters failed to organize an effective political opposition. The RTAA explicitly linked foreign tariff reductions that were beneficial to exporters to lower tariff protection for producers competing against imports. This fostered the development of exporters as an organized group opposing high domestic tariffs because they wanted to secure lower foreign tariffs on their products. In addition, the lower tariffs negotiated under the RTAA increased the size of export sectors and decreased the size of sectors that competed with imports, and thereby increased the political clout of interests supporting renewals of the RTAA.

These features of the RTAA reduced the costs and increased the benefits of organization and lobbying by free trade interests.

The General Agreement on Tariffs and Trade

To officials at the time, the lesson of the 1930s was absolutely clear: like appeasement in the realm of diplomacy, protectionism in the field of economic policy was a serious mistake that helped make the decade of the 1930s a political and economic disaster. World leaders therefore agreed that, after World War II, cooperative actions must be taken to reduce barriers to international trade. Even as World War II raged, American and British officials began exploring postwar trade arrangements. The United States aimed to convert the piecemeal, bilateral RTAA approach into a broader, multilateral system based on nondiscrimination and the reduction of trade barriers.

Unlike plans for the postwar international monetary system, which were completed at the Bretton Woods conference in 1944, the trade arrangements materialized more slowly. Finally, in October 1947 in Geneva, representatives from twenty-three countries, accounting for roughly 80 percent of world trade, agreed on tariff reductions and on the text of a General Agreement on Tariffs and Trade (GATT).

The tariff reductions were negotiated on a bilateral, product-by-product basis. Under the "reciprocal mutual advantage" principle, no country would be forced to make unilateral concessions. If a bilateral agreement on specific commodity tariffs were reached, the lower negotiated rates would then be applied to all other members, through the most-favored nation clause, and considered bound at those rates. The United States reduced its tariff about 20 percent in the first GATT round.[4]

---

[4] But as figure 1.4 illustrated, average U.S. tariffs dropped sharply from about 45 percent in 1933 to just over 10 percent in the early 1950s. Most of this reduction was not the result of negotiated reductions in tariff rates, but the effect of inflation on specific duties. Because these duties were unchanged in terms of nominal amounts, inflation during and after World War II dramatically eroded the ad valorem equivalent of these duties. See Irwin 1998b.

_____*Table 7.1*
Major Provisions of the General Agreement on Tariffs and Trade

Provision	Description
Article 1	General Most-Favored Nation Treatment
Article 2	Schedule of Tariff Concessions
Article 3	National Treatment on Internal Taxes and Regulation
Article 6	Antidumping and Countervailing Duties
Article 10	Transparency of Trade Regulations
Article 11	General Elimination of Quantitative Restrictions
Article 12	Restrictions to Safeguard the Balance of Payments
Article 14	Exceptions to Rule of Nondiscrimination
Article 16	Subsidies
Article 17	State Trading Enterprises
Article 19	Emergency Action on Imports of Particular Products (safeguards)
Article 20	General Exceptions
Article 21	Security Exceptions
Article 23	Nullification and Impairment
Article 24	Customs Unions and Free Trade Areas

These tariff reductions did not require congressional approval because of the authority granted the president in the 1945 renewal of the RTAA. Precise estimates of the degree to which other countries reduced their tariffs are unavailable, but major European countries reduced their import tariffs significantly between the early 1930s and the early 1950s, although quantitative restrictions and exchange controls persisted in many of these countries.

The General Agreement on Tariffs and Trade set out principles for the conduct of commercial policy. The main provisions of the GATT are summarized in table 7.1.[5] First and foremost, Article 1 declared that all GATT signatories would extend unconditional most-favored nation treatment to all other contracting parties. The MFN clause forbids countries from using trade measures to discriminate against other GATT partners. Governments would have discretion in choosing the terms on which they permitted foreign goods into their country, but as a matter of principle (if not always practice) they would not be allowed to treat the

[5] Hoekman and Kostecki (2001) provide an excellent overview of world trade system rules.

goods from one signatory of the GATT differently from the same goods from another.[6]

Similarly, Article 3 requires that countries imposing domestic taxes and regulations adhere to the standard of "national treatment." National treatment is another form of nondiscrimination by which domestic and imported goods should face the same regulatory standards. Under this provision, governments were prevented from setting one standard for domestic products and then imposing a more stringent standard for similar imported products.

The other articles of the GATT deal with more specific trade policy issues. Article 6 condemns dumping if it causes or threatens material injury to an established industry and sets out very general standards for imposing antidumping and countervailing duties. Article 16 mandates that countries avoid the use of subsidies for primary products and proposes that countries limit subsidies. Article 11 is a sweeping prohibition on the use of quantitative restrictions, although Article 12 permits the imposition of import quotas when countries have balance-of-payments difficulties. Article 18 is a general exemption for developing countries from GATT rules to give them flexibility to support infant industries and protect their balance of payments. Other articles of the GATT address such mundane details as the valuation of merchandise for customs purposes, marks of origin, and the transparency of trade regulations.

The Geneva conference that founded the GATT proved to be a tremendous success in establishing international cooperation on matters of trade policy. However, the GATT was not a formal international institution, unlike the World Bank and International Monetary Fund (IMF). The countries signing the GATT were "contracting parties" and not members because the GATT was simply an agreement between governments, not an international organization. The GATT as an institution consisted of an extremely

---

[6] The MFN clause in Article 1 simply reads: "With respect to customs duties and charges of any kind imposed on or in connection with importation or exportation . . . any advantage, favour, privilege or immunity granted by any contracting party to any product originating in or destined for any other country shall be accorded immediately and unconditionally to the like products . . . of all other contracting parties." But Article 24 permits countries to deviate from unconditional MFN in the case of free trade agreements and customs unions. The text of the 1947 GATT is available in World Trade Organization 1999.

_____Table 7.2
GATT Negotiating Rounds

Negotiating Round	Dates	Major Accomplishments
Geneva	1947	GATT established. About 20 percent tariff reduction negotiated.
Annecy	1949	Accession of 11 new contracting parties. Minor tariff reduction (about 2 percent).
Torquay	1950–51	Accession of 7 new contracting parties. Minor tariff reduction (about 3 percent).
Geneva	1955–56	Minor tariff reduction (about 2.5 percent).
Dillon	1960–61	Negotiations involving external tariff of European Community. Minor tariff reduction (4 percent).
Kennedy	1964–67	About 35 percent tariff reduction.
Tokyo	1973–79	About 33 percent tariff reduction. Six codes negotiated (e.g., subsidies, technical barriers).
Uruguay	1986–94	WTO established. Additional tariff reductions. New agreements on dispute settlement, agriculture, clothing, services, investment, and intellectual property
Doha	2001–	To be determined.

small secretariat in Geneva, but its official standing was precarious.[7] The advantage of this situation was that the GATT remained a small body devoted to a single mission: promoting further attempts to liberalize trade and establishing broad rules for commercial policy. In contrast to the World Bank and IMF, the GATT had a narrow focus rather than a multifaceted agenda.

After the establishment of the GATT, the contracting parties met on a regular basis to negotiate further reductions in trade barriers. Because of the passivity of the United States and other countries, the GATT did not achieve much for more than a decade after its establishment. Subsequent negotiating rounds, listed in table 7.2, resulted in the accession of more countries to the GATT, but further tariff reductions were negligible in the 1950s and early 1960s.

[7] Refusing to give it formal recognition, Congress inserted in trade legislation throughout the 1950s the statement that "this Act shall not be construed to determine or indicate the approval or disapproval by the Congress of the Executive Agreement known as the General Agreement on Tariffs and Trade." Hudec 1990, 70.

In 1958, six European countries agreed to eliminate all tariffs on each other's goods, thus forming a common market, the precursor to today's European Union. U.S. exporters were concerned that their sales would suffer because American goods would still be subject to import duties in Europe. To reduce the margin of preference on intra-European trade, Congress took a serious interest in reducing trade barriers between the United States and Europe and authorized the president to undertake new, substantive negotiations. The Kennedy Round, begun in 1962 and concluded in 1967, resulted in a 35 percent reduction in tariffs, on average. These cuts were generally across the board, with each country receiving exemptions for sensitive sectors. The across-the-board approach proved to be more efficient and less cumbersome than the product-by-product negotiations used in previous rounds, although this was not obvious from the length of the negotiations.

The Tokyo Round negotiations (from 1973 to 1979) sliced tariffs by another third. By this time, tariffs on manufactured goods for the major industrialized countries had generally fallen to low levels. As a result, the Tokyo Round began the trend toward even more difficult negotiations about nontariff barriers. The Tokyo Round resulted in several codes dealing with nontariff issues such as subsidies, technical barriers, import licenses, government procurement, customs valuation, and antidumping procedures. These codes substantially broadened the scope of trade rules in certain areas, but also contained wide-ranging exceptions. In addition, countries could pick and choose which, if any, of the codes it wished to adopt, an approach that became known as "GATT à la carte." A majority of GATT members, including most developing countries, chose not to sign the codes. Indeed, developing countries were given "special and differential" treatment, meaning that they were not required to cut their trade barriers and adhere to GATT rules to the same extent as the industrialized countries.

Is the GATT a Success?

Before discussing the sweeping changes reached during the Uruguay Round of trade negotiations, let us pause to consider a basic question: has the GATT been a success?

In terms of its most basic objective, the answer is yes. The architects of the postwar world trading system desperately wanted to avoid

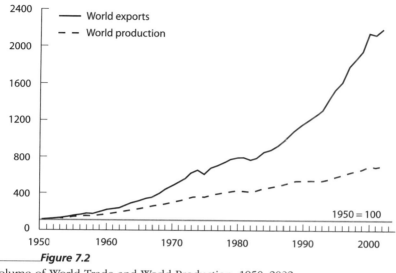

Figure 7.2
Volume of World Trade and World Production, 1950–2002
Source: World Trade Organization 2003, table A.1.

a repeat of the interwar trade policies after World War II. They not only accomplished this goal, but succeeded in undoing many of the high barriers that arose during the 1930s. The reduction in trade barriers and the stability of tariff policy in most countries in the decades after 1947 has permitted the expansion of world trade to proceed unchecked. As figure 7.2 indicates, world trade has grown much more rapidly than world output over the postwar period.

This figure alone does not prove that the GATT was responsible for much or all of this expansion. But statistical evidence indicates that the GATT can take credit for a good deal of the growth in world trade. A detailed study of bilateral trade flows during the half century since 1950 reveals that industrial countries that have participated in the GATT have much larger imports (and exports) than countries that have not participated.[8] This study finds that industrial country bilateral imports are 65 percent greater as a result of the GATT. However, GATT participation by developing countries did not increase their imports, perhaps because they were given "special and differential" treatment for so long and not required to liberalize their trade policies.

[8] Subramanian and Wei 2003.

In fact, according to the study, imports by new developing country members of the WTO are greater by virtue of their membership, but imports by old developing country members of the GATT are not. This is because new members are required to liberalize their trade policies before joining the WTO, whereas long-standing members were protected from changing their policies because of special and differential treatment. Finally, this analysis shows that bilateral trade for GATT participants is not higher in the case of clothing, footwear, and agriculture, precisely the sectors of trade that have been largely exempt from liberalization.[9]

Granting that the GATT and WTO have succeeded in increasing world trade, another question is why multilateral trade agreements have been politically successful in liberalizing trade. From a strictly economic point of view, the GATT's system of reciprocity in tariff reductions and rules for commercial policy is unnecessary because countries are better off pursuing a policy of free trade regardless of the trade policies pursued by others. As set out in chapter 2, the case for free trade is a unilateral one: as the economist Joan Robinson once put it, a country should not throw rocks in its harbors simply because other countries have rocks in theirs. The mercantilist language of international trade negotiations—that a reduction in one's own trade barriers is a 'concession" to others—is wrong from an economic standpoint.

The reason that reciprocity via multilateral trade agreements has worked well since 1947 is that such agreements have both economic and political value for governments seeking to contain protectionist pressures. When countries choose their tariffs alone, the outcome can be inefficient economically because governments are pressured by import-competing producers into maintaining trade restrictions. In addition, the gains from trade are magnified if other countries also reduce their trade barriers.[10]

---

[9] Subramanian and Wei 2003. Rose (2004) originally questioned whether the GATT had any significant impact on trade, and, in his examination of the bilateral trade data, he failed to find much of an effect of GATT participation. However, in his table 1 benchmark regressions, when country fixed effects are included in the analysis (which is generally considered to be the most appropriate specification), GATT participation is indeed related to more trade. Subramanian and Wei replicate Rose's findings and show how a more refined look at the data reveals the importance of the GATT.

[10] If tariff policies are interdependent, such that an increase in one country's tariff leads to an increase in another country's tariff, then a noncooperative equilibrium will include relatively high tariffs and be inefficient. See Bagwell and Staiger 2002.

Multilateral tariff cooperation is a way to avoid an economically inefficient result. Trade agreements are also beneficial politically because they enhance domestic support for open trade. Such agreements make exporters more politically active, counterbalancing the power of interests opposed to imports and thus facilitating trade liberalization.[11] Although unilateral free trade is beneficial, not all unilateral policies are free trade, as our discussion of trade politics in chapter 3 has described.

The GATT's economic and political value is demonstrated in countries' adherence to its provisions even though the agreement has no direct mechanism to enforce them. Under Article 23, if any contracting party fails to carry out its obligation or undertakes an action that "nullifies or impairs" a benefit due to another party, other countries can ask the GATT to allow them to suspend their concessions or waive their obligations to the offending country. In other words, if one country fails to adhere to the rules, then other countries are not obligated to adhere to the rules with respect to it. They can retaliate by raising tariffs against the rule-breaker's goods. In the "chicken war" of 1962, the United States imposed tariffs on $26 million in European goods because Europe violated GATT rules by imposing a high variable levy on poultry imports.

Thus, the countries that have signed the GATT contract are responsible for enforcing the agreement; no independent power resides with the GATT itself, which essentially relies on the goodwill of the signatories. Countries appear to be concerned about their reputation for adhering to agreements. Reputation can be a powerful device for preventing the erosion of agreements because a country that fails to abide by the rules forfeits the right to insist that other countries do so, and thus risks discrimination against its exports.[12] Evidence suggests that countries try to cultivate good reputations and fear retaliation for noncompliance with the agreed-upon rules.[13]

[11] Hillman and Moser (1996) provide a theoretical analysis of this point.

[12] In Hudec's (1998, 36) view, "other governments interested in maintaining the integrity of legal commitments are willing to go to considerable lengths to expose the defendant government to criticism for not keeping its word. . . . To be caught not performing one's own obligation is to lose the right to enforce the obligations on others, thereby losing specific trade opportunities as well as imperiling the entire liberal trading system. Rarely, if ever, does the gain from a violation of GATT obligations make it worth jeopardizing the benefits of the existing trade order."

[13] Bown 2004b.

Despite its success, the GATT legal framework has several notable defects. The agreement is written broadly, often with several exceptions for every rule. These exceptions give countries the flexibility to deal with unexpected contingencies and to maneuver through politically difficult decisions on policy. But they also provide loopholes and excuses for evading the basic principles of the agreement. For example, Article 1 contains the MFN clause, but Article 14 is entitled "Exceptions to the Rule of Nondiscrimination," and Article 24 permits countries to form customs unions and free trade areas, which are inherently discriminatory. Article 11 generally forbids the use of import quotas and quantitative restrictions, but Article 13 states that when they are imposed, they should be administered in a nondiscriminatory way, a provision that would be unnecessary if Article 11 were fully effective.

Another problem has been gaps in the coverage of the rules. For many decades, the agricultural sector and developing countries were exempt from many of the GATT disciplines. After 1952, the United States began imposing quotas on imports of such goods as oats, barley, butter, and milk and in 1955 received a broad waiver from the GATT—which was powerless prevent the quotas—to continue them. (The European Union similarly restricts agricultural trade with the Common Agricultural Policy.) And developing countries were given "special and differential treatment" under the GATT beginning in the mid-1960s. They were allowed greater flexibility in applying rules and were not bound by all of the GATT commitments. For example, reciprocity in tariff reductions was not expected of developing countries. These deficiencies were remedied, however, in the Uruguay Round of negotiations, discussed below.

Despite these deficiencies, over the past half century the multilateral trading system has achieved many of its original goals. Countries that are party to the GATT have generally adhered to the rules. Nondiscrimination has been established as a benchmark for commercial policy, and tariff barriers have been significantly reduced in successive negotiating rounds. In addition, overall trade relations have been good: specific disputes have been contained and policies have been stable, providing an environment in which international commerce has flourished. To be sure, discriminatory policies remain, antidumping actions and some nontariff barriers have surfaced, and disputes still arise and sometimes fester. But on the whole, the postwar system must be judged a great success.

This outcome is a formidable and enduring achievement of the architects of the postwar economic order.

Two other factors have made this outcome possible. First, the postwar economic expansion has been relatively smooth, punctuated only by a few recessions but free of major depressions. This experience has muted demands for protection and reduced the burdens of adhering to the rules. Economic growth and rising income mitigate the pain associated with structural shifts, due to international trade or other factors, by creating new opportunities for those displaced. In short, the economic shocks confronting the trading system have not been strong enough to bring about a systemic collapse, although the system was tested during the severe recession of the early 1980s.

Second, the bipartisan consensus forged in the United States during the 1940s in favor of reciprocal trade agreements has stayed largely intact. The initially tepid Republican support for trade liberalization faded as the postwar economic boom continued and as business interests continued to take an interest in opening up foreign markets for U.S. goods. By the early 1970s, on the other hand, several important Democratic constituencies had become less comfortable with liberalization efforts. Several labor unions, some of which had earlier supported reciprocal trade agreements, now began pressing for limits on trade as competition from imports intensified. The AFL-CIO's decision to support import quotas in the Burke-Hartke bill in 1971 was the first clear signal that organized labor was now opposed to freer trade. By the mid-1970s, union workers in the steel and automobile industries had joined others in taking a more aggressive stand against imports. Trade issues have become increasingly contentious, and the bipartisan consensus has frayed at the edges, and yet both Republican and Democratic administrations have continued to press for trade-liberalizing measures and have passed them through Republican- and Democratic-controlled Congresses.[14]

_____The Uruguay Round

The Uruguay Round of multilateral trade negotiations was launched in Punte del Este in 1986 after a trying decade for the world trading system.

---

[14] To those who believe that getting trade measures passed by Congress has become increasingly difficult, one should recall that such actions were not easy in the 1960s and 1970s either, as Dryden (1995) reminds us.

The Tokyo Round had been only a modest success. Slower economic growth, higher inflation, and persistent unemployment had diminished support for trade liberalization, and the painful recession of the early 1980s had fueled demands for new restrictions. Many observers believed that the GATT system was crumbling and blamed the proliferation of restrictions not covered by trade rules, such as voluntary export restraints. Moreover, countries were increasingly unwilling to adhere to existing rules. The system appeared to be adrift, without leadership or direction.[15]

And yet when the Uruguay Round negotiations were concluded in December 1993 and signed in April 1994, the resulting agreements turned out to be the most successful and comprehensive since the formation of the GATT. They not only liberalized trade in areas that had eluded previous negotiators, notably agriculture and clothing, but extended rules to new areas such as services, investment, and intellectual property. The Uruguay Round also brought about important institutional changes, both creating the World Trade Organization and strengthening the dispute settlement process.[16] At the same time, these far-reaching agreements produced controversy the likes of which the GATT had never seen.

As in previous negotiations, participating countries agreed to reduce tariffs on merchandise goods. Developed countries reduced tariffs on industrial products (excluding petroleum) by about 40 percent on a trade-weighted average basis. This brought average tariff levels in these countries down from 6.3 percent to 3.8 percent. The remaining tariffs are highly uneven across sectors, relatively low on sophisticated manufactured goods but substantially higher on labor-intensive manufactured goods. Developing countries reduced their tariffs by 20 percent on average, bringing their average rates down from 15.3 percent to 12.3 percent.[17] Table 7.3 reports tariffs after the Uruguay Round on industrial, agricultural, and clothing products for selected countries.

More importantly, the Uruguay Round began to incorporate trade in agricultural goods and in textiles and apparel into the GATT

[15] For example, the legal scholar John Jackson (1978) famously warned of the "crumbling institutions of the liberal trade system."

[16] See Schott (1994) and Hoekman and Kostecki (2001) for an overview of the accomplishments of the Uruguay Round and the substance of WTO agreements.

[17] Preeg 1995, 191.

_____Table 7.3
Post–Uruguay Round Average Applied Tariffs for Selected Countries

	Industrial Tariffs	Agricultural Tariffs	Textiles and Clothing
Developed countries			
United States	3.1	2.2	14.8
European Union	2.9	3.7	8.7
Japan	1.4	10.5	7.2
Canada	2.6	1.5	14.2
Australia	9.7	3.3	21.6
Developing countries			
Argentina	10.6	4.9	12.1
India	29.0	60.1	42.4
Korea	7.6	11.6	13.0
Thailand	26.8	26.5	28.9

Source: Finger, Ingco, and Reincke 1996.

system. Since the 1950s, the agricultural policies of many countries had been exempt from the GATT rules. The Multi-Fiber Arrangement (MFA) in textiles and apparel set quantitative limits on trade, product by product, country by country, in a way that GATT rules did not generally permit. The Uruguay Round sought to normalize trade in these sectors, so that protection could only take the form of bound, nondiscriminatory tariffs and not be cloaked in special export restraint deals or country-specific quotas operating outside of GATT disciplines.

Reform of agricultural trade had also eluded negotiators ever since the GATT's formation because of the political sensitivity of domestic support for farmers. A key problem facing negotiators in the Uruguay Round was that countries protected agricultural producers through a complex host of measures, including tariffs, import quotas, domestic price supports, and export subsidies. The Uruguay Round agreement limits the use of export subsidies and internal price supports by capping and reducing these outlays from a given base period. The agreement also seeks to ensure greater market access by requiring countries to convert all nontariff barriers (variable import levies, import quotas and prohibitions, voluntary export restraints, etc.) into a single import tariff. After this "tariffication" of existing restrictions, the tariffs are to be reduced over ten years by an average one-third for developed countries and by one-quarter for developing countries.

The resulting tariffs, however, are incredibly high. Table 7.4 reveals just how imposing the remaining restrictions are. Many countries used the process of converting the complex trade barriers into tariffs as an opportunity to cheat, raising tariffs above the existing combination of nontariff restrictions. This practice, known as "dirty tariffication," means that the actual liberalization in agriculture was slight. In addition, quantitative restrictions and export subsidies that are generally not permissible with manufactured goods persist in agricultural trade.

Subsidies have also persisted. In 2003, OECD countries provided $257 billion in support to agricultural producers, mainly through price supports. About 32 cents of every dollar received by OECD farmers came from taxpayers or consumers.[18] The effort to roll back subsidies received a major setback in 2002 when the United States enacted a new farm bill that expanded rather than contracted support for agricultural producers, a big step backward in terms of reforming agricultural policies. As a result of this farm legislation, one leading agricultural economist wrote,

> America's farm trade policy has become a four-dimensional
> disaster. It attempts to hide huge subsidy increases behind
> semantic claims of "non-product specificity" in order to keep
> them GATT-legal, effectively insulating U.S. producers from
> global markets. It sends exactly the wrong signal to those in
> Europe and developing countries who have struggled for trade
> liberalization, undercutting progress made in the Uruguay
> Round to reduce protectionism and expand agricultural
> markets for all farmers—notably U.S. farmers. Because these
> huge subsidies will quickly be capitalized into farmland values,
> U.S. producers will face higher costs, and younger and less
> landed farmers will be denied entry, aggravating disturbing
> trends toward an aging farm population and fueling division
> between a landed elite and their tenants. And despite increases
> in authorized funding for conservation, the massive infusions of
> subsidies to row crop production are likely seriously to
> aggravate soil and water degradation as the United States
> continues to pay the agricultural polluter.[19]

[18] Organization for Economic Cooperation and Development 2004, 22.
[19] Runge 2003, 93. These subsidies could also be illegal under the provisions of the Agreement on Agriculture reached during the Uruguay Round. Steinberg and Josling 2003.

_____Table 7.4
Border Protection for Selected Agricultural Goods, 1986-1988, 1995, and 2000
(in percent)

Country/Region	Wheat			Sugar		
	Actual Protection	*As Bound in Uruguay Round*		*Actual Protection*	*As Bound in Uruguay Round*	
	1986–88	*1995*	*2000*	*1986–88*	*1995*	*2000*
European Union	106	170	82	234	297	152
United States	20	6	4	131	197	91
Japan	651	240	152	184	126	58
Brazil	98	45	45		55	35
Mexico	−1	74	67	−58	173	156
Other Latin America	−17	34	34	41	85	80
Sub-Saharan Africa	10		133	44		100

Source: Ingco 1996, 437

Still, the WTO's agreement on agriculture is a tremendous achievement because it constitutes a critical first step. Various impediments have been simplified into one single transparent metric: tariffs. Although these tariffs are high and severely distort production and trade, they are finally on the negotiating table. The reform of agricultural trade policies, however, will be an objective for many years to come.[20]

The Uruguay Round also abolished the Multi-Fiber Arrangement, the complex web of bilateral export restraints and import quotas that clogs trade in textiles and apparel. The MFA was phased out over ten years, ending in January 2005, and the elimination of these quantitative restrictions has been a major step toward freer trade in clothing. Yet the United States and other developed countries will continue to protect their textile and apparel producers with high tariffs, as table 7.3 shows. In addition, antidumping and safeguard laws remain a vehicle for blocking textile and apparel imports with the MFA no longer around.[21]

The Uruguay Round made little progress in regulating the use of

[20] See Josling (1998) on the tasks ahead in the agriculture trade negotiations.
[21] On the MFA, see Spinanger (1999) and Reinert (2000).

	Dairy			Meat	
Actual Protection	*As Bound in Uruguay Round*		*Actual Protection*	*As Bound in Uruguay Round*	
1986–88	*1995*	*2000*	*1986–88*	*1995*	*2000*
177	289	178	96	96	76
132	144	93	3	31	26
501	489	326	87	93	50
−21	53	46	−52	25	25
−3	66	54	42	50	45
	75	69		51	47
		100			100

Source: Ingco 1996, 437.

antidumping laws, but countries did pledge not to "seek take or maintain any voluntary export restraints, orderly marketing arrangements or any other similar measures on the export or the import side."[22] These so-called gray measures had been previously used by countries to restrict trade without explicitly violating GATT rules. They are now eliminated, at least in principle. When countries seek to protect domestic industries from foreign competition, they are obligated to follow existing procedures and rules regarding safeguards and escape clauses. If adhered to, this provision also constitutes a major improvement in discipline.

The Uruguay Round also produced a General Agreement on Trade in Services (GATS) and established rules regarding trade-related investment measures (TRIMs) and trade-related intellectual property (TRIPs). Although these agreements are weak by the standards of the GATT, they constitute the first attempt to extend the principle of nondiscrimination to new areas of international commerce. The core obligations in the GATS are set around three principles: most-favored nation treatment, market access, and national treatment. The main sectors include

[22] Article 1:1(b) of the Agreement on Safeguards, in World Trade Organization 1999, 280.

telecommunications, financial services, air and maritime transport and construction. Although the agreement contains specific commitments to liberalization, coverage is incomplete because the important provisions of the GATS apply only to the sectors specified by the member countries. In general, trade in services was freed only slightly, but a framework was established in which liberalization could be pursued in the future.

The TRIMs agreement was even more modest in making national treatment the standard for regulating foreign investment. The agreement aims to eliminate quantitative restrictions on investment, including limits on the share of foreign ownership in certain industries. Because of opposition from developing countries, there was no attempt to consider such issues as the right of firms to establish enterprises in other countries, or the elimination of trade-related performance requirements on foreign investment.

The TRIPs agreement is one of the most controversial elements of the Uruguay Round. It consolidates previous international accords protecting copyrights, trademarks, patents, and industrial designs, and provides for the enforcement of these agreements within the WTO. But protection of intellectual property is not strictly speaking a trade issue that should be under the purview of the WTO, especially given the existence of the World Intellectual Property Organization. Many developing countries complain that, unlike mutually beneficial tariff reductions, the TRIPs agreement merely transfers income from developing to developed countries by strengthening the ability of multinational corporations to charge higher prices in poorer countries.[23] In addition, using instruments of trade policy to protect intellectual property makes it harder to reject demands to use them to enforce other non-trade-related objectives, such as environmental or labor standards. It opens the door to many interests who want to use the threat of trade sanctions to achieve their own non-trade objectives, and thus puts the WTO in the business of enforcing behavior in areas only tangentially related to trade. This dilutes the institution's focus on the reduction of trade barriers.

The Uruguay Round was a "single undertaking," meaning that all participants and future members of the WTO are bound to follow all of

---

[23] Maskus (2000) estimates that the full implementation of the TRIPs agreement would transfer $5.8 billion from developing countries to the United States, and another $2.5 billion to five other developed countries.

the agreements reached. Unlike the "GATT à la carte" approach of the Tokyo Round, countries cannot pick which accords to adhere to, and "special and differential treatment" for developing countries is limited. Although the obligations are extensive, they are less than the costs of remaining outside the agreement and losing the benefits of MFN treatment by other countries. As a result, membership in the WTO has become increasingly attractive. At the start of the Uruguay Round in 1986, the GATT consisted of 91 contracting parties. The WTO was established in 1995 with nearly 130 members, and by late 2004 the membership had risen to 148 nations, accounting for over 90 percent of world trade. About 30 countries are waiting to join the organization.

The Uruguay Round was the first round of multilateral trade negotiations in which developing countries played an active role, and their participation helped shape the outcome. Developed countries agreed to abolish the MFA's clothing quotas and to reform agricultural trade, increasing trade in sectors where developing countries have a comparative advantage. In return, developing countries accepted rules in the new areas of trade where developed countries have a comparative advantage. This exchange of market access came to be known as the "grand bargain." However, developing countries increasingly view the grand bargain as a major disappointment: they took on many new obligations in services, investment, and intellectual property, and yet developed countries have yet to grant significant access to markets in agriculture and clothing. The developing countries are now more suspicious about the benefits of multilateral negotiations, particularly if developed countries force them to consider labor standards in future negotiations, as discussed in chapter 6. As developing countries become more assertive in the WTO, the developed countries will have to be more sensitive to their concerns, or the differences between the two groups of nations could become a serious obstacle to completing the recently commenced Doha Round of trade negotiations.

The Doha Development Round of trade negotiations, launched in Qatar in November 2001, aims to promote the interests of developing countries. The formal agenda includes six broad areas: agriculture, nonagricultural market access, services, the so-called Singapore issues (transparency in government procurement, trade facilitation, investment, and competition policy) and rules (trade remedies), TRIPs, and development-related issues.

Each of these areas presents difficulties—agricultural policy reform is politically difficult in the United States and European Union, developing countries object to negotiations on investment and competition, and the TRIPs agreement remains contentious. The Doha Round is supposed to be completed by 2005, but in the past trade negotiations have rarely met such deadlines, which is why the GATT is sometimes referred to as the "General Agreement to Talk and Talk."

_____The World Trade Organization

The WTO was established in 1995 as a result of the Uruguay Round. The WTO has been a much more visible and controversial organization than the GATT, so it is important to get a sense of what the organization is all about, particularly its dispute settlement mechanism.[24]

The World Trade Organization is something more, but not much more, than the GATT. While the GATT was simply an intergovernmental agreement overseen by a small secretariat, the WTO is an international organization. But like the GATT, it has virtually no independent power and strives to be a neutral party among all the member countries. The director-general of the WTO has no policymaking authority and cannot comment directly on members' policies. The power to make trade policy and to write the rules governing it resides specifically with the member governments, not with the WTO. In negotiating the rules and running the organization, the WTO operates on the basis of a consensus among its members. Reaching any consensus is extremely difficult: a former director-general has likened the WTO to a car with one accelerator and more than 140 handbrakes.[25]

The scope of the WTO is broader than that of the GATT because it oversees multilateral agreements relating not just to goods, but also to services, investment, and intellectual property. The WTO provides the

[24] For a general overview of the WTO, see Jones (2004).

[25] Moore 2003, 110. Of course, not all 147 members have equal input on the negotiations. The United States and European Union carry the most weight. And many small developing countries cannot afford representation in Geneva and hence designate a country, such as India, to represent its interests. For a skeptical view of whether the WTO can serve the interests of developing countries, and an inside look at how negotiations are conducted, see Jawara and Kwa (2003).

forum for consultations and negotiations on these matters, assists with the interpretation of the legal texts, arranges for the arbitration of disputes, and conducts fact-finding surveillance reviews of members' policies, but ultimately the accords are intergovernmental agreements. The WTO has no power to force countries to obey the agreements or to comply with its rulings.

Because it is a forum for the discussion of trade policy more than anything else, the WTO as an institution is extremely small. The support staff and budget are limited in comparison to other international organizations. The WTO secretariat in Geneva consists of only six hundred employees, about a quarter of whom are translators. The WTO's budget in 2004 was about $130 million.[26] These figures are paltry in comparison to other international economic organizations, and even some nongovernmental organizations.[27]

Yet these small figures do not reflect the true importance of the organization as the cornerstone of the world trading system. Indeed, resources may be misallocated among the international economic organizations: the WTO's mission—to keep the international trading system functioning smoothly—is more clearly defined and perhaps even more important than the World Bank's more diffused mission of promoting economic development, but the WTO's budget is a tiny fraction of the bank's. Despite its heavy workload and the importance of its mission, the WTO makes do with relatively few resources. These resources may be insufficient as more nations turn to the organization to resolve trade disputes and handle other commercial matters.[28]

What most distinguishes the WTO from the GATT, aside from the new agreements, is the dispute settlement process. The original GATT agreement made little provision for settling disputes between member countries. When conflicts arose in the early years, an informal and ad hoc process was developed to help resolve them through negotiation. As it

[26] World Trade Organization 2004, 126.

[27] For example, the World Bank employs about 9,000 people and has an administrative budget of about $1.6 billion, the IMF employs 2,700 people and has a budget of $840 million, and the Food and Agriculture Organization (FAO) of the United Nations employs 3,500 people with a budget of $750 million. Many nongovernmental organizations have budgets that rival that of the WTO, such as the World Wildlife Fund ($102 million) and Greenpeace ($140 million).

[28] See Blackhurst (1998) for a discussion.

evolved, the GATT would often convene a panel of experts to arbitrate the dispute and interpret GATT rules. The panel would issue a finding about whether the trade measure in question conformed to the rules, but would leave a solution to the parties themselves. Over time, these flexible procedures became more complicated, and the growing body of case law was interpreted as having established legal precedent.

The Uruguay Round agreement established a dispute settlement mechanism that largely formalized existing practices. But it also strengthened the process by providing for specific timetables to expedite cases and, perhaps most importantly, by preventing countries from blocking the establishment of a panel or the adoption of a panel report. The GATT operated by consensus, meaning that unanimity was required for most decisions. As a result, a country accused of violations could block the establishment of a panel or, if a panel were set up, could object to the adoption of the panel's report. Understandably, this procedure hampered the enforcement of the rules. Under the WTO, the default has changed. The creation of a panel and the adoption of its report now go forward automatically unless, according to a "negative consensus" rule, there is a consensus in opposition.[29]

How does the new dispute settlement mechanism work? Countries may file "violation" complaints, alleging that a specific rule (such as nondiscrimination) has been broken, or "nonviolation" complaints, alleging that a government action "nullifies or impairs" a previous concession even if no specific rule has been broken. If initial consultations to resolve the dispute are not successful, a three-member panel is appointed to determine whether WTO rules have been violated. If it establishes a violation, the panel suggests that the disputed policy be brought into conformity with the rules, but generally leaves to the parties themselves the task of working out a solution. The panel decision can be appealed to an

[29] As a U.S. Trade Representative (2000, 41) report noted, "Under the GATT, panel proceedings took years, the defending party could simply block any unfavorable judgment, and the GATT panel process did not cover some of the agreements. Under the WTO, there are strict timetables for panel proceedings, the defending party cannot block findings unfavorable to it, and there is one comprehensive dispute settlement process covering all of the Uruguay Round Agreements." Despite the weaknesses of the GATT approach, Hudec (1990) argues that the process actually worked reasonably well in practice because countries made serious efforts to resolve disputes.

Appellate Body, which rules on matters of law and legal interpretation in the panel report.

As under the GATT, if the policy in question is found to violate the rules, the country can bring its policy into conformity with the rules, or keep the policy in place and offer compensation (lower tariffs) on other goods exported from the complaining country, which then has the option of accepting or rejecting the compensation offer. If neither alternative has been implemented, the complaining country can seek authorization to "suspend the application to the Member concerned of concessions or other obligations in the covered agreements." In other words, the complainant can retaliate by withdrawing previous tariff "concessions" to the country that has chosen not to comply with the finding. Such retaliations occur infrequently because most disputes are settled through negotiations. Two recent high-profile cases in which the United States was authorized to retaliate concern the European Union's ban on hormone-treated beef, which will be discussed shortly, and its discriminatory banana regime, which was settled in early 2001.

Why was the dispute settlement process strengthened in the Uruguay Round? Largely because Congress insisted. In Section 1101 of the Omnibus Trade and Competitiveness Act of 1988, which set out the objectives of the United States in the Uruguay Round, Congress instructed negotiators to seek the opening of foreign markets, the elimination of trade-distorting policies, and the establishment of "a more effective system of international trading disciplines and procedures." Frustrated with the GATT system, Congress wanted to improve the speed and effectiveness of the dispute settlement mechanisms and procedures.[30]

How has the new dispute settlement process worked? In a report to Congress in 2000, the independent General Accounting Office concluded that the dispute settlement process has worked well for the United States. Examining the cases considered by the WTO up to that time, the GAO found that most led to beneficial changes in foreign regulations and practices and that "none of the changes the United States

---

[30] U.S. House of Representatives 2003, 230. When members of Congress complain about the strong dispute settlement system as impinging on U.S. sovereignty, it is helpful to remember that it was the Congress itself that demanded that the GATT approach be strengthened because of its inherent weaknesses.

has made in response to WTO disputes have had major policy or commercial impact to date, though the stakes in several were important."[31]

In the first five years of the dispute settlement system, the United States brought many more cases against other countries than were brought against it. Since then, however, many more cases have been brought against the United States. In the first nine years of the WTO (1995–2003), the United States filed sixty-four complaints about foreign trade measures and was the subject of seventy-seven complaints. Of the sixty-four complaints, forty-five had been resolved by the early 2004. Of these cases, twenty-one were resolved to U.S. satisfaction without litigation, twenty-one received favorable rulings by WTO panels, and in three the United States lost on core issues at the WTO. Of the seventy-seven complaints brought against the United States, forty-three had been resolved by mid-2004. Of these cases, twelve were resolved without litigation, the United States won nine, and in twenty-two some aspect of U.S. policy was found inconsistent with WTO rules. This reflects a general tendency: countries that bring a complaint to the WTO tend to win their cases, while the defendant countries tend to lose. This probably reflects the fact that countries will only go through the effort of bringing a case if it is a strong one.

Among the politicians in Washington, there is a tendency to judge the dispute settlement mechanism only on the basis of whether the United States "wins" the cases it files and those brought against it. Clearly the mechanism is more important than that. It was established simply to ensure that the rules that countries agreed upon together and pledged to abide by are actually mean something. Sometimes the United States is on the wrong side. For example, in 1995 Costa Rica won a complaint against the United States concerning restrictions on imports of underwear. The fact that small countries can receive fair treatment under the rule of law is a strength of the world trading system.[32] The alternative is that more powerful countries simply dictate outcomes to others.

But even when the United States loses a case, the WTO cannot force change in U.S. laws, regulations, or policies. The WTO cannot strike down any U.S. law, as an American court can. As the General Accounting Office puts it: "The United States maintains that it has the right not to

[31] U.S. General Accounting Office 2000b, 2–3.
[32] Bown (2004a) shows how developing countries have received better treatment from WTO dispute settlement than under the GATT.

comply with WTO rulings. However, the United States recognizes that it may bear a penalty for not complying with WTO rulings, both in the form of retaliatory duties on U.S. exports and in terms of its reputation as a key player in the world trading system."[33] WTO panels merely determine whether disputed policies conflict with WTO rules and, if they do, recommend that members bring those policies into conformity. The disputing countries must still resolve the matter themselves, often through a negotiated settlement.

Some nonparticipants are disturbed by the closed proceedings during disputes and ask whose interests get represented in the panels. Many NGOs, particularly environmental groups, have complained that the WTO is secretive and antidemocratic in its procedures. Although they are now allowed to file amicus (friends of the court) briefs, NGOs are generally barred from the dispute settlement process. This is because the WTO agreements are strictly government-to-government agreements that deal with governmental policy, and not the behavior of private firms. The appropriate way for commercial and noncommercial domestic interests, which are not parties to the negotiated agreements, to influence the WTO is through their member governments.[34] The GATT and WTO have typically operated under a diplomatic veil rather than as an open forum in the past because commercial negotiations involved reducing tariffs in one sector to secure lower foreign tariffs for another sector, thus trading off various domestic interests. The United States wants the institution to become more open and transparent, but other members have strongly resisted. Because the WTO is a consensual body, the issue is not one to decide unilaterally and against the wishes of the other members.[35]

[33] U.S. General Accounting Office 2000b, 16.

[34] Robertson (2000) provides an incisive examination of whether so-called civil society should participate more directly in the WTO.

[35] As Sampson (2000, 42–43) notes, "the view of the significant majority of WTO members is that it would be inappropriate to allow NGOs to participate directly even as observers in the proceedings of WTO meetings." If such groups were allowed, difficult questions would have to be answered: "Which groups of civil society should be represented at different meetings, and who would decide? . . . Should farmers' unions be present during negotiations on the reduction of agricultural subsidies that lead to environmental degradation, or should environmental NGOs? Should consumer groups be present during negotiations when trade liberalization leading to lower consumer prices was being discussed, or should it be the sectoral interests that would be adversely affected by a lowering of trade barriers? . . . Is it not preferable to have a democratically elected government represent the diverse interest groups in a given country."

The dispute settlement process has become one of the most controversial aspects of the WTO. Some legal experts have raised the concern that WTO panels and the Appellate Body have exceeded their mandate to interpret the agreements and have created new rights and imposed new obligations on members. Has the WTO overreached its authority by failing to give sufficient deference to policymakers in member countries? While most legal scholars believe that it has not overreached, with the possible exception of trade remedies, others are concerned that judicial legislation goes on.[36]

Trade remedies, such as antidumping and safeguard measures, discussed in chapter 5, have come under WTO scrutiny, and these reviews have often found problems with the imposition of remedies by domestic authorities. With regard to safeguards, the WTO has found fault with just about every escape clause action undertaken by any member. This creates formidable legal obstacles to using safeguards, which as chapter 5 indicated may be a form of trade intervention superior to antidumping duties. The WTO decisions regarding safeguards sometimes have been unclear and often difficult to implement, particularly regarding how agencies should link increased imports and serious injury to a domestic industry.[37]

If the WTO takes too critical a view of safeguard actions, it risks triggering a backlash in Congress and undermining domestic political support for the institution. A General Accounting Office report on the WTO review of trade remedies found that the United States is the most frequent defendant in such cases. Examining all disputes filed with the WTO from 1995 to 2002, the report indicated that the United States had 12 percent of its 239 trade remedy measures challenged in the WTO, while the EU had only 4 of its 182 measures challenged and India none of its 226 measures. Although the United States has been a defendant more often than a complainant, the GAO found that the WTO ruled similarly in U.S. and non-U.S. trade remedy cases. The GAO found that WTO

---

[36] Davey 2001; McRae 2004.

[37] See Sykes (2003) and Irwin (2003) on safeguards. Antidumping actions have been subject to fewer reviews. Article 17.6 of the WTO Antidumping Agreement indicates that deference should be given to the decisions of national authorities in antidumping determinations, if the domestic agency properly established the facts and evaluated them in an unbiased and objective manner.

rulings "have not required numbers changes to members' laws, regulations, and practices, but have resulted in the revision or removal of a number of trade remedy measures that members imposed."[38] (An example of this is the Bush administration's decision to rescind the steel safeguard tariffs in December 2003 as a result of an adverse WTO ruling.) However, if the United States perceives that it is being singled out and its dumping and escape clause cases given especially strict scrutiny, then Congress will begin to raise serious questions about these WTO reviews.

Environmental Regulations and WTO Rules

Several WTO rulings have also raised questions about whether trade rules take precedent over domestic environmental, health, and safety regulations, thereby impinging on a country's sovereignty. Critics, such as Global Trade Watch, part of Ralph Nader's Public Citizen organization, charge that the WTO has undermined every environmental regulation it has reviewed. Unfortunately, the passionate opposition to certain rulings has given rise to much exaggeration and distortion. For example, Global Trade Watch charges that "in the WTO forum, global commerce takes precedence over everything—democracy, public health, equity, access to essential services, the environment, food safety and more. . . . years of experience under the WTO have confirmed environmentalists' fears: the WTO is undermining existing local, national, and international environmental and conservation policies."[39]

This accusation is clearly wrong. The General Accounting Office points out that "WTO rulings to date against U.S. environmental measures have not weakened U.S. environmental protections."[40] As of late 2004, fewer than 10 of the more than 140 disputes brought before the WTO had dealt with environmental or health issues, and most trade dispute are quite banal. These few environmental cases have mainly focused on whether the regulation in question has been implemented in a nondiscriminatory way, not whether that regulation is justifiable. At the same time, however, some cases illustrate the difficult issues and potential conflicts that can arise when trade and environmental policy intersect.

[38] U.S. General Accounting Office 2003, 5.
[39] Wallach and Woodall 2004, 13, 20.
[40] U.S. General Accounting Office 2000b, 14.

What precisely are the trade rules that affect environmental measures? The most relevant provision of the GATT is Article 20, entitled "General Exceptions":

> Subject to the requirement that such measures are not applied in a manner which would constitute a means of arbitrary or unjustifiable discrimination between countries where the same conditions prevail, or a disguised restriction on international trade, nothing in this Agreement shall be construed to prevent the adoption or enforcement by any contracting party of measures . . . (b) necessary to protect human, animal or plant life or health . . . [or]
> (g) relating to the conservation of exhaustible natural resources if such measures are made effective in conjunction with restrictions on domestic production or consumption.[41]

The key element of Article 20 is the introductory paragraph. This provision allows countries to enact and enforce various measures that may restrict trade in order to achieve various objectives, provided that the measure is nondiscriminatory, does not constitute a disguised restriction on international trade, and is necessary to achieve the stated objective. The subsections of Article 20 specify objectives that would justify measures to constrain trade. The most important subsections, (b) and (g), permit regulatory measures to protect human and animal health and to conserve natural resources.[42]

Three of the WTO's environmental cases have become notorious, concerning imported gasoline, tunas and dolphins, and shrimps and turtles. They are worth considering in some detail because popular

---

[41] World Trade Organization 1999, 455. The remaining provisions relate to the protection of public morals, to protection of national treasures of artistic, historic, or archaeological value, to trade in gold and silver, to products of prison labor, and to other measures such as intergovernmental commodity agreements and customs enforcement.

[42] Wallach and Woodall (2004, 21) complain that the Article 20 exceptions apply only in certain narrowly defined circumstances and that in many cases the "exceptions were so narrowly interpreted as to render them moot." But if this is really the problem, then the members of the WTO should simply amend the Article 20 exceptions to reflect a broader view. After all, those rules are not made up by the WTO as some independent entity, but were agreed upon by the member countries of the WTO, among them the United States and European Union.

discussion of them is highly emotional but superficial, and therefore prone to distortion. Article 20 has been the focus of disputes not so much because of the exceptions specified in subsections (b) and (g), but because any environmental trade measure must be implemented in a nondiscriminatory fashion. As pointed out earlier, the United States has long insisted that nondiscrimination be the basis of international trade relations, which is why the most-favored nation clause is instituted as Article 1, and national treatment is instituted as Article 3, of the GATT. The United States would be understandably upset if foreign regulations discriminated against American exports. If the United States insists upon receiving fair treatment abroad, it cannot be surprised that other countries demand nondiscriminatory treatment from the United States. This appears to be a noncontroversial proposition. Surprisingly, Public Citizen's most widely trumpeted example of the WTO's weakening of U.S. environmental regulations involves precisely this issue.

_____Reformulated Gasoline Case

The Public Citizen book *Whose Trade Organization?* opens by accusing the WTO of forcing the Environmental Protection Agency (EPA) to weaken its environmental standards on imported gasoline. This case "was the first concrete evidence of the WTO's threat to environmental policy" and "an example of how the WTO could be used to skirt a country's democratic policymaking and judicial systems," bringing "credibility to critics' concerns that the WTO could threaten national sovereignty to set and effectively enforce important policies."[43]

Yet the case did not involve the stringency of the EPA's regulation, but simply the nondiscriminatory implementation of the regulation as required by the introductory paragraph of Article 20. Simply put, the U.S. regulation discriminated against imported gasoline to the benefit of domestically refined gasoline. The EPA was free to demand any standard of cleanliness it chose, but was obligated under Article 20 to apply the same standard to domestic and foreign producers.

In December 1993, the EPA issued a regulation to reduce the amount of contaminants in domestic and imported gasoline. Its purpose

[43] Wallach and Woodall 2004, 25.

was to limit harmful emissions from automobile exhaust. Each domestic refiner was required to meet a new, more stringent standard based on its own 1990 benchmark quality level. This individual standard was permitted because a single industry-wide baseline would make compliance very costly for certain domestic oil refiners, which vary in cleanliness. Imported gasoline, however, was subject to a uniform baseline, and foreign refiners were not offered the option of establishing an individual benchmark. And though this was partly for ease of administration, a less publicized reason was deliberate discrimination. As an EPA administrator later testified before Congress, the agency thought "that it was appropriate, if we had a choice, to lean in the direction of doing something that would favor their competitive position [i.e., that of domestic refiners] vis-à-vis the [foreign producers]."[44] In other words, the EPA built in discrimination to help domestic oil refiners compete against foreign refiners.

In 1995, Venezuela and Brazil brought a complaint to the WTO, charging that the United States was applying a more stringent standard on imported gasoline. A WTO panel ruled against the United States, which then appealed to the Appellate Body. The Appellate Body determined that while such regulations were permitted under Article 20, this regulation involved discrimination and therefore violated the introductory provision of the article. The Appellate Body recommended that the regulation be brought into conformity with WTO obligations, but left to the United States how it would comply.

At this point, the United States had three options: it could ignore the Appellate Body finding, let the regulation stand but offer compensation to Venezuela and Brazil in the form of lower tariffs on other products, or bring the regulation into conformity with the WTO obligation.[45] It is useful to consider the implications of each option.

If the United States chose to ignore the ruling, Venezuela and Brazil could legally withdraw previous tariff concessions extended to

[44] Quoted in Palmeter 1999.

[45] Public Citizen makes the options appear more draconian, saying that the "WTO's ruling forced the U.S. to make a 'no-win' choice: repeal the regulation and permit imports of gasoline with higher contamination levels. . . , or keep the policy and face $150 million in trade sanctions each year the U.S. failed to comply" (Wallach and Woodall, 2004, 28). The EPA regulation would not have to be "repealed," just modified to eliminate the discrimination. The regulation would not make imports dirtier as long as the domestic regulation was made as stringent as that on imports.

U.S. goods, equivalent in value to their lost gasoline exports. In signing the GATT, the United States agreed to abide by its rules No authority can force compliance or negotiated settlement, but other countries can retaliate by withdrawing tariff concessions (i.e., raising tariffs) on their imports from the United States.[46] In practice, Venezuela and Brazil might choose not to retaliate against the United States, realizing that such actions would probably fail to accomplish anything. But they might choose this option, which would be permissible under WTO rules.

The second possible U.S. response would be to keep the existing regulation in place, but to compensate Venezuela and Brazil by lowering tariffs against other goods. If this compensation were acceptable to Venezuela and Brazil, the case would be over. But this response requires lowering tariffs on another industry, an unlikely outcome. One trade lawyer pointed to the political difficulty: "imagine the U.S. Trade Representative explaining to an industry why the United States had agreed to lower tariffs on its products in order to keep in place a discriminatory rule that favored the oil industry."[47]

As a result, the United States chose to bring the regulation into conformity with the WTO nondiscrimination requirement. This could have been accomplished by requiring domestic refiners to meet the same statutory baseline that applied to imports, but the domestic industry did not want this option. Instead, in August 1997 the EPA allowed foreign refiners to use individual baselines, as domestic producers were allowed to do. To ensure that imports of "dirty" gas did not increase, the EPA established a benchmark for imported gasoline quality based on the volume-weighted average of individual benchmarks for domestic refiners. The EPA monitors imported gasoline closely and imposes remedies if imports do not meet that benchmark.[48]

Note that compliance with the WTO rules and resolution of this dispute had nothing to do with whether a more or less stringent standard

---

[46] As Palmeter (1999, 90) puts it, "the sole remedy available to a WTO member that wins its case against the measure of another, if that measure is not changed and if adequate compensation is not forthcoming, is, effectively, cancellation of the bargain . . . [In other words,] if some side backs out of its bargain, the other side may do the same."

[47] Palmeter 1999, 86.

[48] For a full description, see the EPA's notice in the August 28, 1997, issue of the Federal Register (45544–68), available on-line at http://www.access.gpo.gov.

was applied. It only required that the *same* standard be applied to domestic and foreign sources of gasoline. The EPA could have resolved the case by raising the domestic standard, rather than lowering the standard applied to imports. Thus, the case is far from one in which the WTO "undermines" domestic environmental regulation, as Global Trade Watch and others have made it out to be. In fact, Public Citizen, which decries corporate influence on government policy, put itself in the position of defending a rule that worked to the advantage of the domestic petroleum industry, one of the nation's most politically powerful special interest groups. The United States may have lost this case, but the system worked exactly as the United States wanted it to. The United States can invoke the same rule against discriminatory regulations in other countries.

Finally, it is important to understand the small proportions of this case. Most of the gasoline consumed in the United States is refined in the United States from imported crude petroleum. The United States imports only a small amount of finished motor gasoline, just 3.7 percent of the total U.S. supply (domestic production plus imports) in 1998. By far the largest foreign supplier of gasoline in that year was the Virgin Islands, followed by Venezuela, with Canada a close third. Other countries such as Brazil supply just a tiny amount.[49]

_____The Tuna-Dolphin Case

The "tuna-dolphin" case is perhaps the most infamous recent trade dispute. In 1991, a GATT panel ruled that a U.S. ban on imported tuna that had been caught without using dolphin-safe methods was inconsistent with GATT rules. In some sense, this case is now completely moot: it was decided under the old GATT (rather than WTO) rules, did not force any change in U.S. policy, and was later resolved through negotiations. But the case is important because the panel's legal interpretation continues to cast a shadow over the debate about conflicts between environmental policies and world trade rules.

Many dolphins are accidentally killed by tuna fisherman who use purse seine fishing nets. Under the Marine Mammal Protection Act, the United States established dolphin protection standards for the American

[49] U.S. Department of Energy 1998, 1:17, 56.

fishing fleet and for countries fishing for yellowfin tuna in parts of the Pacific Ocean. The act required that the United States ban the importation of tuna from countries that failed to meet U.S. standards for dolphin-safe fishing methods.

Mexico objected to the embargo, and in 1991 requested that a panel review the case. Mexico argued that the ban violated Article 11 of the GATT, which prohibits quantitative restrictions or embargoes on the goods from other member countries. Mexico noted that dolphins were not an endangered species and there was no international agreement forbidding the use of purse seine nets. Eleven other countries made representations to the panel, all supporting the Mexican position. The United States was outnumbered in the GATT mainly because other countries objected to the unilateral nature of the ban. They believed that by imposing such standards, the United States was simply trying to force other countries to adhere to America's view of how non-American resources should be protected. They viewed this as bullying, and objected as a matter of principle.

The United States argued that the import restrictions were justified under GATT Article 3, allowing the enforcement of domestic regulations at the border, and Article 20, allowing trade measures to protect health and safety and promote conservation. The GATT panel rejected both defenses. The panel ruled that the trade restrictions justified by Article 3 apply only to products as such, and not to the process by which the product was produced. This distinction became known as the "product-process" doctrine. Because tuna caught by dolphin-safe methods was the same as tuna caught by dolphin-endangering methods, the panel saw no legal basis for differentiating between them.

The panel also rejected the Article 20 defense of the embargo. The United States could not invoke Article 20(b) because the "human, animal or plant life or health" was not within the jurisdiction of the United States, and GATT rules did not allow a country to take trade actions for the purpose of enforcing its own standards in another country (something known as extraterritoriality). Finally, the Article 20 defense failed because the measure was not shown to be "necessary" since other GATT-consistent options (such a multilateral negotiations) had not been explored. A later case brought by the European Community in 1994, known as Tuna-Dolphin II, resulted in a similar panel report regarding

Article 3 but proposed a different interpretation of Article 20, allowing for the regulation of environmental resources that are not in the regulating country.

Under the old GATT dispute system, a panel report was not official until adopted by the GATT Council. Mexico did not pursue the panel decision any further, and the United States blocked the adoption of the Tuna-Dolphin II panel report. All during this time, the U.S. import ban remained in place. The tuna dispute was resolved in 1992 when the United States, Mexico, and eight other tuna-fishing nations signed an international agreement to regulate the conditions of tuna fishing. Since then, incidental dolphin deaths due to tuna fishing have dropped dramatically, according to the National Oceanic and Atmospheric Administration (NOAA). The American import embargo finally ended in 1997, thereby ending the seven-year dispute. Some implications of this case will be discussed shortly, although the ultimate outcome must be judged satisfactory: the import ban was replaced by an international treaty, which has been more effective at saving dolphins than any unilateral import ban.

_____**The Shrimp-Turtle Case**

Another high-profile case, this one involving the WTO, concerns U.S. regulations on imported shrimp. WTO critics charge that a ruling completely undermined U.S. efforts to require foreign shrimp trawlers to use "turtle excluder devices" (TEDs), which helped prevent the accidental drowning of endangered sea turtles. But as with the Venezuelan gasoline case, this WTO ruling did not concern the law itself but rather the way in which the United States implemented the law.[50] The ruling also opened the possibility that Article 20 exceptions could consider the "process" of production in designing trade-related environmental regulations.

In 1989, Congress prohibited imports of shrimp and shrimp products harvested in a way that may harm endangered sea turtles. The prohibition was to be lifted only for countries that the State Department had certified as having a program to prevent accidental turtle deaths (or for countries whose fishermen trawl only in cold waters where there are

[50] See Balton 1999 for details.

no such turtles). For some reason, the State Department initially inter-preted the law as applying only to countries in the Caribbean and At-lantic. As a result of a suit brought by environmental groups, however, in December 1995 the U.S. Court of International Trade determined that the law applied to imports worldwide. The court rejected a request by the State Department to delay the enforcement of the ruling to allow newly affected countries time to comply, and thus the worldwide embargo went into effect in May 1996, less than six months after the ruling.

In September 1996, India, Malaysia, Pakistan, and Thailand, all of which were newly affected by the ban, brought a case to the WTO. They argued that shrimp must be allowed in the U.S. market regardless of the "process" by which they are caught. The dispute settlement panel ruled against the United States on the grounds that the ban was inconsistent with Article 11 (limiting the use of import prohibitions) and could not be justified under Article 20. The United States appealed the verdict to the Appellate Body, which overruled most of the panel's decision. In October 1998, the Appellate Body held that the shrimp certification measure was justified under Article 20(g) relating to the conservation of exhaustible natural resources, but that its implementation was inconsistent with the nondiscrimination requirement. For example, in applying a countrywide standard, the State Department might prohibit all imports of shrimp from a country even if some of the its shrimp was caught by trawlers using TEDs. In addition, the Appellate Body stated that the regulations were not transparent or predictable, and that the United States had negotiated a treaty to protect sea turtles in the Western Hemisphere but had not at-tempted to negotiate a treaty with governments in the Indian Ocean.

The WTO did not require the United States to lift its ban on shrimp imports, but only to implement the ban in a nondiscriminatory way. The import ban was not lifted at any point during the dispute pro-cess. The United States continues to impose an embargo against shrimp imports from countries that have not been certified, but is negotiating with countries that desire to become certified as not endangering turtles.

There is little doubt, however, that the initial panel decision was not just legally questionable, but created immense political problems for the WTO. The initial decision left the impression that the GATT and en-vironmental rules are necessarily in conflict and ruled against amicus briefs by NGOs, fueling their hostility to the WTO. The Appellate Body overruled most of the panel report, but the damage was already done. The fact that the Appellate Body report overturned so many of the legal aspects of the panel report made the panel's findings seem arbitrary, as though "law" could be made up by bad panels, or that the Appellate Body was simply bowing to outside pressure and could change legal interpretations on a whim.

Lessons from the Environmental Cases

These cases convey some sense of the issues involved in trade and environmental disputes. What are the lessons to be learned?

The first lesson is that, although there may be some tensions between trade policy and environmental objectives, world trade rules are not antienvironmental. Several less well publicized decisions reaffirm that Article 20 allows countries to maintain consistent and nondiscriminatory environmental regulations. For example, in 1994, a GATT panel affirmed that the corporate average fuel economy (CAFE) standards, regulating the fuel efficiency of automobiles sold in the United States, were a perfectly acceptable form of product regulation to protect public health and environment, as long as those standards did not explicitly discriminate on the basis of country of origin. Similarly, a WTO panel in 2000 upheld France's ban on asbestos imports, on the grounds that they were hazardous materials, after Canada had challenged the embargo.

Second, the "product-process" distinction that prevents consideration of how tunas or shrimp are fished is a source of great difficulty. Never explicitly propounded or endorsed by WTO members, the doctrine emerged from a creative interpretation of a GATT panel and gradually took on a life of its own. The distinction is arbitrary and unsustainable because process-based regulation has already been introduced in the agreement on trade-related intellectual property. For example, original and copied software are similar products, but the process by which they were produced is quite different.

Many people in developed countries care about how products are made: tuna may be tuna, but tuna fished by dolphin-safe methods is not viewed as identical to tuna fished by dolphin-unsafe methods. Furthermore, as set out in the tuna-dolphin case, the product-process doctrine may not even be legally sound. One leading GATT legal scholar has written that "the underlying conceptual foundation based on 'product' focus of Article 3 tends to crumble on analysis" and that "the suggestion that Article 3 does not apply to ('cover') process-based regulation is just plain wrong."[51] Although the shrimp-turtle ruling weakened the product-process doctrine, it can still pose an obstacle to process-based regulation.

At the same time, there are sound reasons for not allowing any and all process regulations. Developing countries fear that process regulation will open the door to the imposition of standards that other countries cannot afford. They are concerned that if the method of production of a particular good becomes grounds for blocking trade, then labor and environmental conditions of production will be introduced as excuses for keeping out the products of developing countries.[52] The product-process distinction will be one of the most difficult and important issues that the WTO membership has to work out.

The third lesson is that unilateral trade sanctions are a poor instrument for achieving environmental objectives. Simply keeping foreign goods out of the U.S. market may be viscerally satisfying, but it does not solve the problem. The refusal of the United States to buy fish that have been caught in ways that harm other animals does nothing directly to help those other animals. Sanctions do not prevent a country from diverting tuna and shrimp caught with harmful methods away from the U.S. market toward other markets that would accept it. In the end, international agreements on standards are clearly preferable to trade embargoes, and a global approach must be taken in those negotiations because the lack of cooperation by a few key countries can undermine the goal.

While the threat of sanctions can sometimes provide the incentive for countries to join negotiations, it is also true that countries are apt to resent and resist the imposition of U.S. standards. When other nations are reluctant to negotiate about a problem, the carrot of subsidies rather than the stick of sanctions can be used to promote the adoption of safer

[51] Hudec 2000, 198.

[52] As Sampson (2000, 18–19) points out: "in the view of [developing] nations, permitting discrimination among imports on the basis of production methods would profoundly undermine a principle that lies at the heart of the WTO legal system. This concern manifests itself in a resistance to any attempts to provide for the extension of industrial country production standards to developing countries in order for their exports to be acceptable for import in industrial countries. The strength of feeling on this matter on the part of many developing countries cannot be overstated."

production methods. For example, a straightforward solution to the dolphin and turtle problem would have been to subsidize the purchase of dolphin-safe nets and turtle excluder devises for use around the world. These technologies are not expensive. Rather than spending millions of dollars on legal fees over many years in an effort to solve the problem through compulsion, a combination of foreign aid, World Bank assistance, and NGO financial resources should have been pooled to give these dolphin- and turtle-saving technologies to fishermen in developing countries.

Because trade controls are usually ineffective and sometimes counterproductive as environmental regulations, the issue of whether trade restrictions are a necessary part of the environmental effort should be considered. Although relatively few multilateral environmental agreements contain provisions calling for trade restrictions, those that do include the Convention on International Trade in Endangered Species (CITES), the Basle Convention on the Control of Transboundary Movements of Hazardous Wastes and Their Disposal, and the Montreal Convention on Fluorocarbons.

CITES bans trade in ivory and other products to help save endangered animals. But an ivory trade ban is not the best policy to protect endangered African elephants because such a ban fails to deal with the underlying problem of domestic resource management. The convention hurts countries that manage their resources well, such as Zimbabwe, Botswana, and South Africa, where the number of elephants has risen. The sale of ivory from herd culls in these countries could generate valuable revenue that the cash-starved game reserves could use to improve the situation even more. Meanwhile, the decline in elephant populations in Kenya and Tanzania is not directly due to the ivory trade, but to poor national management that has failed to prevent local farmers from attempting to use reserve lands for commercial cultivation. These incursions, more than the ivory trade, result in animal deaths. Simply banning trade is no substitute for strong domestic measures that protect species, and a well-regulated and well-managed trade can prove better than import bans.[53]

The Basle convention bans illegal trade in toxic waste to prevent its dumping in developing countries. But illegal dumping was very

[53] As Morris (2000, 279) puts it, "CITES imposes trade restrictions on trade in certain species. The ostensible ground for such restrictions is that demand for parts of those species outside the territory of the nations in which those species live is encouraging

infrequent in the past, and the ban did nothing to solve the underlying problem: that national laws that already regulated toxic waste dumping were not enforced. According to some analysts, the convention may even have impeded recycling efforts in developing countries.[54] The Montreal Protocol seeks to limit the production and use of chlorofluorocarbons (CFCs), but also imposes bans on the export or import of controlled substances and requires trade sanctions against nonsignatory countries. While the protocol has been effective in limiting CFC production, the question is how effective trade sanctions are against countries that choose not to comply with the agreement, since production and not trade is the main problem.

In the case of trade in ivory and trash, the problem is not that the WTO poses a barrier to effective environmental management, but that the multilateral agreements substitute trade restrictions for solutions that more effectively address the underlying problem. The Montreal Protocol is a more difficult issue. A global consensus could emerge that trade measures are an effective component of an international economic agreement. If provisions of an environmental agreement conflict with WTO rules on nondiscrimination, then the governments agreeing to the environmental accord could also form a consensus in the WTO that discrimination in certain products was acceptable for environmental reasons.[55] There should be enough common ground between the trade policy and the environmental community to work out these differences.

What has become clear is that it will not be acceptable for the world trade community to ignore or undermine environmental concerns when there is a global consensus on those concerns. Effective environmental and safety regulations should not be blocked simply because they reduce international trade. The notion that all trade must be kept free at

---

people to poach those species, leading to dwindling stocks. However, this characterization of the problem misses what for most species is the most important factor in determining numbers, namely the opportunity cost of their continued existence to those people who live nearby. Indeed, by reducing the value of various species to the locals, CITES may in fact discourage conservation."

[54] See Montgomery 1995.

[55] As Sampson (2000, 97) argues, "If the agreed solution involves a loss of rights under the WTO (that is, being discriminated against), then providing all WTO members agree to forgo those rights, it is difficult to see where there could be a problem."

all costs is simply wrong. As Thomas Babington Macaulay put it in a par-
liamentary speech in 1845,

> I am, I believe, as strongly attached as any member of this
> House to the principle of free trade, rightly understood. Trade,
> considered merely as trade, considered merely with reference
> to the pecuniary interest of the contracting parties, can hardly
> be too free. But there is a great deal of trade which cannot be
> considered merely as trade, and which affects higher than
> pecuniary interests. And to say that government never ought to
> regulate such trade is a monstrous proposition, a proposition at
> which Adam Smith would have stood aghast.[56]

_____Public Health and the Beef Hormones Case

World trade rules do not stand in the way of government action to protect the public health. When the United States banned imports of live-
stock and meats from Europe in 2001 because of fears of mad cow and
foot-and-mouth disease, the action was legal according to WTO rules. At
the same time, public health is sometimes used as a justification for regulations intended only to protect special interests. International negotiators have attempted to allow health and safety regulations even if they
restrict trade, while trying to discourage regulatory protectionism, that is,
trade barriers designed to protect domestic producers but cloaked under
a health or safety rationale. Distinguishing these two cases, however, can
be extremely difficult.

    The use of public health as an excuse for protectionist regula-
tions is not a new problem. In the late 1880s, for example, many European countries banned the sale of American pork after rumors spread
that it was tainted with trichinosis. Even though there proved to be no
evidence of such a problem, the ban was enormously beneficial to European pork farmers, who had well-known difficulties competing against
low-priced American pork.[57] Today, the United States and other countries

---

[56] Macaulay 1900, 102.

[57] According to one historian of the incident, "the general fear of trichinosis was
a godsend for European protectionists." The American consulate in Le Havre reported that
French inspectors were instructed to find trichinae in at least 25 percent of American pork

maintain trade barriers that are ostensibly designed to protect the public health, but upon further examination are actually maintained for the benefit of producers. The Department of Agriculture estimates that questionable foreign regulations cost the United States about $5 billion in agricultural, forestry, and fishery exports in 1996.[58]

The U.S.-EU dispute over hormone-treated beef is a classic example of the extreme difficulty in drawing the line between regulations to protect consumers and regulations to protect producers. The long-festering dispute remains unresolved despite countless attempts to negotiate a settlement. The conflict began in 1985, when Europe restricted the use of natural hormones for therapeutic purposes and banned the use of synthetic hormones for growth purposes in cattle and meat sold in the EU. At the same time, the EU prohibited the importation of animals or meat from animals that had been treated with such hormones. Thus, the regulation was seemed to be nondiscriminatory because the same standard was applied to domestic and imported meat. In such cases, the regulation cannot be held in violation of Article 1 or Article 20 of the GATT.

Implemented in 1989, the measure wiped out about $100 million in American beef exports to Europe. The United States strenuously objected, arguing that the EU ban was unjustifiable because the hormones had been found safe when used in accordance with good practices of animal husbandry. The safety of the hormones had been accepted not just by the U.S. Food and Drug Administration, but by numerous international scientific panels. Efforts to resolve the dispute under the Tokyo Round's Agreement on Technical Barriers failed because it deals only with end-product characteristics, and cattle with naturally occurring hormones cannot be distinguished from cattle and beef treated with supplemental hormones. As a result, the United States retaliated in 1989 by imposing 100 percent tariffs on $100 million of agricultural imports from Europe.

The United States sought to clarify international rules on health and safety regulations during the Uruguay Round, and the result was

---

that they examined. The foreign minister of Austria-Hungary publicly admitted that protection to domestic producers was a determining factor in the exclusion though it was ostensibly imposed for sanitary reasons. See Gignilliat 1961.

[58] Roberts and DeRemer 1997.

the Agreement on the Application of Sanitary and Phytosanitary Measures (SPS). The SPS agreement provides that trade-related sanitary measures should be based on scientific principles and maintained with sufficient scientific evidence (Article 2.2) or be based on international standards (if they exist). Sanitary measures should be nondiscriminatory and not be more trade-restrictive than required to achieve the appropriate level of sanitary protection. In addition, Article 5.5 of the SPS states that governments should strive to achieve consistency in the protection of health risks and "shall avoid arbitrary or unjustifiable distinctions in the levels it considers to be appropriate in different situations, if such distinctions result in discrimination or a disguised restriction on international trade."[59]

The United States (supported by Australia, Canada, and New Zealand) used the SPS to challenge the EU ban on beef imports, arguing that the ban failed to meet any of these requirements. The WTO panel convened experts, two chosen by the United States, two chosen by the European Union, and another chosen by those four, to evaluate the scientific evidence regarding the hormones. The five scientists unanimously concluded that there was no public health risk. In 1995 the United Nations Codex Alimentarius Commission and a scientific panel convened by the EU declared that there is no human health risk from the hormones when used in accordance with proper animal husbandry, confirming what other international science bodies had stated.

The record also showed that high levels of several of the hormones occurred naturally in animal products, and yet these products were not regulated. For example, of the six hormones at issue, the one identified as most dangerous by the EU is found from ten times to hundreds of times more concentrated in such products as eggs, cabbage, broccoli, and soybean oil than in hormone-treated beef. If the objective was to protect the public from exposure to specific hormones, then why was the sale of eggs not banned? In the view of the U.S. government, these facts made the ban arbitrary and inconsistent. According to the United States, the real motivation for the measure was to protect domestic beef producers from foreign competition and to reduce surplus beef supplies in the EU. If consumer health were the true motivation, then the EU should not have

---

[59] World Trade Organization 1999, 62. For an evaluation of the SPS Agreement, see Roberts (1998) and Josling, Roberts, and Orden (2004).

allowed the use of growth additives by its competitive pork producers while disallowing it in its less competitive beef industry.[60]

The EU countered by arguing that the ban was justified under Article 20(b) of the GATT and claimed that the United States was simply attacking the "level" of protection provided. The EU maintained that the WTO could not rule on the appropriate level of protection provided by any regulation, but merely whether the measure itself was in conformity with the SPS. The EU argued that the ban was based on the "precautionary" principle, which took the view that if scientific evidence did not establish beyond a doubt that the hormone residues were safe for humans, then a ban was appropriate.[61] The EU stressed that it did not ban all meat imports, and that hormone-free beef could be sold in Europe.

In 1997, the WTO panel ruled that the hormone ban was not based on scientific evidence or a risk assessment and therefore was inconsistent with the EU's obligations under the SPS agreement. The Appellate Body reaffirmed that decision in 1998. In 1999, after the EU failed to implement any changes in policy, the United States imposed 100 percent tariffs on European imports valued at nearly $120 million, the estimated annual amount of lost U.S. beef exports. Proposals to resolve the impasse by replacing the import ban with a labeling requirement, allowing consumers to make the choice about whether to purchase hormone-treated beef, ran into difficulties. As of late 2004, a negotiated settlement had yet to be reached and the tariffs remained in place.

As already noted, Article 20 allows trade restrictions with the proviso that they be imposed in a nondiscriminatory fashion, but also that they are not "a disguised restriction on international trade." Discrimination

[60] The United States noted that Europe introduced milk quotas in 1984 to reduce the oversupply of dairy products, and this resulted in an increase in cattle slaughter, which more than doubled the stock of surplus beef (World Trade Organization 1997, 20). As Roberts (1998, 394) points out, "It was no coincidence, the United States argued, that EC officials were willing to allow the use of productivity-enhancing inputs in the internationally competitive pork sector, but substantially more conservative about allowing the use of such inputs in a sector which relied on costly domestic price support measures, import protection, and export subsidies to maintain producer profitability."

[61] Article 5.7 of the SPS states, "In cases where relevant scientific evidence is insufficient, a Member may provisionally adopt sanitary or phytosanitary measures on the basis of available pertinent information." The EU did not formally invoke this provision because its ban was permanent, and as the record made clear, there was abundant scientific evidence that judicious use of hormones was not harmful.

was never an issue in this case because the use of hormones was forbidden in domestic as well as imported meat. The question is whether the measure was a "disguised restriction" on trade. The problem is that this standard is virtually impossible to determine because it gets to the unobserved motives behind a trade action. If the intention was not disguised, it would be obvious. The head of the European Alliance for Safe Meat, and a member of the European Parliament, admitted that "the decision to ban these substances was made for political and commercial reasons and not, as the public was led to believe, for consumer protection."[62] Such admissions fuel the suspicion that there was no compelling health or safety reason for the ban, but that it was designed to help special interests, namely European beef producers.

The challenge confronting trade policymakers is to distinguish health and safety protection from regulatory protectionism enacted under the name of health and safety. As it turns out, there are tangible benefits to giving many of the existing regulations a hard look. As a result of the SPS agreement, the United States lifted a controversial eighty-three-year ban on Mexican avocados and allowed the importation of uncooked Argentine beef for the first time in eighty years (from regions of Argentina recognized as free of foot-and-mouth disease). In addition, Japan removed its forty-six-year ban on U.S. tomatoes, New Zealand citizens are now able to purchase Canadian salmon, and Australians are now able to buy cooked poultry meat. In each case, the restriction's public health rationale was questionable.

And yet merely writing rules (such as SPS) is not going to end such trade disputes. Negotiated rules are a useful way of finding common ground, but countries are bound to have different assessments of the risk trade-offs involved in any given regulation. For example, the United States and European Union have different assessments of the risks of genetically modified foods, such as corn and other agricultural crops. In Europe, the food is under suspicion until proven safe, whereas in the United States, the food is acceptable until proven harmful. There is little scientific evidence that such foods are harmful, but Europe invokes the precautionary principle to justify restrictions on its use. These different principles cannot be easily bridged simply by writing down rules. The

---

[62] Quoted in Aaronson 2001, 153.

question is how far WTO members want to go in limiting the ability of governments to adopt trade restrictions when scientific evidence does not exist or is ambiguous. One approach is to allow countries complete freedom in choosing their own product safety standards because they benefit the most from proper regulation and bear the cost of regulatory protectionism. Governments and the business community, however, appear to benefit from common ground, rules that provide a transparent and stable system for distinguishing appropriate from inappropriate standards.

The WTO may have a limited role in such conflicts. Some trade disputes are not a matter for litigation and a legal solution, but negotiation and a diplomatic solution. As one observer of the WTO has put it: "Too much policy in the WTO is now formulated on the basis of finding legal 'solutions' to problems, often through legal interpretations of the GATT and WTO agreements, instead of through decisions taken by all members after a full-fledged policy debate. Today's WTO is moving toward being a 'House of Litigation,' lost in the intricacies of legal rulings, rather than an institution based on widely accepted principles that have produced time-tested policies."[63] This is a critical issue that the WTO membership will have to confront in coming years.

Preferential Trade Agreements

Aside from unilateral trade actions and multilateral trade agreements, countries sometimes pursue bilateral or regional trade initiatives as well. The United States began undertaking such agreements in the early 1980s, at a time when the multilateral process had stalled. U.S. bilateral and regional trade negotiations are listed in table 7.5. This approach paused after NAFTA in 1994, but started up again under President Bush.

The motivation for these agreements varies. In some cases, a diplomatic or foreign policy objective is at stake; in others cases, economic or sectoral interests are advanced. Whatever the case, economists have

[63] Sampson 2000, 7. Sampson (111) has also noted that "perhaps [legal] rulings such as this have some short-term political merit in finding immediate 'solutions' to politically sensitive matters, but in the long term, policy choices as important as the legitimacy of the unilateral application of trade measures to enforce domestic societal preferences extraterritorially should not be left to litigation of this nature, with confusing and uncertain outcomes."

_____Table 7.5
U.S. Regional and Bilateral Trade Agreements

Country or Region	Status (as of December 2004)
Israel	In effect since April 1985
North American Free Trade Agreement (Canada and Mexico)	In effect since January 1994
Jordan	In effect since December 2001
Singapore	In effect since January 2004
Chile	In effect since January 2004
Australia	In effect since January 2005
Central American Free Trade Agreement (Costa Rica, El Salvador, Guatemala, Honduras, Nicaragua)	Signed May 2004
Morocco	Signed June 2004
Bahrain	Signed September 2004
Free Trade Area of the Americas (34 Western Hemisphere countries)	In negotiation
Dominican Republic	In negotiation
Southern African Customs Union (Botswana, Lesotho, Namibia, South Africa, Swaziland)	In negotiation
Thailand	Announced intention to negotiate
Panama	Announced intention to negotiate
Andean Free Trade Agreement (Colombia, Peru, Bolivia, Ecuador)	Announced intention to negotiate

Source: Office of the U.S. Trade Representative.

viewed these preferential agreements with skepticism, particularly in comparison to unilateral and multilateral approaches to trade liberalization. The problem is that these so-called free trade agreements are really preferential and discriminatory trade arrangements.[64] Although Article 24 of the GATT permits them, they are contrary to the most-favored nation treatment (MFN) embodied in Article 1. And they could actually harm economic welfare.

The classic analysis of preferential trade arrangements distinguishes two effects: trade creation and trade diversion. When the United States and Mexico eliminate tariffs on each other's goods, prices to consumers fall and trade is created. However, U.S. and Mexican exporters are also given preference over other countries in the two partners' markets, possibly diverting existing trade away from nonmember countries. In other words, the tariff preferences may shift trade not on the basis of

[54] Bhagwati and Panagariya (1996) stress this point

economic efficiency, but on the basis of preferential tax treatment. Countries may be induced to purchase their imports from less efficient producers, possibly harming economic welfare. Preferential agreements create a distortion because a tax incentive is given for trade with certain countries and not with others.

The precise magnitudes of trade creation and trade diversion are hard to determine. In the case of NAFTA, for example, it is extremely difficult to distinguish the effects of the slowly phased-in tariff preferences on United States–Mexico trade from those of the peso crisis in December 1994 and the ongoing rise of the maquiladoras.[65] The welfare effects of the preferences are even harder to gauge. Assessment hinges on whether (pretariff) import prices were actually higher than they would have been in the absence of the preferential treatment. There is precious little empirical evidence on this crucial point: some research suggests that preferences might harm the welfare of nonmembers by forcing them to reduce their export prices.[66]

Rules of origin are a potentially more serious distortion to trade that can arise in preferential agreements. In a preferential agreement, each member country retains its own tariff schedule that it applies to imports from nonmembers countries.[67] This gives rise to transshipment: the incentive to bring imports into the country with the lowest tariff and then ship them into the high-tariff country. To avoid transshipment, NAFTA mandates that duty-free treatment extends only to goods with sufficient "North American" content About two hundred pages of the two-thousand-page NAFTA text is devoted to rules of origin, which are stricter than those in the U.S.-Canada Free Trade Agreement. In the Canadian agreement, automobiles must have 50 percent North American content to receive duty-free treatment, but this standard was raised to 62.5 percent in NAFTA. In the original agreement with Canada, textile and apparel goods must be made from North American fabric to be eligible, but under NAFTA the yarn from which the fabric is woven must also be of North American content. Thus, Mexican garments receive duty-free treatment

---

[65] According to one assessment (Krueger 2000), there is not much empirical support for the concern that NAFTA has resulted in substantial trade diversion.

[66] Winters and Chang 2000.

[67] In a customs union such as the EU, all member countries have a common external tariff.

in the United States only if the yarn is made, the cloth woven, and the cutting and sewing done primarily in North America.

Rules of origin can bring about trade distortions when exporters strive to achieve enough North American content. For example, Mexican producers may shift their imports from third-country suppliers to higher-cost U.S. sources. This diversion raises the North American content so that the goods can qualify for duty-free treatment in United States.[68]

Although preferential trade agreements have been subject to valid criticisms, such agreements may have countervailing benefits. The concerns about trade creation and trade diversion take a purely static view of trade, ignoring the beneficial effects on U.S. and Mexican pro ductivity as a result of greater competition. Furthermore, trade diversion is not a serious concern from the standpoint of the United States because the margins of preferences are minimal due to the low average tariffs. (The story may be different for high-tariff countries signing an agreement with the United States.) And sometimes regional trade agreements can provide templates that can be later adopted at the multilateral level, as was the case with the U.S.-Canada agreement on services trade.

One of the most important issues concerning regional trade arrangements is whether they are stepping-stones to multilateral liberalization of trade, or stumbling blocks that detract from the multilateral system and distort trade flows into artificial regional patterns. It is difficult to know, a priori, whether regional and multilateral trade arrangements are complements or substitutes. This depends upon the intention of the participants and upon reaction of other countries, whether they wish to join the agreement or respond by forming their own preferential arrangements.

Fortunately, the preferential trade agreements are fundamentally different from the pernicious bilateralism of the 1930s: the momentum is entirely toward removing trade barriers, resulting in smaller preferential margins, rather than in creating even greater degrees of discrimination. The Bush administration's trade representative, Robert Zoellick, argues that bilateral agreements are a part of a "competitive liberalization" strategy that will induce other countries to sign agreements and reduce trade barriers to nonparticipants, who will seek to reduce discrimination against their exports. For example, shortly after the United States signed NAFTA

---

[68] Krueger 1999.

with Mexico, the European Union sought a similar trade agreement with
Mexico to keep its exports competitive in the country.

Bilateral and regional trade agreements have proliferated in recent years. The World Bank reports that the number of regional trade
agreements in force has risen from 50 in 1990 to nearly 230 as of late
2004.[69] These agreements are complex and overlapping. There are sound
reasons to be concerned about the effect of these agreements on the
multilateral system. Many of the agreements, particularly among developing countries, liberalize trade only marginally and lack much substance. The political effort vested in these schemes could be better de-
ployed at the multilateral level. And because of their overlapping nature,
to say nothing of their complexity, preferential trade arrangements detract from the simplicity that was part of the multilateral system's design.
Large regional trade arrangements are generally concluded no more
quickly than multilateral initiatives, and thus the advantages of pursuing
them are questionable.

In many instances, however, these arrangements are pursued for
their political importance rather than for their economic effects. The formation of the European Economic Community, the precursor to the
present-day European Union, was driven by a desire to solidify political
and economic ties in a way not possible without some discrimination.
When Mexico signaled that it was interested in pursuing a free trade
agreement with the United States as a way of promoting closer political
ties and economic integration, it would have been nearly impossible for
any U.S. administration to snub the request.

Despite these regional diversions, the United States has a much
greater stake in the multilateral system of the WTO and continues to play
a pivotal role in shaping that system.

[69] World Bank 2005, 28.

No nation was ever ruined by trade.
—Benjamin Franklin, 1774

Conclusion

In a recent speech at Dartmouth College, former senator George Mitchell said that he had drawn two conclusions from his role as mediator in the conflict in Northern Ireland: that economic opportunity is a prerequisite for peace, and that America's vision of that economic opportunity is the basis of its influence in the world.

These simple lessons have some connection to trade policy. For nearly three-quarters of a century, the United States has nurtured a rules-based world trading system centered on the principle of nondiscrimination and the goal of gradually reducing trade barriers. The United States is admired around the world as a place of economic opportunity, where individuals are given a chance to succeed regardless of their background. America's commitment to a system of open trade and willingness to accept products from around the world is one reason it is so highly regarded. The choices that the United States makes in its own trade policies have ramifications far beyond America's shores and have implications well beyond economics.

Today, the open world trading system supported by the United States faces challenges from two different sources. The first is the threat of protectionism. Protectionist pressures are always present because, as this book has noted many times, economic interests that are adversely affected by trade always seek to limit it. But given the rapid increase in trade integration over the past few decades, it is surprising that these pressures are so weak.[1]

---

[1] Pastor (1983) analyzes what he calls the "cry and sigh" cycle that has consistently exaggerated the threat of protectionism. The cry is the consistent refrain since the

Why have protectionist demands been so muted? Postwar economic growth and macroeconomic stability have tempered such demands by creating new opportunities for those displaced by imports. Transfer payments and social insurance have also mitigated the cost to those adversely affected by economic change. Businesses that depend upon imported intermediate goods have become a countervailing force against those that demand new trade restrictions. Finally, many industries facing foreign competition, such as televisions and automobiles and semiconductors, have found that international diversification or joint ventures with foreign partners are a more profitable way of coping with global competition than simply stopping goods at the border. Firms that have failed to adjust, diversify, or join with foreign partners, such as the integrated steel industry and the footwear industry, either continue to resist foreign competition or have shrunk to the point where they have lost their political strength to lobby for import restrictions.

These factors have sustained political support for an open trading system and have prevented a globalization backlash on the basis of economic interests. As a result, the political appeal of economic nationalism, with protectionism as a central part of its program, has not been strong. A century ago, protectionism was associated with industrial strength and independence. As the robust Theodore Roosevelt once quipped, "Thank God I am not a free-trader. In this country pernicious indulgence in the doctrine of free trade seems inevitably to produce fatty degeneration of the moral fibre."[2] But today, protectionism is taken as a sign of weakness. As Senator John McCain put it, building walls is for cowards.

While those supporting the liberal trading system should always remain vigilant with respect to protectionist demands, the second challenge facing the world trading system is perhaps a more difficult one. This new challenge comes from NGOs who do not represent sectional interests, but stand for particular causes. These "public interest" groups include "consumer associations, conservation and environmental groups, societies concerned with development in poor countries, human rights

---

1940s that protectionist pressures are on the rise and the sighing is when these pressures are diffused and markets are opened even further.

[2] Quoted in Viner 1991, 246.

groups, movements for social justice, humanitarian societies, organizations representing indigenous people, and church groups from all denominations." Together, they are said to comprise "civil society."[3]

In most instances, these groups are opposed to the current system of world trade. "With some exceptions, they are hostile to, or highly critical of, capitalism, multinational corporations, freedom of crossborder trade and capital flows, and the idea of a market economy. They are a force on the side of interventionism."[4] The antagonism of these groups goes well beyond international trade to include most forms of market-based commerce. Despite differences of interest and emphasis among these groups, the more radical elements "share a vision of the world in which past history and present-day market-based economic systems are portrayed in terms of patterns of oppression and abuses of power. Free markets and capitalism are seen as embodying and furthering environmental destruction, male dominance, class oppression, racial intolerance, imperialist coercion and colonial exploitation."[5]

The charges made by these groups against the world economy are wide-ranging and serious. "If the critics were right," Martin Wolf points out, "supporters of the global market economy would be in favour of mass poverty, grotesque inequality, destruction of state-provided welfare, infringement of national sovereignty, subversion of democracy, unbridled corporate power, environmental degradation, human rights abuses and much more."[6] Of course, this is not true. As chapters 2 and 6 have argued, growing world trade can improve growth prospects and thereby help reduce poverty, can check corporate power through greater competition, can improve the environment by allowing the spread of new cleaner technologies, and may even unleash a process that promotes democracy, as we have seen in Chile, Mexico, South Korea, Taiwan, and elsewhere.

[3] From Henderson (2001, 19), whose incisive analysis I have drawn upon here. See also Robertson 2000.

[4] Henderson 2001, 20.

[5] Henderson 2001, 30. Alan Greenspan (2000, 5) has also referred to this unease, stating that "even among liberal democracies, one can still find deep-seated antipathy toward free market capitalism and its partner, creative destruction. . . . While recognizing the efficacy of capitalism to produce wealth, there remains considerable unease among some segments about the way markets distribute that wealth and about the effects of raw competition on the civility of society."

[6] Wolf 2004, 23.

Economic fragmentation, on the other hand, would exacerbate rather than ameliorate many of the problems that the critics identify.

Although these anti-globalization groups have not been represented in the corridors of power, they cannot be dismissed as insignificant. The more radical groups have gained respectability by positioning themselves with mainstream organizations, such as moderate NGOs, UN agencies, labor unions, and some political leaders and other public figures. They have been able to achieve a broader appeal by focusing on human rights, corporate responsibility, and sustainable development, all of which are agreeable in principle but behind which are very different views of policy.[7] As a result, these groups have not only been politically active, but have become an increasingly influential part of the public debate.

International agencies, national governments, and even corporations that in the past have had a stake in promoting markets have begun to acquiesce to their demands. Yet reconciling their interests with much of the NGO agenda will be difficult because of fundamental incompatibilities in outlook. For many of the more militant NGOs, the attack on trade is simply an attack on the most visible part of the market economy. They are starting with the easiest target, but the objective is much bigger. As the *Economist* put it several years ago:

> It is no coincidence that the keenest economic reformers
> among the developing and ex-communist countries are the
> new champions of free trade. It is also no coincidence that
> those in the industrial countries who are most fearful about the
> future seek to lessen the rich world's reliance on the market
> economy, and have made it their first goal to smash the GATT
> and the other institutions of liberal trade. Both sides, in their
> different ways, are right. Each has recognized that the market
> economy is ultimately inseparable from a liberal order of
> international trade.[8]

[7] "All three appear, and are presented, as proof against doubt and objections: who could want to oppose, deny or restrict human rights, to prefer that corporations should act non-responsibly, or to advocate development that was unsustainable? Yet all these virtuous-seeming notions, as now interpreted, bear a collectivist message" (Henderson 2001, 31).

[8] "Battle Lines," *Economist*, December 24, 1994, 14.

Although the classical liberal conception of a market economy is not compromised by prudent government regulation or transfer payments to the less fortunate, it will become compromised if open markets are closed by governments. Dealing with this challenge may prove extremely difficult in the years to come.

Trade policy has always been one of the most contentious areas of economic policy and is therefore the subject of a never-ending debate. Though the postwar period has been marked by a concerted reduction in trade barriers, the matter is not settled because the pressures to weaken the commitment to open markets never abate. The world trading system is far from perfect, and many reforms and changes in rules should be under discussion. Although much remains to be done, the cause of trade liberalization is worthy of continued support, including a defense of what has been accomplished.

References

Aaronson, Susan A. 2001. *Taking Trade to the Streets: The Lost History of Public Efforts to Shape Globalization.* Ann Arbor: University of Michigan Press.

Ades, Alberto, and Rafael Di Tella. 1999. "Rents, Competition, and Corruption." *American Economic Review* 89: 982–93.

Addison, John T., Douglas A. Fox, and Christopher J. Ruhm. 1995. "Trade and Displacement in Manufacturing." *Monthly Labor Review*, April, 58–67.

Aitken, Brian, Ann Harrison, and Robert E. Lipsey. 1996. "Wages and Foreign Ownership: A Comparative Study of Mexico, Venezuela, and the United States." *Journal of International Economics* 40 (May): 345–71.

Anderson, Kym. 1992. "Effects on the Environment and Welfare of Liberalizing World Trade: The Cases of Coal and Food." In Kym Anderson and Richard Blackhurst, eds., *The Greening of World Trade Issues.* Ann Arbor: University of Michigan Press.

———. 1998. "Agricultural Trade Reforms, Research Initiatives, and the Environment." In E. Lutz, ed., *Agriculture and the Environment: Perspectives on Sustainable Rural Development.* Washington D.C.: World Bank.

Anderson, James, and Eric van Wincoop. 2003. "Gravity with Gravitas: A Solution to the Border Puzzle." *American Economic Review* 93 (March): 170–92.

———. 2004. "Trade Costs." *Journal of Economic Literature*, forthcoming.

Antweiler, Werner, Brian R. Copeland, and M. Scott Taylor. 2001. "Is Free Trade Good for the Environment?" *American Economic Review* 91 (September): 877–908.

Audley, John J. 1997. *Green Politics and Global Trade: NAFTA and the Future of Environmental Politics.* Washington, D.C.: Georgetown University Press.

Audley, John J., Demetrios G. Papademetriou, Sandra Polaski, and Scott Vaughan. 2003. *NAFTA's Promise and Reality: Lessons from Mexico for the Hemisphere.* Carnegie Endowment for International Peace.

Baffes, John. 2004. "Cotton: Market Setting, Trade Policies, and Issues." World Bank Policy Research Working Paper No. 3218, February.

Bagwell, Kyle, and Robert W. Staiger. 2002. *The Economics of the World Trading System.* Cambridge: MIT Press.

Baicker, Katherine, and Marit Rehavi. 2004. "Trade Adjustment Assistance." *Journal of Economic Perspectives* 18 (Spring): 239–55.

Baier, Scott L., and Jeffrey H. Bergstrand. 2001. "The Growth of World Trade: Tariffs, Transport Costs, and Income Similarity." *Journal of International Economics* 53 (February): 1–27.

Bailey, Michael, Judith Goldstein, and Barry Weingast. 1997. "The Institutional Roots of American Trade Policy: Politics, Coalitions, and International Trade." *World Politics* 49 (April): 309–38.

Baldwin, Robert E. "The Inefficacy of Trade Policy." 1988. In *Trade Policy in a Changing World Economy.* Chicago: University of Chicago Press.

Baldwin, Robert E., and Jeffrey W. Steagall. 1994. "An Analysis of ITC Decisions in Antidumping, Countervailing Duty, and Safeguard Cases." *Weltwirtschaftliches Archiv* 130, no. 2: 290–308.

Balke, Norman, and Robert J. Gordon. 1989. "The Estimation of Prewar Gross National Product: Methodology and New Evidence." *Journal of Political Economy* 97 (February): 38–92.

Balton, David. 1999. "Setting the Record Straight on Sea Turtles and Shrimp." Remarks to the Eleventh Annual Judicial Conference of the U.S. Court of International Trade on Social Justice Litigation: The CIT and WTO, New York, December 7. Available at http://www.state.gov/www/policy_remarks/1999/991207_balton_turtles.html.

Barbier, Edward B., Nancy Bockstael, Joanne C. Burgess, and Ivar Strand. 1995. "The Linkage between the Timber Trade and Tropical Deforestation— Indonesia." *World Economy* 12 (May): 411–42.

Barbieri, Katherine. 2002. *The Liberal Illusion: Does Trade Promote Peace?* Ann Arbor: University of Michigan Press.

Barfield, Claude. 2003. *High Tech Protectionism: The Irrationality of Antidumping Laws.* Washington, D.C.: AEI Press.

Barringer, William H., and Kenneth J. Pierce. 2000. *Paying the Price for Big Steel: $100 Billion in Trade Restraints and Corporate Welfare.* Washington, D.C.: American Institute for International Steel.

Beason, Richard, and David Weinstein. 1996. "Growth, Economies of Scale, and Targeting in Japan (1955–1990)." *Review of Economics and Statistics* 78 (May): 286–95.

Beghin, John C., Barbara El Osta, Jay R. Cherlow, and Samarendu Mohanty. 2003. "The Cost of the U.S. Sugar Program Revisited." *Contemporary Economic Policy* 21 (January): 106–16.

Berman, Eli, John Bound, and Zvi Griliches. 1994. "Changes in the Demand for Skilled Labor within U.S. Manufacturing: Evidence from the Annual

Survey of Manufacturers." *Quarterly Journal of Economics* 109 (May): 367–97.

Bernard, Andrew B., Jonathan Eaton, J. Bradford Jenson, and Samuel Kortum. 2003. "Plants and Productivity in International Trade." *American Economic Review* 93 (September): 1269–90.

Bernard, Andrew B., and J. Bradford Jensen. 1995. "Exporters, Jobs, and Wages in U.S. Manufacturing: 1976–1987." *Brookings Papers on Economic Activity: Microeconomics,* 67–112.

———. 1999. "Exceptional Exporter Performance: Cause, Effect, or Both?" *Journal of International Economics* 47 (February): 1–26.

Bernhofen, Daniel M., and John C. Brown. 2004. "Estimating the Comparative Advantage Gains from Trade: Evidence from Japan." *American Economic Review,* forthcoming.

Bhagwati, Jagdish. 1996. "The Demands to Reduce Domestic Diversity among Trade Nations." In Jagdish Bhagwati and Robert Hudec, eds., *Fair Trade and Harmonization: Prerequisites for Free Trade?* Cambridge: MIT Press.

———, ed. 2002. *Going Alone: The Case for Relaxed Reciprocity in Freeing Trade.* Cambridge: MIT Press.

Bhagwati, Jagdish, and Arvind Panagariya. 1996. "Preferential Trading Areas and Multilateralism: Strangers, Friends, or Foes?" In Jagdish Bhagwati and Arvind Panagariya, eds., *The Economics of Preferential Trading Areas.* Washington, D.C.: AEI Press.

Bhagwati, Jagdish, and T. N. Srinivasan. 2002. "Trade and Poverty in the Poor Countries." *American Economic Review* 92 (May): 180–83.

Blackhurst, Richard. 1998. "The Capacity of the WTO to Fulfill Its Mandate." In Anne O. Krueger, ed., *The WTO as an International Organization.* Chicago: University of Chicago Press.

Blonigen, Bruce A. 2003. "Evolving Discretionary Practices of U.S. Antidumping Activity." NBER Working Paper No. 9625, April.

Blonigen, Bruce A., and Thomas J. Prusa. 2003. "Antidumping." In E. Kwan Choi and James Harrigan, eds., *Handbook of International Trade.* Oxford: Blackwell.

Bolaky, Bineswaree, and Caroline Freund. 2004. "Trade, Regulations, and Growth." World Bank Policy Research Working Paper No. 3255, April.

Bordo, Michael D., Barry Eichengreen, and Douglas A. Irwin. 1999. "Is Globalization Today Really Different from Globalization a Hundred Years Ago?" In Susan Collins and Robert Z. Lawrence, eds., *Brookings Trade Forum, 1999.* Washington, D.C.: Brookings Institution.

Borga, Maria, and Michael Mann. 2003. "U.S. International Services: Cross Border Trade in 2002 and Sales through Affiliates in 2001." *Survey of Current Business* 83 (October): 58–118.

Borjas, George J., Richard B. Freeman, and Lawrence F. Katz. 1997. "How Much Do Immigration and Trade Affect Labor Market Outcomes?" *Brookings Papers on Economic Activity*, 1–67.

Bovard, James. 1991. *The Fair Trade Fraud*. New York: St. Martin's Press.

Bown, Chad P. 2004a. "Developing Countries as Plaintiffs and Defendants in GATT/WTO Trade Disputes." *World Economy* 27 (January): 59–80.

———. 2004b. "Trade Disputes and the Implementation of Protection under the GATT: An Empirical Assessment." *Journal of International Economics* 62 (March): 263–94.

Brander, James A. 1995. "Strategic Trade Policy." In Gene M. Grossman and Kenneth Rogoff, eds., *Handbook of International Economics*, vol. 3. New York: Elsevier.

Branstetter, Lee G. 2001. "Are Knowledge Spillovers International or Intranational in Scope? Microeconometric Evidence from the U.S. and Japan." *Journal of International Economics* 53 (February): 53–80.

Broda, Christian, and David Weinstein. 2004. "Globalization and the Gains from Variety." NBER Working Paper No. 10314, February.

Brown, Drusilla K. 2000. "International Trade and Core Labor Standards: A Survey of the Recent Literature." Discussion Paper No. 2000-05, Department of Economics, Tufts University, January.

Brown, Drusilla K., Alan V. Deardorff, and Robert M. Stern. 2003. "Developing Countries' Stake in the Doha Round." Research Seminar in International Economics, Discussion Paper No. 495, University of Michigan, June.

Buchanan, Patrick. 1998. *The Great Betrayal: How American Sovereignty and Social Justice Are Being Sacrificed to the Gods of the Global Economy*. Boston: Little, Brown.

Bureau of Labor Statistics. 2004. "Extended Mass Layoffs Associated with Domestic and Overseas Relocations, First Quarter 2004, Summary." June 10.

Burtless, Gary, Robert Z. Lawrence, Robert E. Litan, and Robert J. Shapiro. 1998. *Globaphobia: Confronting Fears about Open Trade*. Washington, D.C.: Brookings Institution, Progressive Policy Institute, and Twentieth Century Fund.

Casas, Francois R. 1991. "Lerner's Symmetry Theorem Revisited." *Keio Economic Studies* 28 (January): 15–19.

Clark, Gregory, and Robert C. Feenstra. 2003. "Technology in the Great Divergence." In Michael Bordo, Alan Taylor, and Jeffrey Williamson, eds., *Globalization in Historical Perspective*. Chicago: University of Chicago Press.

Clerides, Sofronis K., Saul Lach, and James R. Tybout. 1998. "Is Learning by Exporting Important? Micro-dynamic Evidence from Colombia, Mexico, and Morocco." *Quarterly Journal of Economics* 113 (August): 903–47.

Collins, Susan, ed. 1998. *Imports, Exports, and the American Worker*. Washington, D.C.: Brookings Institution.

Congressional Budget Office. 1994. *How the GATT Affects U.S. Antidumping and Countervailing Duty Policy.* Washington, D.C., September.

———. 1998. *Antidumping Action in the United States and around the World: An Analysis of International Data.* Washington, D.C., June.

———. 2004. *Economic Analysis of the Countervailing Duty and Subsidy Offset Act of 2000.* Washington, D.C., March 2.

Cooper, Helene. 2000. "A Trade Deal Helps Cambodian Workers, but Payoff Is Withheld." *Wall Street Journal,* February 28, A1.

Corden, W. Max. 1974. *Trade Policy and Economic Welfare.* Oxford: Clarendon Press.

Council of Economic Advisers. 2004. *Economic Report of the President, February 2004.* Washington, D.C.: GPO.

Dai, Xiudian, Alan Cawson, and Peter Holmes. 1996. "The Rise and Fall of High Definition Television: The Impact of European Technology Policy." *Journal of Common Market Studies* 34 (June): 149–66.

Das, Gurcharan. 2001. *India Unbound.* New York: Knopf.

Davey, William J. 2001. "Has the WTO Dispute Settlement System Exceeded Its Authority?" *Journal of International Economic Law* 4:79–110.

Davis, Steven J., John C. Haltiwanger, and Scott Schuh. 1995. *Job Creation and Destruction.* Cambridge: MIT Press.

de Melo, Jaime, and David Tarr. 1992. *A General Equilibrium Analysis of U.S. Foreign Trade Policy.* Cambridge: MIT Press.

———. 1993. "Industrial Policy in the Presence of Wage Distortions: The Case of the U.S. Auto and Steel Industries." *International Economic Review* 34 (November): 833–51.

Decker, Paul T., and Walter Corson. 1995. "International Trade and Worker Displacement: Evaluation of the Trade Adjustment Assistance Program." *Industrial and Labor Relations Review* 48 (July): 758–74.

Destler, I. M. 1998. "Trade Politics and Labor Issues, 1953–1995." In Susan Collins, ed., *Imports, Exports, and the American Worker.* Washington, D.C.: Brookings Institution Press.

Dickens, William T. 1995. "Do Labor Rents Justify Strategic Trade and Industrial Policy?" NBER Working Paper No. 5137, May.

Dollar, David, and Aart Kraay. 2004. "Trade, Growth, and Poverty." *Economic Journal* 114 (February): F22–F49.

Dollar, David, and Borje Ljunggren. 1997. "Vietnam." In Padma Desai, ed., *Going Global: Transition from Plan to Market in the World Economy.* Cambridge: MIT Press.

Dollar, David, and Kenneth Sokoloff. 1990. "Patterns of Productivity Growth in South Korean Manufacturing Industries, 1963–1979." *Journal of Development Economics* 33 (October): 309–27.

Dryden, Steve. 1995. *Trade Warriors: USTR and the American Crusade for Free Trade.* New York: Oxford University Press.

Eaton, Jonathan, and Samuel Kortum. 2001. "Trade in Capital Goods." *European Economic Review* 45 (June): 1195–235.

Edmonds, Eric, and Nina Pavcnik. 2005a. "The Effect of Trade Liberalization on Child Labor." *Journal of International Economics*, forthcoming.

———. 2005b. "Child Labor in the Global Economy." *Journal of Economic Perspectives*, forthcoming.

Edwards, Sebastian, and Daniel Lederman. 2002. "The Political Economy of Unilateral Trade Liberalization: The Case of Chile." In Jagdish Bhagwati, ed., *Going Alone: The Case for Relaxed Reciprocity in Freeing Trade*. Cambridge: MIT Press.

Elliott, Kimberly Ann, Dabayani Kar, and J. David Richardson. 2004. "Assessing Globalization's Critics: 'Talkers Are No Good Doers?'" In Robert E. Baldwin and L. Alan Winters, eds., *Challenges to Globalization: Analyzing the Economics*. Chicago: University of Chicago Press.

Faini, Riccardo, Jaime de Melo, and Wendy Takacs. 1995. "A Primer on the MFA Maze." *World Economy* 18 (January): 113–35.

Feenstra, Robert C. 1984. "Voluntary Export Restraint in U.S. Autos, 1980–81: Quality, Employment, and Welfare Effects." In Robert Baldwin and Anne Krueger, eds., *The Structure and Evolution of Recent U.S. Trade Policy*. Chicago: University of Chicago Press.

———. 1998. "Integration of Trade and Disintegration of Production in the Global Economy." *Journal of Economic Perspectives* 12 (Fall): 31–50.

———. (ed.) 2000. *The Impact of International Trade on Wages*. Chicago: University of Chicago Press.

Feenstra, Robert C., and Gordon H. Hanson. 2003. "Global Production and Rising Inequality: A Survey of Trade and Wages." In E. Kwan Choi and James Harrigan, eds., *Handbook of International Trade*. New York: Basil Blackwell.

Feenstra, Robert C., James R. Markusen, and William Zeile. 1992. "Accounting for Growth with New Inputs." *American Economic Review* 82 (May): 415–21.

Fernandez, Raquel, and Dani Rodrik. 1991. "Resistance to Reform: Status Quo Bias in the Presence of Individual-Specific Uncertainty." *American Economic Review* 81 (December): 1146–55.

Ferreira, Pedro C., and Jose L. Rossi. 2003. "New Evidence from Brazil on Trade Liberalization and Productivity Growth." *International Economic Review* 44 (November): 1383–405.

Ferreira, Susana. 2004. "Deforestation, Property Rights, and International Trade." *Land Economics* 80 (May): 174–93.

Field, Alfred J., and Edward M. Graham. 1997. "Is There a Special Case for Import Protection for the Textile and Apparel Sectors Base on Labour Adjustment?" *World Economy* 20 (March): 137–57.

Finger, J. Michael. 1996. "Legalized Backsliding: Safeguard Provisions in GATT."

In Will Martin and L. Alan Winters, eds., *The Uruguay Round and Developing Countries*. New York: Cambridge University Press.

———, ed. 1993. *Antidumping: How It Works and Who Gets Hurt*. Ann Arbor: University of Michigan Press.

Finger, J. Michael, Merlinda D. Ingco, and Ulrich Reincke. 1996. *The Uruguay Round: Statistics on Tariff Concessions Given and Received*. Washington, D.C.: World Bank.

Flam, Harry. 1985. "A Heckscher-Ohlin Analysis of the Law of Declining International Trade." *Canadian Journal of Economics* 18 (August): 602–15.

Flamm, Kenneth. 1996. *Mismanaged Trade? Strategic Policy and the Semiconductor Industry*. Washington, D.C.: Brookings Institution.

Food and Agriculture Organization. 2002. *FAO Annual Yearbook: Fertilizer, 1999*. Rome: FAO.

Francois, Joseph F., and Laura M. Baughman. 2001. "Estimated Economic Effects of Proposed Import Relief Remedies for Steel." Washington, D.C.: Trade Partnership. December.

Francois, Joseph F., Hans van Meiji, and Frank van Tongeren. 2003. "Trade Liberalization and Developing Countries under the Doha Round." Center for Economic Policy Research Discussion Paper Series No. 4032, October.

Frank, Charles R., Jr., Kwang S. Kim, and Larry E. Westphal. 1975. *Foreign Trade Regimes and Economic Development. South Korea*. New York: National Bureau of Economic Research.

Frankel, Jeffrey. 2000. "Globalization of the Economy." In Joseph Nye and John Donahue, eds., *Governance in a Globalizing World*. Washington, D.C.: Brookings Institution.

Frankel, Jeffrey A., and David Romer. 1999. "Does Trade Cause Growth?" *American Economic Review* 89 (June): 379–99.

Freeman, Richard B., and Morris M. Kleiner. 1998. "The Last American Shoe Manufacturers: Changing the Method of Pay to Survive Foreign Competition." NBER Working Paper No. 6750, October.

Gallaway, Michael P., Bruce A. Blonigen, and Joseph E. Flynn. 1999. "Welfare Costs of the U.S. Antidumping and Countervailing Duty Laws." *Journal of International Economics* 49 (December): 211–44.

Gates, Scott, Torbjørn Knutsen, and Jonathon Moses. 1996. "Democracy and Peace: A More Skeptical View." *Journal of Peace Research* 33 (February): 1–10.

General Agreement on Tariffs and Trade. 1953. *International Trade, 1952*. Geneva: GATT, June.

Gibbons, Robert, and Lawrence Katz. 1992. "Does Unmeasured Ability Explain Inter-industry Wage Differentials?" *Review of Economic Studies* 59 (July): 515–35.

Gignilliat, John L. 1961. "Pigs, Politics, and Protection: The European Boycott of American Pork." *Agricultural History* 35 (January): 3–24.

Glewwe, Paul. 2000. "Are Foreign Owned Businesses in Vietnam Really Sweatshops?" *Agricultural Economist Newsletter*, University of Minnesota Extension Service, No. 701, Summer.

Golub, Stephen S. 1999. *Labor Costs and International Trade.* Washington, D.C.: AEI Press.

Golub, Stephen S., and Chang-Tai Hsieh. 2000. "Classical Ricardian Theory of Comparative Advantage Revisited." *Review of International Economics* 8 (May): 221–34.

Greenspan, Alan. 2000. "Opening Remarks." In *Global Economic Integration: Opportunities and Challenges.* Kansas City: Federal Reserve Bank of Kansas City.

———. 2004. "The Critical Role of Education in the Nation's Economy." Speech at Greater Omaha Chamber of Commerce Annual Meeting, February 20.

Gresser, Edward. 2002. "Toughest on the Poor: America's Flawed Tariff System." *Foreign Affairs* 81 (November–December): 9–14.

Groombridge, Mark A. 2001. "America's Bittersweet Sugar Policy." Trade Briefing Paper, Center for Trade Policy Studies, Cato Institute, December.

Grossman, Gene M., and Alan B. Krueger. 1993. "Environmental Impacts of a North American Free Trade Agreement." In Peter Garber, ed., *The Mexico-U.S. Free Trade Agreement.* Cambridge: MIT Press.

Grossman, Gene M., and Giovanni Maggi. 1998. "Free Trade vs. Strategic Trade: A Peak into Pandora's Box." In R. Sato, R. V. Ramachandran and K. Mino, eds., *Global Competition and Integration.* Boston: Kluwer Academic Publishers.

Guest, Robert. 2004. *The Shackled Continent: Power, Corruption, and African Lives.* Washington, D.C.: Smithsonian Books.

Hall, Robert E., and Charles I. Jones. 1999. "Why Do Some Countries Produce So Much More Output per Worker Than Others? *Quarterly Journal of Economics* 114 (February): 83–116.

Hansen, Wendy L., and Thomas J. Prusa. 1996. "Cumulation and ITC Decision-Making: The Sum of the Parts Is Greater Than the Whole." *Economic Inquiry* 34 (October): 746–69.

———. 1997. "The Economics and Politics of Trade Policy: An Empirical Analysis of ITC Decision Making." *Review of International Economics* 5 (May): 230–45.

Harrison, Ann E. 1994. "Productivity, Imperfect Competition and Trade Reform: Theory and Evidence." *Journal of International Economic* 36 (February): 53–73.

Harrison, Ann E., and Jason Scorse. 2004. "Moving Up or Moving Out? Anti-sweatshop Activists and Labor Market Outcomes." NBER Working Paper No. 10492, May.

Hart, Jeffrey A. 1993. "The Antidumping Petition of the Advanced Display Manufacturers of America: Origin and Consequences." *World Economy* 16
(January): 85–109.

———. 1994. "The Politics of HDTV in the United States." *Policy Studies Journal* 22 (Summer): 213–28.

Hausmann, Ricardo, and Dani Rodrik. 2003. "Economic Development as Self-
Discovery." *Journal of Development Economics* 72 (December):
603–33.

Heckman, James. 1999. "Doing It Right: Job Training and Education." *Public
Interest* 135 (Spring): 86–107.

Henderson, David. 2001. *Anti-liberalism, 2000: The Rise of New Millennium
Collectivism.* London: Institute of Economic Affairs.

Hicks, John R. 1969. *A Theory of Economic History.* Oxford: Clarendon Press.

Hillman, Arye, and Peter Moser. 1996. "Trade Liberalization as Politically Opti-
mal Exchange of Market Access." In Matthew Canzoneri, Wilfred
Ethier, and Vittorio Grilli, eds., *The New Transatlantic Economy.*
New York: Cambridge University Press.

Hinojosa-Ojeda, Raul, David Runsten, Fernando De Paolis, and Nabil Kamel.
2000. "This U.S. Employment Impacts of North American Integration
after NAFTA." Working paper, School of Public Policy and Social Research, University of California at Los Angeles, January.

Hoekman, Bernard, and Michel Kostecki. 2001. *The Political Economy of the
World Trading System: From GATT to WTO.* 2d ed. New York: Oxford
University Press.

Hoekman, Bernard, Francis Ng, and M. Olarreaga. 2004. "Reducing Agricultural
Tariffs versus Domestic Support: What Is More Important for Developing Countries?" *World Bank Economic Review* 18(2): 175–204.

Hudec, Robert. 1990. *The GATT Legal System and World Trade Diplomacy.*
2d ed. Salem, N.H.: Butterworth Legal Publishers.

———. 1998. "Does the Agreement on Agriculture Work? Agricultural Disputes
after the Uruguay Round." International Agricultural Trade Research
Consortium Working Paper No. 98-2, April. http://iatrcweb.org.

———. 2000. "The Product-Process Doctrine in GATT/WTO Jurisprudence." In
Marco Bronckers and Reinhard Quick, eds., *New Directions in Inter-
national Economic Law: Essays in Honour of John H. Jackson.* Boston:
Kluwer Law International.

Hufbauer, Gary C., and Kimberly A. Elliott. 1994. *Measuring the Costs of Protection in the United States.* Washington, D.C.: Institute for International
Economics, January.

Hufbauer, Gary C., and Jeffrey J. Schott. 1993. *NAFTA: An Assessment.* Rev. ed.
Washington, D.C.: Institute for International Economics, October.

Hummels, David. 2000. "Time as a Trade Barrier." Working paper, Department
of Economics, Purdue University, October.

Hummels, David, Jun Ishii, and Kei-Mu Yi. 2001. "The Nature and Growth of Vertical Specialization in World Trade." *Journal of International Economics* 54 (June): 75–96.

Hummels, David, Dana Rapoport, and Kei-Mu Yi. 1998. "Vertical Specialization and the Changing Nature of World Trade." *Federal Reserve Bank of New York Economic Policy Review* 4 (June): 79–99.

Ianchovichina, Elena, and Will Martin. 2002. "Economic Impacts of China's Accession to the WTO." World Bank Working Paper, December.

Ikenson, Dan. 2004. "Zeroing In: Antidumping's Flawed Methodology under Fire." Center for Trade Policy Studies, Cato Institute, Free Trade Bulletin No. 11, April 27.

Ingco, Merlinda D. 1996. "Tariffication in the Uruguay Round: How Much Liberalization?" *World Economy* 19 (July): 425–46.

International Monetary Fund. 2000. *International Financial Statistics Yearbook, 2000.* Washington, D.C.: IMF.

———. 2002. *World Economic Outlook.* Washington, D.C.: IMF, September.

Irwin, Douglas A. 1996a. *Against the Tide: An Intellectual History of Free Trade.* Princeton: Princeton University Press.

———. 1996b. "Trade Politics and the Semiconductor Industry." In Anne O. Krueger, ed., *The Political Economy of American Trade Policy.* Chicago: University of Chicago Press.

———. 1998a. "From Smoot-Hawley to Reciprocal Trade Agreements: Changing the Course of U.S. Trade Policy in the 1930s." In Michael Bordo, Claudia Goldin, and Eugene White, eds., *The Defining Moment: The Great Depression and the American Economy.* Chicago: University of Chicago Press.

———. 1998b. "Changes in U.S. Tariffs: The Role of Import Prices and Commercial Policies." *American Economic Review* 88 (September): 1015–26.

———. 2001. "Welfare Cost of Autarky: Evidence from the Jeffersonian Trade Embargo, 1807–1809." NBER Working Paper No. 8692, December.

———. 2003. "Causing Problems? The WTO Review of Causation and Injury Attribution in U.S. Section 201 Cases." *World Trade Review* 2 (November): 297–325.

———. 2004. "The Rise of U.S. Antidumping Actions in Historical Perspective." NBER Working Paper No. 10582, July.

Irwin, Douglas A., and Peter J. Klenow. 1994. "Learning-by-Doing Spillovers in the Semiconductor Industry." *Journal of Political Economy* 102 (December): 1200–1227.

Irwin, Douglas A., and Randall S. Kroszner. 1999. "Interests, Institutions, and Ideology in Securing Policy Change: The Republican Conversion to Trade Liberalization after Smoot-Hawley." *Journal of Law and Economics* 42 (October): 643–73.

Irwin, Douglas A., and Nina Pavcnik. 2004. "Airbus versus Boeing Revisited: International Competition in the Aircraft Market." *Journal of International Economics* 64 (December): 223–45.

Irwin, Douglas A., and Marko Terviö. 2002. "Does Trade Raise Income? Evidence from the Twentieth Century." *Journal of International Economics* 58 (October): 1–18.

Jackson, John H. 1978. "The Crumbling Institutions of the Liberal Trade System." *Journal of World Trade Law* 12 (March–April): 93–106.

Jacobson, Louis. 1998. "Compensation Programs." In Susan Collins, ed., *Imports, Exports, and the American Worker*. Washington, D.C.: Brookings Institution.

Jaffe, Adam B., Steven R. Peterson, Paul R. Portney, and Robert Stavins. 1995. "Environmental Regulation and the Competitiveness of U.S. Manufacturing: What Does the Evidence Tell Us?" *Journal of Economic Literature* 33 (March): 132–63.

Jawara, Fatoumata, and Aileen Kwa. 2003. *Behind the Scenes at the WTO: The Real World of International Trade Negotiations*. New York: Zed Books.

Jomo, K. S. 2001. "Rethinking the Role of Government Policy in Southeast Asia." In Joseph Stiglitz and Shahid Yusuf, eds., *Rethinking the East Asian Miracle*. New York: Oxford University Press.

Jones, Charles I. 2001. "Comment on Rodríguez and Rodrik." In Ben S. Bernanke and Kenneth Rogoff, eds., *NBER Macroeconomics Annual, 2000*. Cambridge: MIT Press.

Jones, Kent. 2004. *Who's Afraid of the WTO?* New York: Cambridge University Press.

Josling, Timothy. 1998. *Agricultural Trade Policy: Completing the Reform*. Washington, D.C.: Institute for International Economics, April.

Josling, Timothy, Donna Roberts, and David Orden. 2004. *Food Regulation and Trade: Toward a Safe and Open Global System*. Washington, D.C.: Institute for International Economics.

Kahn, Matthew. 2000. "United States Pollution Intensive Trade Trends from 1972 to 1992." Working paper, Department of Economics, Tufts University, February.

Katz, Lawrence F., and Lawrence H. Summers. 1989. "Industry Rents: Evidence and Implications." *Brookings Papers on Economic Activity: Microeconomics,* 209–75.

Kehoe, Timothy J., and Kim J. Ruhl. 2002. "How Important Is the New Goods Margin in International Trade?" Working paper, University of Minnesota, October.

Keller, Wolfgang. 2002. "Trade and the Transmission of Technology." *Journal of Economic Growth* 7:5–24.

———. 2004. "International Technology Diffusion." *Journal of Economic Literature* 42 (September): 752–83.

Kim, Euysung. 2000. "Trade Liberalization and Productivity Growth in Korean Manufacturing Industries: Price Protection, Market Power, and Scale Efficiency." *Journal of Development Economics* 62 (June): 55–83.

King, Neil. 2002. "Trade Imbalance: Why Uncle Sam Wrote a Big Check to a Sparkler Maker." *Wall Street Journal*, December 5.

Klenow, Peter, and Andrés Rodríguez-Clare. 1997. "Quantifying Variety Gains from Trade Liberalization." Working paper, University of Chicago, September.

Kletzer, Lori G. 1998a. "Job Displacement." *Journal of Economic Perspectives* 12 (Winter): 115–36.

———. 1998b. "Trade and Job Displacement in U.S. Manufacturing: 1979–1991." In Susan Collins, ed., *Imports, Exports, and the American Worker*. Washington, D.C.: Brookings Institution.

———. 2000. "Trade and Job Loss in U.S. Manufacturing, 1979–1994." In Robert Feenstra, ed., *The Impact of International Trade on Wages*. Chicago: University of Chicago Press for the NBER.

———. 2001. *Job Loss from Imports: Measuring the Costs*. Washington, D.C.: Institute for International Economics.

Kose, M. Ayhan, Guy Meredith, and Christopher Towe. 2004. "How Has NAFTA Affected the Mexican Economy? Review and Evidence." *Weltwirtschaftliches Archiv*, forthcoming.

Krishna, Pravin, and Devashish Mitra. 1998. "Trade Liberalization, Market Discipline, and Productivity Growth: New Evidence from India." *Journal of Development Economics* 56 (August): 447–62.

Kristof, Nicholas D., and Sheryl WuDunn. 2000. "Two Cheers for Sweatshops." *New York Times Magazine*, September 24, 70–71.

Krueger, Alan B. 1997. "International Labor Standards and Trade." In Michael Bruno and Boris Pleskovic, eds., *Annual World Bank Conference on Development Economics, 1996*. Washington, D.C.: World Bank.

Krueger, Anne O. 1990. "Free Trade Is the Best Policy." In Robert Z. Lawrence and Charles L. Schultze, eds., *An American Trade Strategy: Options for the 1990s*. Washington, D.C.: Brookings Institution.

———. 1997. "Trade Policy and Economic Development: How We Learn." *American Economic Review* 87 (March): 1–22.

———. 1999. "Free Trade Agreements as Protectionist Devices: Rules of Origin." In James R. Melvin, James C. Moore, and Raymond Reizman, eds., *Trade, Theory, and Econometrics: Essays in Honor of John S. Chipman*. New York: Routledge.

———. 2000. "NAFTA's Effects: A Preliminary Assessment." *World Economy* 23 (June): 761–75.

———, ed. 1996. *The Political Economy of American Trade Policy*. Chicago: University of Chicago Press.

Krugman, Paul. 1994. "Competitiveness: A Dangerous Obsession." *Foreign Affairs* 73 (March–April): 28–44.

———. 1995. "Dutch Tulips and Emerging Markets." *Foreign Affairs* 74 (July–August): 28–44.

———. 1998a. "Ricardo's Difficult Idea: Why Intellectuals Don't Understand Comparative Advantage." In Gary Cook, ed., *The Economics and Politics of International Trade.* London: Routledge.

———. 1998b. *The Accidental Theorist.* New York: Norton.

Kull, Steven. 2000. "Americans on Globalization." University of Maryland, Program on International Policy Attitudes, March 28.

———. 2004. "Americans on Globalization, Trade, and Farm Subsidies." University of Maryland, Program on International Policy Attitudes, January 22.

Lardy, Nicholas. 1992. *Foreign Trade and Economic Reform in China, 1978–1990.* New York: Cambridge University Press.

Lawrence, Robert Z., and Robert E. Litan. 1986. *Saving Free Trade: A Pragmatic Approach.* Washington, D.C.: Brookings Institution.

Lawrence, Robert Z., and Matthew J. Slaughter. 1993. "International Trade and American Wages in the 1980s: Giant Sucking Sound or Small Hiccup?" *Brookings Papers on Economic Activity,* no. 2: 161–211.

League of Nations. 1933. *World Economic Survey.* Geneva: League of Nations.

Lee, Jong-Wha. 1995. "Capital Goods Imports and Long-Run Growth." *Journal of Development Economics* 48 (October): 91–110.

———. 1996. "Government Interventions and Productivity Growth." *Journal of Economic Growth* 1 (September): 391–414.

Lerner, Abba P. 1936. "The Symmetry between Import and Export Taxes." *Economica* 3 (August): 306–13.

Levine, Ross, and David Renelt. 1992. "A Sensitivity Analysis of Cross-Country Growth Regressions." *American Economic Review* 82 (September): 942–63.

Levinsohn, James. 1993. "Testing the Imports-as-Market-Discipline Hypothesis." *Journal of International Economics* 35 (August): 1–22.

Levinsohn, James, and Wendy Petropoulos. 2001. "Creative Destruction or Just Plain Destruction? The U.S. Textile and Apparel Industry since 1972." NBER Working Paper No. 8348, June.

Lewis, William W. 2004. *The Power of Productivity.* Chicago University of Chicago Press.

Limão, Nuno, and Anthony J. Venables. 2001. "Infrastructure, Geographical Disadvantage, Transport Costs, and Trade." *World Bank Economic Review* 15:451–79.

Lindsey, Brink. 2001. "Poor Choice: Why Globalization Didn't Cause 9/11." *New Republic,* November 12.

————. 2004. "Job Losses and Trade: A Reality Check." Trade Policy Briefing Paper No. 19, Center for Trade Policy Studies, Cato Institute, March 17.

Lindsey, Brink, Daniel T. Griswold, and Aaron Lukas. 1999. "The Steel 'Crisis' and the Costs of Protectionism." Trade Briefing Paper, Center for Trade Policy Studies, Cato Institute, April 16.

Lindsey, Brink, Mark A. Groombridge, and Prakash Loungani. 2000. "Nailing the Homeowner: The Economic Impact of Trade Protection of the Softwood Lumber Industry." Trade Policy Analysis No. 11, Cato Institute, July.

Lindsey, Brink, and Daniel J. Ikenson. 2003. *Antidumping Exposed: The Devilish Details of Unfair Trade Law.* Washington, D.C.: Cato Institute.

Lipsey, Robert E., and Fredrik Sjöholm. 2001. "Foreign Direct Investment and Wages in Indonesian Manufacturing." NBER Working Paper No. 8299, May.

Lizza, Ryan. 2000. "Silent Partner: The Man behind the Anti–Free Trade Revolt." *The New Republic* 222 (January 10): 22–25.

Lopez-Cordova, J. Ernesto, and Christopher Meissner. 2004. "Globalization and Democracy, 1870–2000." Working paper, Cambridge University.

Low, Patrick. 1993. *Trading Free: The GATT and U.S. Trade Policy.* New York: Twentieth Century Fund.

Lowe, Jeffrey H. 2004. "An Ownership-Based Framework of the U.S. Current Account, 1992–2002." *Survey of Current Business* 84 (January): 66–68.

Macaulay, Thomas Babington. 1900. *The Complete Writings of Lord Macaulay.* Vol. 18, *Speeches and Legal Studies.* Boston: Houghton, Mifflin.

Mansfield, Edward D., Helen V. Milner, and B. Peter Rosendorff. 2000. "Free to Trade: Democracies, Autocracies, and International Trade." *American Political Science Review* 94 (June): 305–21.

Marshall, Alfred. 1926. *Official Papers of Alfred Marshall.* Edited by J. M. Keynes. London: Macmillan.

Maskus, Keith. 1997. "Should Core Labor Standards Be Imposed through International Trade Policy?" World Bank Policy Research Paper No. 1817, August.

————. 2000. *Intellectual Property Rights in the Global Economy.* Washington, D.C.: Institute for International Economics.

Mayda, Anna M., and Dani Rodrik. 2005. "Why Are Some Individuals (and Countries) More Protectionist Than Others?" *European Economic Review,* forthcoming.

Mayer, Jane, and Jose de Cordoba. 1991. "Sweet Life: First Family of Sugar Is Tough on Workers, Generous to Politicians." *Wall Street Journal,* July 29.

Mayer, Wolfgang. 1984. "Endogenous Tariff Formation." *American Economic Review* 74 (December): 970–85.

Mazumdar, Joy. 2001. "Imported Machinery and Growth in LDCs." *Journal of Development Economics* 65 (June): 209–24.

McKinsey Global Institute. 1993. *Manufacturing Productivity*. Washington, D.C.: McKinsey and Co., October.

McLean, Ian, and Kris Mitchener. 1999. "U.S. Economic Growth and Convergence, 1880–1980." *Journal of Economic History* 59 (December): 1016–42.

McRae, Donald. 2004. "What Is the Future of WTO Dispute Settlement?" *Journal of International Economic Law* 7 (March): 3–21.

Messerlin, Patrick A. 2001. *Measuring the Costs of Protection in Europe*. Washington, D.C.: Institute for International Economics, May.

Milazzo, Matteo. 1998. *Subsidies in World Fisheries: A Reexamination*. World Bank Technical Paper No. 406.

Mill, John Stuart. 1909. *Principles of Political Economy*. London: Longmans.

———. 1982. *On Liberty*. New York: Penguin.

Montesquieu. 1989. *The Spirit of the Laws*. Translated by A. M. Cohler, B. C. Miller, and H. S. Stone. New York: Cambridge University Press.

Montgomery, Mark. 1995. "Reassessing the Waste Trade Crisis: What Do We Really Know?" *Journal of Environment and Development* 4 (winter): 1–28.

Moore, Michael. 2003. *A World without Walls: Freedom, Development, Free Trade, and Global Governance*. New York: Cambridge University Press.

Moore, Michael O. 1992. "Rules or Politics? An Empirical Analysis of ITC Antidumping Decisions." *Economic Inquiry* 30 (July): 449–66.

———. 1996. "Steel Protection in the 1980s: The Waning Influence of Big Steel?" In Anne O. Krueger, ed., *The Political Economy of American Trade Policy*. Chicago: University of Chicago Press.

———. 1999. "Antidumping Reform in the United States: A Faded Sunset." *Journal of World Trade* 33 (August): 1–17.

———. 2000. "VERs and Price Undertakings in the WTO." Working paper, George Washington University.

Morris, Julian. 2000. "International Environmental Agreements: Developing Another Path." In Terry L. Anderson and Henry I. Miller, eds., *The Greening of U.S. Foreign Policy*. Stanford, Calif.: Hoover Institution Press.

Mussa, Michael. 1982. "Government Policy and the Adjustment Process." In Jagdish Bhagwati, ed., *Import Competition and Response*. Chicago: University of Chicago Press.

Nader, Ralph, ed. 1993. *The Case against Free Trade: GATT, NAFTA, and the Globalization of Corporate Power*. San Francisco: Earth Island Press.

Oneal, John, and Bruce Russett. 2000. *Triangulating Peace: Democracy, Interdependence, and International Organizations*. New York: Norton.

Oneal, John, Bruce Russett, and Michael L. Berbaum. 2003. "Causes of Peace: Democracy, Interdependence, and International Organizations, 1885–1992." *International Studies Quarterly* 47 (September): 371–91.

Organization for Economic Cooperation and Development. 1981. *Statistics of Foreign Trade*. Paris: OECD, June.

———. 1994. *The OECD Jobs Study: Facts, Analysis, Strategy*. Paris: OECD.

————. 1996. *Trade, Employment, and Labour Standards: A Study of Core Workers' Rights and International Trade.* Paris: OECD.

————. 2000a. *Agricultural Policies in OECD Countries: Monitoring and Evaluation 2000.* Paris: OCED.

————. 2000b. *International Trade and Core Labour Standards.* Paris: OECD.

————. 2001. *Monthly Statistics of International Trade.* Paris: OECD, April.

————. 2004. *Agricultural Policies, 2004.* Paris: OCED.

Orme, William A., Jr. 1996. *Understanding NAFTA: Mexico, Free Trade, and the New North America.* Austin: University of Texas Press.

Oxfam. 2002. *Rigged Rules and Double Standards: Trade, Globalisation, and the Fight against Poverty.* London: Oxfam.

Palmeter, N. David. 1999. "National Sovereignty and the World Trade Organization." *Journal of World Intellectual Property* 2 (January): 77–91.

Panagariya, Arvind. 2004a. "Miracles and Debacles: Do Free Trade Skeptics Have a Case?" *World Economy* 27 (August): 1149–72.

————. 2004b. "India in the 1980s and 1990s: A Triumph of Reforms." IMF Working Paper 04/43, March.

Panagariya, Arvind, Shekhar Shah, and Deepak Mishra. 2001. "Demand Elasticities in International Trade: Are They Really Low?" *Journal of Development Economics* 64 (April): 313–42.

Pareto, Vilfredo. 1971. *Manual of Political Economy.* Translated by Ann S. Schwier. New York: Augustus M. Kelley.

Pastor, Robert. 1983. "The Cry-and-Sigh Syndrome: Congress and Trade Policy." In Allen Shick, ed., *Making Economic Policy in Congress.* Washington, D.C.: American Enterprise Institute.

Pavcnik, Nina. 2002. "Trade Liberalization, Exit, and Productivity Improvements: Evidence from Chilean Plants." *Review of Economic Studies* 69 (January): 245–76.

Pierce, Richard J. 2000. "Antidumping Law as a Means of Facilitating Cartelization." *Antitrust Law Journal* 67:725–43.

Preeg, Ernest H. 1995. *Traders in a Brave New World: The Uruguay Round and the Future of the International Trading System.* Chicago: University of Chicago Press.

Prusa, Thomas J. 1997. "The Trade Effects of U.S. Antidumping Actions." In Robert C. Feenstra, ed., *The Effects of U.S. Trade Protection and Promotion Policies.* Chicago: University of Chicago Press.

————. 1998. "Cumulation and Antidumping: A Challenge to Competition." *World Economy* 21 (November): 1021–33.

————. 2001. "On the Spread and Impact of Antidumping." *Canadian Journal of Economics* 34 (August): 591–611.

Revenga, Ana L. 1992. "Exporting Jobs? The Impact of Import Competition on Employment and Wages in U.S. Manufacturing." *Quarterly Journal of Economics* 107 (February): 255–84.

Reich, Robert B. 1994. "Keynote Address." In *International Labor Standards and Global Economic Integration: Proceedings of a Symposium.* Washington, D.C.: U.S. Department of Labor.

Reid, Peter C. 1990. *Made Well in America: Lessons from Harley-Davidson on Being the Best.* New York: McGraw-Hill.

Reinert, Kenneth A. 2000. "Give Us Virtue, but Not Yet: Safeguard Actions under the Agreement on Textiles and Clothing." *World Economy* 23 (January): 25–56.

Renaud, Jean-Paul. 2004. "Steep Cost Overruns, Delays Plague Efforts to Rebuild Bay Bridge." *Los Angeles Times,* May 29.

Richards, Bill. 1997. "Shaky Numbers: Layoffs Not Related to NAFTA Can Trigger Special Help Anyway." *Wall Street Journal,* June 30, A1.

Roberts, Donna. 1998. "Preliminary Assessment of the Effects of the WTO Agreement on Sanitary and Phytosanitary Measures Trade Regulations." *Journal of International Economic Law* 2 (December): 377–405.

Roberts, Donna, and Kate DeRemer. 1997. *An Overview of Technical Barriers to U.S. Agricultural Exports.* Economic Research Service, U.S. Department of Agriculture, Staff Paper AGES-9705, March.

Roberts, Mark J., and James R. Tybout. 1996. *Industrial Evolution in Developing Countries: Micro Patterns of Turnover, Productivity, and Market Structure.* New York: Oxford University Press for the World Bank.

Robertson, David. 2000. "Civil Society and the WTO." *World Economy* 23 (September): 1119–34.

Rodríguez, Francisco, and Dani Rodrik. 2001. "Trade Policy and Economic Growth: A Skeptic's Guide to Cross-National Evidence." In Ben S. Bernanke and Kenneth Rogoff, eds., *NBER Macroeconomics Annual, 2000.* Cambridge: MIT Press.

Rodrik, Dani. 1989. "Optimal Trade Taxes for a Large Country with Non-atomistic Firms." *Journal of International Economics* 26 (February): 157–67.

———. 1995. "Political Economy of Trade." In Gene M. Grossman and Kenneth Rogoff, eds., *The Handbook of International Economics,* vol. 3. Amsterdam: Elsevier Publishers.

———. 1996. "Labor Standards in International Trade: Do They Matter and What Do We Do about Them?" In Robert Lawrence et al., *Emerging Agenda for Global Trade: High Stakes for Developing Countries.* Washington, D.C.: Overseas Development Council.

———. 1999. "Democracies Pay Higher Wages." *Quarterly Journal of Economics* 114:707–38.

Rodrik, Dani, and Arvind Subramanian. 2004. "From 'Hindu Growth' to Productivity Surge: The Mystery of the Indian Growth Transition." NBER Working Paper No. 10376, March.

Roland-Holst, David, Kenneth Reinhart, and Clinton Schiells. 1992. "North American Trade Liberalization and the Role of Non-tariff Barriers." In U.S. International Trade Commission, *Economy-Wide Modeling of the Economic Implication of an FTA with Mexico and a NAFTA with Canada and Mexico.* USITC Publication 20436. Washington, D.C.: USITC.

Romer, Paul. 1994. "New Goods, Old Theory, and the Welfare Costs of Trade Restrictions." *Journal of Development Economics* 43 (February): 5–38.

Rose, Andrew K. 2004. "Do We Really Know That the WTO Increases Trade?" *American Economic Review* 94 (March): 98–114.

Rosenberg, Nathan. 1960. "Some Institutional Aspects of the 'Wealth of Nations.'" *Journal of Political Economy* 68 (December): 557–70.

Rosenthal, Elisabeth. 2002. "Buicks, Starbucks, and Fried Chicken. Still China?" *New York Times*, February 25.

Ruffin, Roy J. 2002. "David Ricardo's Discovery of Comparative Advantage." *History of Political Economy* 34 (winter): 727–48.

Runge, C. Ford. 2003. "Agri-vation: The Farm Bill from Hell." *National Interest* 72 (summer): 85–93.

Rutherford, Thomas F., and David G. Tarr. 2002. "Trade Liberalization, Product Variety, and Growth in a Small, Open Economy: A Quantitative Assessment." *Journal of International Economics* 56 (March): 247–72.

Sachs, Jeffrey D., and Andrew M. Warner. 1995. "Economic Reform and the Process of Global Integration." *Brookings Papers on Economic Activity*, no. 1: 1–95.

Sampson, Gary P. 2000. *Trade, Environment, and the WTO: The Post-Seattle Agenda.* Washington, D.C.: Overseas Development Council.

Samuelson, Paul A. 1972. *The Collected Scientific Papers of Paul A. Samuelson.* Vol. 3. Cambridge: MIT Press.

Sanchez, Julian. 2003. "Lou's Blues: Lou Dobbs and the New Mercantilism.' *Reason*, October 30, http://www.reason.com.

Sazanami, Yoko, Shujiro Urata, and Hiroki Kawai. 1995. *Measuring the Costs of Protection in Japan.* Washington, D.C.: Institute for International Economics, January.

Scheiber, Noam. 2004. "As a Center for Outsourcing, India Could Be Losing Its Edge." *New York Times*, May 2.

Scheve, Kenneth F., and Matthew J. Slaughter. 2001a. *Worker Perceptions and Pressures in the Global Economy.* Washington, D.C.: Institute for International Economics, March.

———. 2001b. "What Determines Individual Trade-Policy Preferences?" *Journal of International Economics* 54 (August): 267–92.

Schoepfle, Gregory K. 2000. "U.S. Trade Adjustment Assistance Policies for Workers." In Alan V. Deardorff and Robert M. Stern, eds., *Social*

Dimensions of U.S. Trade Policies. Ann Arbor: University of Michigan Press.

Schott, Jeffrey J. 1994. *The Uruguay Round: An Assessment.* Washington, D.C.: Institute for International Economics.

Scott, Robert E. 1999. "NAFTA's Pain Deepens: Job Destruction Accelerates in 1999 with Losses in Every State." Washington, D.C.: Economic Policy Institute Briefing Paper, November.

Shin, Hyun Ja. 1998. "Possible Instances of Predatory Pricing in Recent U.S. Antidumping Cases." In Robert Z. Lawrence, ed., *Brookings Trade Forum, 1998.* Washington, D.C.: Brookings Institution.

Shirk, Susan L. 1994. *How China Opened Its Door: The Political Success of the PRC's Foreign Trade and Investment Reforms.* Washington, D.C.: Brookings Institution.

Sivadasan, Jagadeesh. 2003. "Barriers to Entry and Productivity: Micro-evidence from Indian Manufacturing Sector Reforms." Working paper, University of Chicago Graduate School of Business, November.

Smith, Adam. 1976. *An Inquiry into the Nature and Causes of the Wealth of Nations.* Oxford: Clarendon Press.

———. 1977. *Correspondence of Adam Smith.* Oxford: Clarendon Press.

———. 1978. *Lectures on Jurisprudence.* Oxford: Clarendon Press.

———. 1980. *Essays on Philosophical Subjects.* Oxford: Clarendon Press.

Spinanger, Dean. 1999. "Textiles beyond the MFA Phase-Out." *World Economy* 22 (June): 455–76.

Srinivasan, T. N. 1998. *Developing Countries and the Multilateral Trading System.* Boulder, Colo.: Westview Press.

Srinivasan, T. N., and Suresh Tendulkar. 2003. *Reintegrating India with the World Economy.* Washington, D.C.: Institute for International Economics.

Steinberg, Richard E., and Timothy E. Josling. 2003. "When the Peace Ends: The Vulnerability of EC and US Agricultural Subsidies to WTO Legal Challenge." *Journal of International Economic Law* 6 (July): 369–417.

Stolper, Wolfgang F., and Paul A. Samuelson. 1941. "Protection and Real Wages." *Review of Economic Studies* 9 (November): 58–73.

Subramanian, Arvind, and Shang-Jin Wei. 2003. "The WTO Promotes Trade, Strongly but Unevenly." NBER Working Paper No. 10024, October.

Suomela, John W. 1993. *Free Trade versus Fair Trade: The Making of American Trade Policy in a Political Environment.* Turku, Finland: Institute for European Studies.

Swagel, Phillip. 2000. "Union Behavior, Industry Rents, and Optimal Policies." *International Journal of Industrial Organization* 18 (August): 925–47.

Sykes, Alan O. 1998. "Antidumping and Antitrust: What Problems Does Each Address?" In Robert Z. Lawrence, ed., *Brookings Trade Forum, 1998.* Washington, D.C.: Brookings Institution.

————. 2003. "The Safeguards Mess: A Critique of WTO Jurisprudence." *World Trade Review* 2 (November): 261–96.

Taylor, Christopher T. 2004. "The Economic Effects of Withdrawn Antidumping Investigations: Is There Evidence of Collusive Settlements?" *Journal of International Economics* 62 (March): 295–312.

Tempest, Rohn. 1996. "Barbie and the World Economy." *Los Angeles Times*, September 22, A-1.

Tonelson, Alan. 1994. "Beating Back Predatory Trade." *Foreign Affairs* 73 (July–August): 123–35.

Tornell, Aaron. 1991. "Time Inconsistency of Protectionist Programs." *Quarterly Journal of Economics* 106 (August): 963–74.

Tornell, Aaron, Frank Westermann, and Lorenza Martinez. 2004. "NAFTA and Mexico's Less-Than-Stellar Performance." NBER Working Paper No. 10289, February.

Trefler, Daniel. 1993. "Trade Liberalization and the Theory of Endogenous Protection: An Econometric Study of U.S. Import Policy." *Journal of Political Economy* 101 (February): 138–60.

————. 2004. "The Long and Short of the Canada-U.S. Free Trade Agreement." *American Economic Review* 94 (September): 870–95.

Tybout, James R. 2000. "Manufacturing Firms in Developing Countries: How Well Do They Do, and Why?" *Journal of Economic Literature* 38 (March): 11–44.

————. 2003. "Plant and Firm Level Evidence on 'New' Trade Theories." In E. Kwan Choi and James Harrigan, eds., *Handbook of International Trade*. New York: Basil Blackwell.

Tybout, James R., and M. Daniel Westbrook. 1995. "Trade Liberalization and the Dimensions of Efficiency Change in Mexican Manufacturing Industries." *Journal of International Economics* 39 (August): 53–78.

United Nations. 1962. *Yearbook of International Trade Statistics, 1960*. New York: United Nations.

United Nations Development Program. 2002. *Arab Human Development Report, 2002: Creating Opportunities For Future Generations*. New York: United Nations.

U.S. Bureau of the Census. 1975. *Historical Statistics of the United States, from Colonial Times to 1970*. Washington, D.C.: GPO.

————. 2004. *Statistical Abstract of the United States, 2003*. Washington, D.C.: GPO.

U.S. Department of Commerce, International Trade Administration. 1988. *United States Sugar Policy: An Analysis*. Washington, D.C.: GPO, April.

U.S. Department of Commerce, Office of Inspector General. 1993. "Import Administration's Investigations of Steel Industry Petitions." Report No. TTD-5541-4-0001, December.

U.S. Department of Energy, Energy Information Administration. 1998. *Petroleum Supply Annual, 1998.* Washington, D.C.: GPO.

U.S. General Accounting Office. 1993. *Sugar Program: Changing Domestic and International Conditions Require Program Changes.* RCED/93/84. Washington, D.C.: GAO.

———. 2000a. *Sugar Program: Supporting Sugar Prices Has Increased Users' Costs While Benefiting Producers.* RCED/00/126. Washington, D.C.: GAO, June.

———. 2000b. *World Trade Organization: Issues in Dispute Settlement.* NSIAD-00-210. Washington, D.C.: GAO, August.

———. 2003. *World Trade Organization: Standard of Review and Impact of Trade Remedy Rulings.* GAO-03-824. Washington, D.C.: GAO, July.

U.S. House of Representatives, Committee on Ways and Means. 1994. *Hearings: North American Free Trade Agreement (NAFTA) and Supplemental Agreements to the NAFTA.* Washington, D.C.: GPO.

———. 2003. *Overview and Compilation of U.S. Trade Statues: 2003 Edition.* Washington, D.C.: GPO, June.

U.S. International Trade Commission. 1995. *The Economic Effects of Antidumping and Countervailing Duty Orders and Suspension Agreements.* Investigation No. 332-344. Publication 2900. Washington, D.C.: USITC, June.

———. 1997. *Likely Impact of Providing Quota-Free and Duty-Free Entry to Textiles and Apparel from Sub-Saharan Africa.* Investigation 332-379. Publication 3056. Washington, D.C.: USITC, September.

———. 1999. *Production Sharing: Use of U.S. Components and Materials in Foreign Assembly, Operations 1995–1999.* USITC Publication 3265. Washington, D.C.: USITC, December.

———. 2003. *Steel Consuming Industries: Competitive Conditions with Respect to Steel Safeguard Measures.* Vol. 3, *Executive Summaries.* Investigation No. 332-452. Publication 3632. Washington, D.C.: USITC, September.

———. 2004. *The Economic Effects of Significant U.S. Import Restraints.* Fourth update, 2004. Investigation No. 332-325. Publication 3701. Washington, D.C.: USITC, June.

U.S. Trade Representative. 2000. *2000 Trade Policy Agenda and 1999 Annual Report.* Washington, D.C.: USTR.

Viner, Jacob. 1991. *Essays on the Intellectual History of Economics.* Princeton: Princeton University Press.

Wacziarg, Romain. 2001. "Measuring the Dynamic Gains from Trade." *World Bank Economic Review* 15 (October): 393–429.

Wacziarg, Romain, and Karen H. Welch. 2003. "Trade Liberalization and Growth: New Evidence." NBER Working Paper No. 10152, December.

Wade, Robert. 2004. *Governing the Market: Economic Theory and the Role of Government in East Asian Industrialization.* Princeton: Princeton University Press.

Wallach, Lori, and Patrick Woodall. 2004. *Whose Trade Organization?* New York: New Press.

Watkins, Ralph. 2003. "Production-Sharing Update: Developments in 2002." *Industry Trade and Technology Review.* Washington, D.C.: U.S. International Trade Commission Publication No. 3534, November.

Watson, James L. 1997. *Golden Arches East: McDonald's in East Asia.* Stanford: Stanford University Press.

Wei, Shang-Jin, and Yi Wu. 2003. "The Life-and-Death Consequences of Globalization." International Monetary Fund Working Paper, June.

Westphal, Larry E. 1990. "Industrial Policy in an Export Propelled Economy: Lessons from South Korea's Experience." *Journal of Economic Perspectives* 4 (summer): 41–59.

Winters, L. Alan, and Won Chang. 2000. "Regional Integration and Import Prices: An Empirical Investigation." *Journal of International Economics* 51 (August): 363–78.

Winters, L. Alan, Neil McCulloch, and Andrew McKay. 2004. "Trade Liberalization and Poverty: The Evidence So Far." *Journal of Economic Literature* 42 (March): 72–115.

Wolf, Martin. 2004. *Why Globalization Works: The Case for the Global Market Economy.* New Haven: Yale University Press.

World Bank. 1993. *The East Asian Miracle: Economic Growth and Public Policy.* New York: Oxford University Press.

———. *World Tables, 1995.* Baltimore: Johns Hopkins University Press.

———. 2000. *World Development Indicators, 2000.* Washington, D.C.: World Bank.

———. 2001. *Global Economic Prospects and the Developing Countries.* Washington, D.C.: World Bank.

———. 2003a. *Global Economic Prospects: Realizing the Development Promise of the Doha Agenda.* Washington, D.C.: World Bank.

———. 2003b. *India: Sustaining Reform, Reducing Poverty.* Washington, D.C.: World Bank.

———. 2004a. *Doing Business in 2004: Understanding Regulation.* Washington, D.C.: World Bank.

———. 2004b. *World Development Indicators 2004.* Washington D.C.: World Bank.

———. 2005. *Global Economic Prospects: Trade, Regionalism, and Development.* Washington, D.C.: World Bank.

World Resources Institute. 1999. *World Resources.* Washington, D.C.: World Resources Institute.

World Trade Organization. 1997. "Report of the Panel: EC Measures concerning Meat and Meat Products (Hormones), Complaint by the United States." WT/DS26/R/US. Geneva: WTO, August 18.

———. 1998. *Annual Report, 1998.* Geneva: WTO.

———. 1999. *The Legal Texts: The Results of the Uruguay Round of Multilateral Trade Negotiations.* New York: Cambridge University Press.

———. 2003. *Trade Policy Review: United States.* WT/TPR/S/26. Geneva: WTO, December 17.

———. 2004. *Annual Report, 2004.* Geneva: WTO, June.

Yoon, Carol K. 2000. "Simple Method Found to Increase Crop Yields Vastly." *New York Times*, August 22.

Zeile, William J. 2003a. "U.S. Affiliates of Foreign Companies: Operations in 2001." *Survey of Current Business* 83 (August): 38–56.

———. 2003b. "Trade in Goods within Multinational Companies: Survey Based Data and Findings for the United States of America." Paper for OECD Committee on Industry and Business Environment, Working Party on Statistics, November.

Index

AFL-CIO, 201, 216
Africa, 201; political power in, 183,
    183n. 43; transport costs in, 177; West
    Africa, 175
African Growth and Opportunity Act
    (2000), 201; as "NAFTA for Africa," 201
agriculture, 54–55; crop production, 55,
    55n. 57
Airbus, 18, 92
aircraft and aerospace industry, 108
Aitken, Brian, 193n. 59
American Electronics Association, 91
Anderson, James, 22n. 21
Anderson, Kym, 55n. 57
Angell, Norman, 50
antidumping (AD), 6, 83, 86, 131, 133–41,
    146–49, 150, 151, 221; costs of, 141–45;
    determination of "material injury," 137–
    38, 140; duties, 77–78, 135n. 7, 138–39,
    142; and evidence of trade diversion,
    140; legal fees associated with, 134; or-
    ders, 138; typical investigation of,
    148n. 39; and the WTO, 230, 230n. 37.
    See also dumping
Apple, 78
Arab world, 165–66
Argentina, 55, 145, 174, 175, 177
Australia, 54, 55, 145
autarky, 35
automobile industry, 9, 15, 16, 16n. 11,
    18, 31, 109–11, 109n. 22, 110n. 23, 150,
    153, 156

balance-of-payments accounting, 124–27
"balance of payments deficit," 125n. 51
Baldwin, Robert E., 153n. 48

Bangladesh, 163, 183, 188, 197n. 63
Barbaum, Michael L., 50n. 50
Barbieri, Katherine, 50n. 50
Barringer, William H., 155n. 51
Basle Convention on the Control of
    Transboundary Movements of
    Hazardous Wastes and Their Disposal,
    242–43
Benin, 187
Bharti Tele-Ventures, 106
Bic, 141
Blonigen, Bruce A., 134n. 5
Boeing, 92, 132n. 1
Bonier, David, 58n. 66
border effect, 22n. 21
Bordo, Michael D., 9n. 1
Bown, Chad P., 228n. 32
Brachs Candy Company, 77
Branstetter, Lee G., 90n. 50
Brazil, 43, 55, 74, 142, 187n. 52, 234–35,
    236
Bretton Woods system, 127–28
Buchanan, Patrick, 2
Bureau of Labor Statistics, 97, 105, 106
Burke-Hartke bill, 216
Burkina Faso, 187
Burma, 165
Bush, George W., 85, 151, 154, 249
"Buy America" rules, 67
Byrd, Robert, 144

California transit authority, 67
Cambodia, 164, 188, 201
Canada, 16, 17, 55, 59, 77, 145, 151, 197,
    199n. 68, 236, 240
Caribbean Basin, 17

Carnegie Endowment for International
Peace, 174
Caterpillar, 78
Chad, 187
child labor, 196–98; in Bangladesh,
197n. 63; in the United States, 198n. 65
Chile, 44, 45, 51, 73–74, 74n. 27, 87,
139–40, 172–73, 183
China, 1, 73, 87, 140, 141, 166–72, 178,
178n. 31; and central planning, 166,
166n. 8; Commerce's estimation of
costs of crawfish farming in, 137; ex-
tension of Permanent Normalized
Trade Relations to, 51; in the fourteenth century, 165; and rice blast,
42–43
Chrysler, 31
Chung Hee Park, 181
Clark, Gregory, 9n. 2
Clerides, Sofronis K., 44n. 34
Clinton, Bill, 71n. 24, 85, 144, 196, 199n. 68
Coalition for Fair Preserved Mushroom
Trade, 140
Coalition of American Steel-Using Manufacturers (CASUM), 78–79, 79n. 33
Colombia, 71, 143, 174, 175, 183
comparative advantage, 28–34, 29n. 6,
32n. 8; and developing countries, 32;
and the opportunity costs of produc-
tion, 29; sources of, 32
competition, 38, 43–45, 107–8, 146, 157
computable general equilibrium models,
36, 38, 38n. 16
Congressional Budget Office, 143, 145
consumer electronics industry, 153
consumer price index, 106n. 18
consumer utility, 38–39
Consuming Industries Trade Action Coalition (CITAC), 79–80
Convention on International Trade in
Endangered Species (CITES), 242,
242–43n. 53
Corden, W. Max, 88n. 47
Costa Rica, 40, 183, 228
Côte d'Ivoire, 43
countervailing duties (CVDs), 132–33
Cuba, 51

Daley, Richard, Jr., 77
Davis, Steven J., 98n. 5
deadweight loss, 64

deforestation, 55–56
Deng Xiaoping, 166
developed countries, and trade policies,
184–88
developing countries, 59, 127n. 54; and
antidumping actions, 145; and comparative advantage, 32; high costs of business regulation in, 176n. 27; as price-
takers, 89n. 48; and trade policy,
160–66
Dickens, William T., 111n. 26
"dirty industry migration" hypothesis, 58
displaced worker assistance: efficiency
rationale and, 117–18; equity rationale
and, 118; political argument for, 118.
See also trade adjustment assistance
division of labor, 27–28
Dollar, David, 164, 176n. 28
Dominican Republic, 71, 164
doux commerce, 49
Dryden, Steve, 216n. 14
dumping, 131–41, 209; and constructed
value method of determination, 136–
37; government definition of, 6; margin, 135–36; and price comparison
method of determination, 135–36

East Asian miracle, 177–84
Economic Policy Institute, 99
Economist, 257
economy, the: goods-producing sector,
13; service sector, 10–11, 12, 102, 105;
traded goods sector, 10–11
educational attainment, 23, 84,
84–85n. 42, 109n. 21, 111–12, 113
Egypt, 164
Eichengreen, Barry, 9n. 1
Elliott, Kimberly Ann, 193n. 58
empirical models of bilateral trade, 21–22
Environmental Protection Agency (EPA),
environmental standards on imported
gasoline, 233–36
escape clause, 131, 149–52, 149n. 41, 159;
and advantages over antidumping, 152;
and the WTO, 230
European Community (EC), 91
European Economic Community (EEC),
253
European Union (EU), 55, 145, 151–52,
199n. 68; and Common Agricultural
Policy, 215; costs of protection in,

69n. 20; dispute of with United States over hormone-treated beef, 245–48
exchange rate, 75, 75n. 28
Export-Import Bank, 132n. 1
export taxes, 89
exports, "optimal" reduction in, 89n. 49

Fair Employment Act (1938), 198n. 65
"fair trade" laws, 131
Fanjul, Alfonso, 70–71, 71n. 24
Federal Reserve Board, 98
Feenstra, Robert C., 9n. 2, 112n. 28
Ferreira, Susana, 53n. 55
"fin de siècle déjà vu" view, 8–9
Finger, J. Michael, 150n. 43
Food and Agricultural Organization (FAO), 53, 225n. 27
footwear industry, 68, 154n. 50, 255
forest products, 55–56
"40 to 1" coalition, 79
"four tigers," 178
France, 188, 240
Frankel, Jeffrey A., 46, 46n. 37
Franklin, Benjamin, 254
free trade, 2, 3, 27n. 3, 59–60; Adam Smith's argument for, 26–28; and company ownership, 15; economic case for, 3–4; effect of on employment, 94–101; and the environment, 52–59; factors shaping, 21–22; increase of in the postwar period, 19–22. *See also* trade
Freeman, Richard B., 154n. 50
Friends of the Earth, 58

General Accounting Office, 227–28, 228–29, 230–31, 231
General Agreement on Tariffs and Trade (GATT), 188, 203, 207–11, 219n. 19, 224–26, 226n. 29; Article 1, 208–9, 209n. 6, 215, 250; Article 3, 209, 237–38, 241; Article 5, 209; Article 11, 109, 215, 232, 237; Article 12, 209; Article 13, 215; Article 14, 213; Article 16, 209; Article 18, 209, Article 20, 232–33, 232n. 42, 234, 239, 240, 247–48; Article 23, 214; Article 24, 209n. 6, 215, 250; and the "chicken war" of 1962, 214; Congress's refusal to recognize in the 1950s, 210n. 7; and "contracting parties," 209; Doha Round, 36, 145, 223–24; evaluation of, 211–16; as the

"General Agreement to Talk and Talk," 224; impact of on trade, 213n. 9; Kennedy Round, 211; major provisions of, 208–9, 209n. 6; most-favored nation (MFN) clause, 208–9; negotiating rounds of, 210; origins of, 203–7; and the "product-process" distinction, 237, 240–41; and the "reciprocal mutual advantage" principle, 207; and standard of "national treatment," 209; Tokyo Round, 211, 217, 245; —, "GATT à la carte" approach of, 211, 223; Uruguay Round, 66, 132, 137, 142, 143, 203, 215, 218–19, 220–24, 226, 227, 245–46; —, Agreement on the Application of Sanitary and Phytosanitary Measures (SPS), 246–48, 247n. 61; —, Agreement on Subsidies and Countervailing Measures, 132; —, General Agreement on Trade in Services (GATS), 221–22; —, as a "single undertaking," 222–23; —, trade-related intellectual property (TRIPs) agreement, 222, 222n. 23; —, trade-related investment measures (TRIM), 222. *See also* World Trade Organization
General Electric, 132n. 1
General Motors, 79
Gephardt, Richard, 58n. 66
Global Trade Watch, 231, 236
globalization, 164; public views on, 22–24
"globalization backlash," 2–3, 255
goods: automotive, 12; capital, 12, 42; consumer, 12; industrial materials and supplies, 12; manufactured, 11–12; nontraded, 9; perishable, 11; traded, 9
gravity equations. *See* empirical models of bilateral trade
Great Depression, 203–4
Greece, 166
Greenpeace, 58, 225n. 27
Greenspan, Alan, 95, 256n.5
Grossman, Gene M., 93n. 55
Guatemala, 71

Hall, Robert E., 46n. 37
Haltiwanger, John C., 98n. 5
Hanson, Gordon H., 112n. 28
Harley-Davidson, 157–59, 157n. 54, 158nn. 55 and 56, 159n. 57
Harrison, Ann, 193n. 59

Heckman, James, 120–21n. 45
Hicks, John, 40n. 20
high-definition television (HDTV), 91
Hoekman, Bernard, 186n. 48, 208n. 5,
   217n. 16
Holiday Rambler Corp., 159n. 57
Hollings, Ernest, 151
home ownership, 85n. 42
Honda, 157, 158
Hong Kong, 178, 179, 183
Hoover, Herbert, 4, 204
Hudec, Robert, 214n. 12, 226n. 29
Hudson, Stewart, 58

Iacocca, Lee, 31
IBM, 106
Iceland, 54
import substitution, 74, 178
imports: and destruction of jobs, 94–101;
   temporary relief from, 152–59
India, 1, 43, 105, 140, 166–72, 168n. 12,
   169–70n. 14, 178, 189–90, 239; and
   "license raj" system, 169
Indonesia, 56, 140, 141, 182, 183,
   193n. 59
industrial policy, 90–91, 178–83
Institute for International Economics, 99
interest groups, 82–83, 161; and the "free
   rider" problem, 84. *See also* nongovernmental organizations
International Labor Organization (ILO),
   195–96, 199; Declaration on Fundamental Principles and Rights, 195; enforcement of charters of, 200
international trade. *See* free trade
International Trade Commission (ITC),
   138n. 12
Irwin, Douglas A., 9n. 1, 46n. 37, 88n. 47,
   90n. 51, 92n. 54
Israel, 151

Jackson, John, 217n. 15
Jacobson, Louis, 122nn. 48 and 49
Japan, 1, 55, 129, 129n. 55, 139, 140, 155,
   178, 179, 183; average productivity of
   workforce in, 33–34; cost of trade pro-
   duction in, 69n. 20; and HDTV, 91; in-
   dustry-level productivity in, 20–31;
   Japanese investors in U.S. assets, 128;
   and Ministry of International Trade and
   Industry (MITI), 180; opening of to the
   world economy, 35; U.S. limits on ex-
   ports to, 67–68
Jawara, Fatoumata, 224n. 25
Jefferson, Thomas, 35
job-training programs, 120, 120–21n. 45
Jones, Charles L., 46n. 37
Jones Act, 68–69
Jordan, 151

Kant, Immanuel, 50
Kantor, Mickey, 100
Kaptur, Marcy, 58n. 66
Kar, Dabayani, 193n. 58
Katz, Lawrence F., 109n. 22, 109–10n. 23
Kawasaki, 157, 158
Kenya, 174
Kleiner, Morris M., 154n. 50
Klenow, Peter, 90n. 50
Kletzer, Lori G., 98n. 4
Kostecki, Michel, 208n. 5, 217n. 16
Kraay, Aart, 164, 176n. 28
Krueger, Anne O., 93n. 56, 153n. 48,
   161n. 2
Krugman, Paul, 3–4, 29n. 6, 90n. 50, 199,
   199n. 67
Kwa, Aileen, 224n. 25

labor standards: core, 195–200; economic,
   195, 200; and trade agreements,
   195–202
Lach, Saul, 44n. 34
Latvia, 140
"law of diminishing international trade," 9
Lawrence, Robert Z., 112n. 28
League of Nations, 204
learning-by-doing, 90
Lee, Jong-Wha, 42n. 28
Lequesne, Caroline, 197n. 63
Lerner, Abba, 72n. 26
Lerner symmetry theorem, 72–73, 76
Levine, Ross, 46n. 38
LifeSavers company, 76
Lipsey, Robert E., 193n. 59
London School of Economics, 168n. 11
Long Term Arrangement on Cotton Tex-
   tiles, 156

Macaulay, Thomas Babington, 1, 5, 59–60,
   244
machine tool industry, 105
macroeconomic policy, 98

Maggi, Giovanni, 93n. 55
Malaysia, 137, 182, 183, 239
Mali, 187
Marine Mammal Protection Act, 236–37
Maskus, Keith, 222n. 23
Maui Pineapple Company, 140–41
Mayda, Anna M., 84n. 41
Mazumdar, Joy, 42n. 28
McCain, John, 255
McDonald's, in foreign countries, 49–50, 50n. 49
McKinsey consulting firm, 180–81
median voter, 84–85, 84n. 40
mercantilism, 62–63
Messerlin, Patrick A., 69n. 30
Mexico, 1, 17, 43, 51, 57–58, 101, 141, 145, 151, 237, 238, 253; effects of NAFTA on, 173–74
Micron Technology, 139, 145
Mill, James, 30n. 7
Mill, John Stuart, 4, 34, 41, 43, 49, 49n. 47, 52
Milliken, Roger, 42
Mishra, Deepak, 89n. 48
Mitchell, George, 254
Moldova, 140
Mongolia, 188
Montesquieu, 49, 50
Montreal Convention on Fluorocarbons, 243
Moore, Michael O., 79n. 33, 160n. 1
Morris, Julian, 242–43n. 53
Multi-Fiber Arrangement (MFA), 65–66, 104, 156, 187, 218, 220; phaseout of, 66; restrictiveness of across commodity products, 66n. 12
multinationals, 18; and relocation of business back in the United States, 190n. 55. *See also* sweatshops

Nader, Ralph, 2
National Oceanic and Atmospheric Administration (NOAA), 238
"new global economy" view, 9
New Zealand, 45, 54
Ng, Francis, 186n. 48
Nicaragua, 174
Nigeria, 164
Nike, 188, 193
nongovernmental organizations (NGOs), 6, 184, 255–57

North American Free Trade Agreement (NAFTA), 1, 17, 85, 101n. 11, 251–52; debate over in the early 1990s, 98–101; effect of on Mexico, 173–74; and the environment, 57–58; environmental groups and, 58, 58n. 65; evaluation of impact of through general equilibrium simulations, 37
Norway, 139, 188

ocean fishing, 53–54
Olarreaga, M., 186n. 48
Omnibus Trade and Competitiveness Act (1988), 227
Oneal, John, 50n. 50
Organization for Economic Cooperation and Development (OECD), 21, 120, 193, 193n. 57; and subsidization of farmers, 184–85, 219
Organization of Petroleum Exporting Countries (OPEC), 89
outsourcing, 1, 13–14, 17n. 13, 105
Oxfam, 163, 184

Pakistan, 239
Palmeter, N. David, 235n. 36
Panagariya, Arvind, 89n. 48, 170n. 14
Pareto, Vilfredo, 81–82
Pastor, Robert, 254–55n. 1
Pavcnik, Nina, 92n. 52
Pension Benefit Guaranty Corporation, 155
Perot, Ross, 99
"Perpetual Peace" (Kant), 50
Philippines, 189–90, 191–92
Pierce, Kenneth J., 155n. 51
pollution, 56–57
Precision Metalforming Association, 78
predatory pricing, 146–47
price discrimination, 133, 146, 148
price distortion, 64
Principles of Political Economy (J. S. Mill), 34
production sharing, 17–18
productivity, 27–28, 106–7, 110n. 24, 190n. 55; gains in, 41–45
Program on International Policy Attitudes (PIPA), 22–23, 22n. 22
property rights, 53, 59
protectionism, 12, 254–55; and the "cry and sigh" cycle, 254–55n. 1; and

protectionism (*cont.*)
　　domestic industries, 153n. 48; eco-
　　nomic benefits of, 88–93; and "legal-
　　ized backsliding," 150n. 43; politics of,
　　81–88; and the public health excuse,
　　244–45. *See also* trade barriers
Prusa, Thomas J., 134n. 4
Public Citizen, 2, 58, 233, 234n. 45,
　　236

quotas, 5, 61; costs of, 61–71; import, 66–
　　67, 209; quota rents, 67–68; tariff-rate,
　　158

Reagan, Ronald, 158
Reciprocal Trade Agreements Act (RTAA/
　　1934), 149; as basis of U.S. trade pol-
　　icy, 204; most-favored nation (MFN)
　　clause, 205; tipping of the political bal-
　　ance of power in favor of lower tariffs,
　　205–7
Reich, Robert, 200n. 69
Renelt, David, 46n. 38
research and development (R&D), 42–43,
　　90, 90n. 51
Ricardo, David, 5, 28–29
Richardson, J. David, 193n. 58
Roberts, Donna, 247n. 60
Robertson, David, 229n. 34
Robertson, Dennis, 9
Robinson, Joan, 213
Rodríguez, Francisco, 46n. 37, 47nn. 39
　　and 42
Rodrik, Dani, 46n. 37, 47nn. 39 and 42,
　　83n. 39, 84n. 41, 170n. 14, 189n. 54
Romer, David, 46, 46n. 37
Roosevelt, Franklin, 204
Roosevelt, Theodore, 255
Rose, Andrew K., 213n. 9
Russett, Bruce, 50n. 50

Sachs, Jeffrey D., 47n. 42
Sampson, Gary P., 229n. 35, 241n. 52,
　　243n. 55, 249n. 63
Samuelson, Paul, 29n. 6, 111n. 27
Schott, Jeffrey J., 217n. 16
Schuh, Scott, 98n. 5
semiconductor industry, 68, 77–78, 86,
　　90n. 51, 149, 153
Shah, Shekhar, 89n. 48
Sharp, 78

Short Term Arrangement on Cotton Tex-
　　tiles, 156
Sierra Club, 58, 58n. 66
simulation models. *See* computable gen-
　　eral equilibrium models
Singapore, 178, 183, 188
Sjöholm, Fredrik, 193n. 59
Slaughter, Matthew J., 112n. 28
Smith, Adam, 5, 25, 26–28, 27n. 3,
　　59–60n. 67, 61–63, 63n. 5, 88n. 46, 130,
　　180n. 34, 184n. 44
Smoot-Hawley tariff (1930), 4, 76, 204
software industry, 105
South Africa, 145
South Korea, 41, 43, 51, 55, 87, 139, 140,
　　172, 178, 179, 183, 191; industrial pol-
　　icy in, 181–82
Spain, 45
Spirit of the Laws, The (Montesquieu), 49
Srinivasan, T. N., 169–70n. 14
steel industry, 68, 71, 78–80, 86, 109–11,
　　109n. 22, 110n. 23, 149, 154–55, 156,
　　255; Big Steel, 154–55; and escape
　　clause actions, 151–52; and filing of
　　antidumping cases, 140; and minimills,
　　111, 154–55; and the "steel triangle,"
　　155
Stolper, Wolfgang, 111n. 27
subcontracting, 103n. 13
Subramanian, Arvind, 170n. 14
subsidies, 90, 131–41, 184–87, 209,
　　241–42; cotton, 186–87
sugar industry, 64, 68, 70–71, 76–77,
　　77n. 30, 82, 105
Summers, Lawrence H., 109n. 22,
　　109–10n. 23
Suzuki, 158
sweatshops, 188–95
Switzerland, 55
Sykes, Alan O., 150n. 43

Taiwan, 51, 129, 178, 179
tariff code, production-sharing provision,
　　17, 17n. 13
"tariffication," 218; "dirty tariffication,"
　　219
tariffs, 5, 20, 38–40, 63, 87; average ap-
　　plied tariff rate on industrial products,
　　162; costs of, 61–71; import, 47–
　　48n. 43, 66–67; in the OECD markets,
　　187–88; U.S. drop in from 1933 to the

early 1950s, 207n. 4. *See also* countervailing duties
Taylor, Christopher C., 143n. 26
Teamsters, the, 201
Tendulkar, Suresh, 169–70n. 14
terms of trade, 88–89
Terviö, Marko, 46n. 37
textile and apparel industry, 68, 86, 104–5,
108, 115–17, 155, 156–57
Thailand, 137, 140–41, 182, 239
Topel, Robert, 110n. 24
Torrens, Robert, 9
Torrington Company, 144
Toshiba, 77–78
trade: benefits from, 45–47, 49–52; as a
conduit for the transfer of foreign technology, 42–43; effect of on income,
46n. 37; gains from, 34–41; "home
bias" in, 21; impediments to, 18; link
between growth and, 46n. 38; and the
manufacturing sector, 101–6; measuring
gains from, 45–49; in services, 13–14;
and specialization, 25–28; trade-democ-
racy link, 51–52; trade-peace link, 50–
51, 50n. 50; and wages, 106–13. *See
also* free trade
trade adjustment assistance (TAA),
118n. 38; Alternative Trade Adjustment
Assistance (ATAA), 121; and displaced
workers, 118–23; NAFTA assistance
program, 119–20; trade readjustment
allowance (TRA), 119, 119n. 40
trade agreements: and labor standards,
195–202; multilateral, 213–14; preferential, 249–53; regional, 253; and safeguard provisions, 150–51
trade barriers, 39, 46n. 38, 48n. 43; and
corruption, 52n. 54; costs of, 69–70;
and developing countries, 65n. 4; and
import barriers, 64; —, harm to downstream industries, 76–81; —, harm to
exports, 72–76; reduction of, 20–21, 40;
statistical measurement of effects, 70;
and the status quo bias in maintaining
trade barriers, 87; welfare costs of,
39–40, 70. *See also* protectionism
trade deficit, 123–30, 129n. 55; and unemployment, 123
Trade Deficit Review Commission,
123n. 50
Trade Expansion Act (1962), 118

trade facilitation, 177
trade policy, 24, 71; difficulty in changing,
86; difficulty in measuring, 47–48; and
economic interests, 85–86; and environmental problems, 53; and lobbyists,
71; reform of, 172–77; —, "back-end
loaded" phaseouts, 66; and identifica-
tion of externalities, 90n. 50; in representative democracies, 93; strategic
trade policy, 92–93; and trade-offs,
80–81
trade restrictions. *See* trade barriers
trade sanctions, 241
transactions costs, 19–20
transportation costs, 19
transshipment, 251
trichinosis, 244, 244–45n. 57
Turkey, 38
Tybout, James R., 38n. 36, 44n. 34

Uganda, 163, 154
UN Arab Human Development Report,
165–66
Union of Needletrades, Industrial and
Textile Employees (UNITE), 201
unions, 109, 110–11, 196, 201
United Kingdom, 87
United States, 54, 145; and bipartisan consensus in favor of reciprocal trade
agreements, 216; and child labor laws,
198n. 65; civilian labor market and employment in, 95; and convergence of
income, 33n. 9; and cotton production,
88–89; as a "debtor" country, 126–
27n. 54; decline of manufacturing jobs
in, 101–2; dispute of with EU over hormone-treated beef, 245–48; and 1807
trade embargo, 35–36; exports, 7, 8,
11–12, 14, 108–9; farm trade policy of,
219; and ILO conventions, 196, 200;
import barriers of, 59; and imports, 7,
8, 11–12, 14, 108; importance of trade
in merchandise goods to economy of,
7–15; industry-level productivity in,
30–31; and international trade, 7; labor
market in, 96–97; labor productivity
and compensation in, 107; as major net
exporter of services, 106; manufacturing production and employment in,
102, 104; mass layoffs in, 97; pattern of
imports and exports, 75–76; production

United States (*cont.*)
sharing in U.S. trade, 15–19; products the United States specializes in, 26; protectionist policies of, 68–69; regional and bilateral trade agreements of, 250; tariff system of, 20, 65, 87; and trade by category of commodity, 11; trade policy of, 254; unemployment in, 95–96; and the WTO, 228, 230
University of Chicago Graduate School of Business, 15
U.S.-Canada Free Trade Agreement (FTA), 44–45, 251
U.S. Court of International Trade, 147–48, 239
U.S. Department of Commerce, 132, 133, 134–37, 138, 141, 142, 143, 144. *See also* antidumping; dumping
U.S. Department of the Treasury, 137
U.S. Food and Drug Administration, 245
U.S. International Trade Commission (ITC), 64, 69, 80, 132, 134, 134n. 5, 137–38, 140, 143, 143–44, 150, 151, 158. *See also* antidumping; dumping
U.S. Trade Representative (USTR), 201
Uzbekistan, 187

van Wincoop, Eric, 22n. 21
Venezuela, 234–35, 236
vertical specialization, 16
Vietnam, 163, 164, 173, 193–94, 197
Virgin Islands, 236
voluntary restraint agreements (VRAs), 78, 79n. 33, 154

Wacziarg, Romain, 48
wages: and import prices, 107n. 19; wage distribution, 108, 111n. 27; wage premiums, 109nn. 21 and 22, 110–12, 110n. 23
Wallach, Lori, 232n. 42
Warner, Andrew M., 47n. 42
Watson, James L., 50n. 49
Wealth of Nations, The (Smith), 26, 28, 62
Welch, Karen, 48
Westbrook, M. Daniel, 38n. 16
Whose Trade Organization? (Public Citizen), 233
Wolf, Martin, 256
women, and employment, 114, 114n. 32
Woodall, Patrick, 232n. 42
Worker Rights Consortium, 193
World Bank, 175–76, 176n. 27, 179, 225, 225n. 27
World Trade Organization (WTO), 1, 6, 145, 151–52, 165, 199n. 68, 200, 203, 213, 224–31, 224n. 25, 253; attractiveness of membership in, 223; and the beef hormones case, 244–49; and the corporate average fuel economy (CAFE) case, 240; and dispute settlement process, 225–30; and environmental regulations, 231–33, 240–44; as a "House of Litigation," 249; and labor standards, 198–99; mission of, 225; and NGOs, 229, 229n. 35; and the protection of intellectual property, 222; and the reformulated gasoline case, 233–36; scope of, 224–25; and the shrimp-turtle case, 238–40; size of, 225; and trade facilitation, 177; and the tuna-dolphin case, 236–38
World Wildlife Fund, 225n. 27

Yamaha, 158

Zambia, 164
Zoellick, Robert, 252